Irven M. Resnick is professor of philosophy and religion and Chair of Excellence in Judaic Studies at the University
of Tennessee at Chattanooga.

THE FATHERS
OF THE CHURCH

MEDIAEVAL CONTINUATION

VOLUME 8

THE FATHERS
OF THE CHURCH

MEDIAEVAL CONTINUATION

PETRUS ALFONSI

DIALOGUE AGAINST THE JEWS

Translated by

IRVEN M. RESNICK
University of Tennessee
Chattanooga, Tennessee

THE CATHOLIC UNIVERSITY OF AMERICA PRESS
Washington, D.C.

The paper used in this publication meets the minimum requirements of the
American National Standards for Information Science—Permanence of Paper
for Printed Library Materials, ANSI z39.48 - 1984.

LIBRARY OF CONGRESS CATALOGING-IN-PUBLICATION DATA
Petrus Alfonsi, 1062–1110?
[Dialogus contra Iudaeos. English]
Dialogue against the Jews / Petrus Alfonsi ; translation and notes by
Irven M. Resnick.
p. cm. — (Fathers of the church. Mediaeval continuation ; no. 8)
Includes bibliographical references and index.
ISBN-13: 978-0-8132-1390-3 (cloth : alk. paper)
ISBN-10: 0-8132-1390-8 (cloth : alk. paper)   1. Judaism—Controversial
literature—Early works to 1800.   2. Apologetics—Early works to 1800.
I. Resnick, Irven Michael.   II. Title.   III. Series.
BM585.P483513 2006
239—dc22
2006004117

CONTENTS

ACKNOWLEDGMENTS

A number of individuals are due special thanks and acknowledgment. I would like to thank John Tolan, whose own work on Petrus Alfonsi was so useful to me, for having kindly responded to my inquiries. Also, thanks to Jeremy Cohen, who encouraged me to translate a substantial portion of the *Dialogue*, which he utilized in his presentations to a summer institute for college and university faculty supported by the National Endowment for the Humanities. The institute, which I directed, entitled "Representations of the 'Other': Jews in Medieval Christendom," met from July 9–August 13, 2003, at the Oxford Centre for Hebrew and Jewish Studies (Yarnton, England). The twenty-five institute participants also forced me to investigate more fully the sources and background to the *Dialogue*. In addition, I would be remiss were I to neglect the administration and staff at the Oxford Centre for Hebrew and Jewish Studies itself, which has opened its doors to me on numerous occasions. I completed this project during 2003 while in residence at the Centre as a visiting scholar. Oxford offers remarkable library resources, and during my stay I had the opportunity to examine manuscripts housed in Oxford's Bodleian Library, St. John's College (Cambridge), and the British Library. Librarians at each institution are due my thanks. Finally, I would like to acknowledge the corrections suggested by Professor Charles Burnett of the Warburg Institute, who kindly read my translation of *tituli* one and five. I am also indebted to The Catholic University of America Press staff editor, Dr. Carole Burnett, whose improvements to the translation are too numerous to count. For whatever errors remain I am, of course, solely responsible.

Illustrations were provided by the following institutions:

Diagram of the *climata*, page 62, by permission of the British Library, Additional MS 15404 fol. 41r

Diagram of the *climata*, page 63, by permission of the Bodleian Library, University of Oxford, MS. Laud Misc. 356, fol. 120r

Diagram of the sun's orbit, page 65, also by permission of the Bodleian Library, University of Oxford, MS. Laud Misc. 356, fol. 120r

Representation of the Tetragrammaton, page 173, by permission of the Master and Fellows of St. John's College, Cambridge, from MS E.4, fol. 153v.

ABBREVIATIONS

B.T.	Babylonian Talmud
CC CM	*Corpus Christianorum Continuatio Mediaevalis*
CC SL	*Corpus Christianorum Series Latina*
CSEL	*Corpus Scriptorum Ecclesiasticorum Latinorum*
FOTC, MC	Fathers of the Church, Mediaeval Continuation
NRSV	New Revised Standard Version
PL	*Patrologiae Cursus Completus, Series Latina*
RTAM	*Recherches de théologie ancienne et médiévale*
S.I.E.P.M.	Société Internationale pour l'Étude de la Philosophie Médiévale
Vulg.	Vulgate

SELECT BIBLIOGRAPHY

Primary Sources

Abraham bar Hayya. *The Meditation of a Sad Soul.* Translated by Geoffrey Wigoder. London: Routledge & Kegan Paul, 1969.

Abraham ibn Ezra (possible author). *Sefer Hanisyonot: The Book of Medical Experiences Attributed to Abraham ibn Ezra.* Edited and translated by J. O. Leibowitz and S. Marcus. Jerusalem: The Magnes Press, 1984.

Abu Ma'ashar. *On Historical Astrology.* Edited by Charles Burnett and Keiji Yamamoto. 2 vols. Leiden: E. J. Brill, 2000.

Agobard of Lyons. *De judaicis superstitionibus.* In *Agobardi Lugdunensis opera omnia.* Edited by L. Van Acker. CC CM 52. Turnholt: Brepols, 1981.

Al-Andalusi, Sa'id. *Science in the Medieval World: 'Book of the Categories of Nations.'* Translated by Sema'an I. Salem and Alok Kumar. Austin: University of Texas Press, 1991.

Alan of Lille. *Theologicae regulae.* PL 210: 617–84.

Albert the Great. *De vegetabilibus libri VII.* Edited by Ernst Meyer and Charles Jessen. Berlin: Georgius Reimeris, 1867.

————. *Quaestiones super de animalibus.* Edited by Ephrem Filthaut. Vol. 12 in *Alberti Magni . . . Opera omnia.* Monasterii Westf.: Aschendorff, 1955.

————. *De sacramentis.* Edited by Albert Ohlmeyer. Monasterii Westf.: Aschendorff, 1958.

Alexander Nequam. *Speculum speculationum.* Edited by Rodney M. Thomson. Auctores Britannici medii aevi, 11. Oxford: Oxford University Press, 1988.

Amédée de Lausanne. *Huit homélies mariales.* Edited by Jean Deshusses and translated by Antoine Dumas. Sources chrétiennes 72. Série des Textes Monastiques d'Occident 5. Paris: Les Éditions du Cerf, 1960.

Augustine. *Epistola 71.* In *Selecta veterum Scriptorum Testimonia de Hieronymianis versionibus Latinis SS. Bibliorum.* PL 28: 139–41.

————. *De ordine.* Edited by Pius Knöll. CSEL 63. Vienna and Leipzig: Hölder-Pichler-Tempsky, 1922.

————. *De civitate Dei.* CC SL 47 and 48. Edited by Bernard Dombart and Alphonse Kalb. Turnholt: Brepols, 1955.

————. *Enarrationes in Psalmos LI–C.* CC SL 39. Edited by E. Dekkers and J. Fraipont. Turnholt: Brepols, 1956.

————. *De quantitate animae.* Edited by Wolfgang Hörmann. CSEL 89, 1.4. Vienna: Hölder-Pichler-Tempsky, 1986.

Bede. *De temporum ratione liber.* CC SL 123B. Edited by Ch. W. Jones and Th. Mommsen. Turnholt: Brepols, 1977.

Belli sacri historia. In *Museum Italicum seu Collectio veterum scriptorum ex bibliothecis italicis*. Edited by Johanne Mabillon and Michaele Germain. Paris: Edmund Martin, John Boudot, and Stephen Martin, 1687.

Benedict of Nursia. *Benedicti regula*. CSEL 75. Edited by Rudolph Hanslik. Vienna: Hölder-Pichler-Tempsky, 1975.

Boethius. *Commentaria in Porphyrium a se translata*. PL 64: 71–158.

————. *In Categorias Aristotelis*. PL 64: 159–293.

————. *In librum De interpretatione, Editio prima*. PL 64: 293–393.

————. *In Porphyrium dialogi*. PL 64: 9–70.

————. *Liber de divisione*. PL 64: 875–91.

————. *Philosophiae consolatio*. Edited by Ludovicus Bieler. CC SL 94. Turnholt: Brepols, 1984.

Bonaventure. *Commentaria in quatuor libros Sententiarum: In primum librum Sententiarum*. Vol. 1 in *Opera omnia*. Quaracchi: Collegii St. Bonaventurae, 1882.

Bruno of Segni. *Expositio in Genesim*. PL 164: 147–234.

Cassiodorus (?). *De oratione et de octo partibus orationis*. PL 70: 1219–39.

Celsus. *On the True Doctrine: A Discourse Against the Christians*. Translated by Joseph Hoffmann. New York and Oxford: Oxford University Press, 1987.

Constantine the African. *Constantini Africani de communibus medico cognitu necessariis locis*. Basel: Henri cum Petrum, 1536.

————. *L'Arte universale della medicina (Pantegni)*. Translated by Marco T. Malato and Umberto de Martini. Rome: Istituto di storia della medicina dell'università di Roma, 1961.

————. *Tratado médico de Constantino el Africano. Constantini Liber de elephancia*. Edited and translated by Ana Isabel Martín Ferreira. Valladolid: Universidad de Valladolid, 1996.

Costa ben Luca. *De differentia animae et spiritus liber translatus a Johanne Hispalensi*. In *Excerpta e libro Alfredi Anglici* De motu cordis *item Costa-ben-Lucae* De differentia animae et spiritus liber *translatus a Johanne Hispalensi*. Edited by Carl Sigmund Barach. Innsbruck: Wagner'schen Universitäts-Buchhandlung, 1876. Pp. 120–39.

Hermann of Cologne. *A Short Account of His Own Conversion*. In *Conversion and Text: The Cases of Augustine of Hippo, Herman-Judah, and Constantine Tsatsos*. Translated by Karl F. Morrison. Charlottesville, VA: University of Virginia Press, 1992. Pp. 76–113.

Honorius of Autun. *De philosophia mundi*. PL 172: 41–102.

Hugh of St. Victor. *Didascalicon de studio legendi*. Edited by Charles H. Buttimer. Washington, DC: The Catholic University of America Press, 1939.

Isidore of Seville. *Etymologiarum*. PL 82: 73–728.

————. *Etymologiarum sive originum libri xx*. Edited by W. M. Lyndsay. Oxford: Clarendon Press, 1911. Repr. 1985.

Jacobus de Voragine. *The Golden Legend: Readings on the Saints*. Translated by William Granger Ryan. 2 vols. Princeton, NJ: Princeton University Press, 1995.

Jacques de Vitry. *Historia Orientalis.* Edited by Franciscus Moschus. Douai, 1597.

————. *Lettres de Jacques de Vitry.* Edited by R. B. C. Huygens. Leiden: E. J. Brill, 1960.

Joseph Kimhi. *Book of the Covenant.* Translated by Frank Talmage. Toronto: Pontifical Institute of Mediaeval Studies, 1972.

Martini, Raymund. *Pugio fidei.* Leipzig, 1687. Repr. Farnsborough, 1967.

Michael Scot. *Liber phisionomiae.* Venice, 1477.

Midrash on Psalms. Translated by William G. Braude. 2 vols. New Haven and London: Yale University Press, 1959.

Midrash Rabbah: Exodus. Translated by S. M. Lehrman. London, 1939.

Midrash Rabbah: Numbers. Translated by J. Slotki. London, 1939.

Nestor the Priest. *The Polemic of Nestor the Priest.* Translated by Daniel J. Lasker and Sarah Stroumsa. 2 vols. Jerusalem: Ben-Zvi Institute for the Study of Jewish Communities in the East, 1996.

Odo of Tournai. *Two Theological Treatises of Odo of Tournai: On Original Sin, and a Debate with the Jew, Leo, Concerning the Advent of Christ, the Son of God.* Translated by Irven M. Resnick. Philadelphia: University of Pennsylvania Press, 1994.

Paul Alvarus. *Indiculus luminosus. Corpus Scriptorum Muzarabicorum.* Edited by Joannes Gil. Vol. 1. Madrid: Consejo superior de investigaciones cientificas, 1973. Pp. 270–315.

Peter Abelard. *Dialogus inter Philosophum, Iudaeum, et Christianum.* Edited by Rudolf Thomas. Stuttgart-Bad Cannstatt: Friedrich Frommann Verlag, 1970.

————. *Dialogue of a Philosopher with a Jew and a Christian.* Translated by Pierre J. Payer. Toronto: Pontifical Institute of Medieval Studies, 1979.

Peter Damian. *Die Briefe des Petrus Damiani.* Edited by Kurt Reindel. MGH, Die Briefe der Deutschen Kaiserzeit. 4 vols. Munich: Monumenta Germaniae Historica, 1983–93.

————. *The Letters of Peter Damian, 1–30.* Translated by Owen J. Blum. FOTC, MC 1. Washington, DC: The Catholic University of America Press, 1989.

————. *The Letters of Peter Damian, 121–150.* FOTC, MC 6. Translated by Owen Blum and Irven M. Resnick. Washington, DC: The Catholic University of America Press, 2004.

Peter the Venerable. *Adversus Judeorum inveteratam duritiem.* Edited by Yvonne Friedman. CC CM 58. Turnholt: Brepols, 1985.

————. *Contra petrobrusianos haereticos.* Edited by James Fearns. CC CM 10. Turnholt: Brepols, 1968.

————. *Liber contra sectam sive haeresim Saracenorum.* In James Kritzeck, *Peter the Venerable and Islam.* Princeton, NJ: Princeton University Press, 1964. Pp. 220–91.

Petrus Alfonsi. *The Scholar's Guide: A Translation of the Twelfth-Century Disciplina clericalis of Pedro Alfonso.* Translated by Joseph Ramon Jones and John Esten Keller. Toronto: Pontifical Institute of Mediaeval Studies, 1969.

————. *The* Disciplina Clericalis *of Petrus Alfonsi.* Edition and German translation by Eberhard Hermes. English translation by P. R. Quarrie. London: Routledge Kegan & Paul, 1977.

————. *Der Dialog des Petrus Alfonsi: seine Überlieferung im Druck und in den Handschriften Textedition.* Edited by Klaus-Peter Mieth. Inaug. diss. Freien Universität Berlin, 1982.

————. *Diálogo contra los Judíos.* Translated by Esperanza Ducay. Edited by Klaus-Peter Mieth. Huesca: Instituto de Estudios Altoaragoneses, 1996.

Pirke de Rabbi Eliezer. Edited by G. Friedlander. London: 1916.

Pseudo-Bede. *De mundi celestis terrestrisque constitutione: A Treatise on the Universe and the Soul.* Edited and translated by Charles Burnett. London: Warburg Institute, 1985.

Ratramnus of Corbie. *Liber de anima ad Odonem Bellovacensem.* Edited by D. C. Lambot. Analecta mediaevalia Namurcensia 2. Namur: Centre d'Études Médiévales, 1951.

Saadia Gaon. *The Book of Beliefs and Opinions.* Translated by Samuel Rosenblatt. New Haven: Yale University Press, 1976.

Salmon ben Yeruham. *Sefer Milhamot Adonai.* Edited by Israel Davidson. New York: Beit Midrash ha-Rabanim de Amerikah, 1934. Quoted in Marc Saperstein. *Decoding the Rabbis: A Thirteenth-Century Commentary on the Aggadah.* Cambridge, MA: Harvard University Press, 1980.

Samuel of Morocco. *Liber de adventu messiae praeterito.* PL 149: 333–68.

Thomas of Cantimpré. *De natura rerum (Lib. IV–XII): Tacuinum sanitatis,* codice C-67 (fols. 2v-116r) de la Biblioteca Universitaria de Granada, commentarios a la edición facsimil. Edited by Luis García Ballester. 2 vols. Granada: Universidad de Granada, 1974.

Vincent of Beauvais. *Speculum historiale.* Douai: Bellerus, 1624. Repr. Graz: Akademische Druck- u. Verlagsanstalt, 1965.

Walcher of Malvern. *Sententia Petri Ebraei . . . de dracone.* In J. M. Millás Vallicrosa, "La aportación astronómica de Pedro Alfonso." *Sefarad* 3 (1943), Appendix I. Pp. 87–97.

William of Conches. *Dragmaticon.* Edited by Italo Ronca. CC CM 152. Turnholt: Brepols, 1997.

William of St. Thierry. *Nature of the Body and Soul.* Translated by Benjamin Clark. In *Three Treatises on Man: A Cistercian Anthropology.* Edited by Bernard McGinn. Kalamazoo, MI: Cistercian Publications, 1977.

Secondary Literature

Abulafia, Anna Sapir. "Twelfth-Century Christian Expectations of Jewish Conversion: A Case Study of Peter of Blois." *Aschkenas* 8/1 (1998): 45–70.

————. "Jewish Carnality in Twelfth-Century Renaissance Thought." In *Christianity and Judaism. Papers Read at the 1991 Summer Meeting and the 1992 Winter Meeting of the Ecclesiastical History Society.* Edited by Diana Wood. Oxford: Blackwell Publishers, 1992. Pp. 59–75.

————. "Bodies in the Jewish-Christian Debate." In *Framing Medieval Bod-*

ies. Edited by Sarah Kay and Miri Rubin. Manchester: Manchester University Press, 1994. Pp. 123–37. Repr. Abulafia, Anna Sapir. *Christians and Jews in Dispute. Disputational Literature and the Rise of Anti-Judaism in the West (c. 1000–1150).* Aldershot: Ashgate, 1998. XVI.

_____. "Twelfth-Century Renaissance Theology and the Jews." In *From Witness to Witchcraft: Jews and Judaism in Medieval Christian Thought.* Edited by Jeremy Cohen. Wolfenbütteler Mittelalter-Studien 11. Wiesbaden: Harrassowitz Verlag, 1996. Pp. 125–39.

_____. *Christians and Jews in the Twelfth Century.* London and New York: Routledge, 1995.

Albert, Bat-Sheva. "*Adversus Iudaeos* in the Carolingian Empire." In *Contra Iudaeos. Ancient and Medieval Polemics Between Christians and Jews.* Edited by Ora Limor and Guy G. Stroumsa. Tübingen: J. C. B. Mohr, 1996. Pp. 119–42.

Aragüés Aldaz, José. "*Fallacia dicta*: narración, palabra y experiencia en la *Disciplina Clericalis.*" In *Estudios sobre Pedro Alfonso de Huesca.* Edited by María Jesús Lacarra. Colección de Estudios Altoaragoneses 41. Huesca: Instituto de Estudios Altoaragoneses, 1996. Pp. 235–60.

Ashtor, Eliayahu. *The Jews of Moslem Spain.* Translated by Aaron Klein and Jenny Machlowitz Klein. 3 vols. Philadelphia: Jewish Publication Society, 1979.

Bar-Ilan, Meir. "The Hand of God: A Chapter in Rabbinic Anthropomorphism." In *Rashi 1040–1090. Hommage à Ephraïm E. Urbach.* Edited by Gabrielle Sed-Rajna. Paris: Les Éditions du Cerf, 1993. Pp. 321–35.

Berger, David, editor and translator. *The Jewish-Christian Debate in the High Middle Ages: A Critical Edition of the* Nizzhon Vetus. Philadelphia: Jewish Publication Society, 1979.

_____. "Gilbert Crispin, Alan of Lille, and Jacob ben Reuben." *Speculum* 49 (1974): 34–47.

_____. "St. Peter Damian: His Attitudes toward the Jews and the Old Testament." *Yavneh* (1965): 80–112.

Blumenkranz, Bernhard. "Augustin et les Juifs—Augustin et le Judaïsme." *Recherches augustiniennes* 1 (1958): 225–41.

Bono, James J. "Medical Spirits and the Medieval Language of Life." *Traditio* 40 (1984): 91–130.

Brody, Saul Nathaniel. *The Disease of the Soul: Leprosy in Medieval Literature.* Ithaca: Cornell University Press, 1974.

Büchler, Alfred. "A Twelfth-Century Physician's Desk Book: The *Secreta secretorum* of Petrus Alphonsi quondam Moses Sephardi." *Journal of Jewish Studies* 37/2 (1986): 206–12.

Burman, Thomas. "'Tathlîth al-wahdânîyah' and the Twelfth-Century Andalusian-Christian Approach to Islam." In *Medieval Christian Perceptions of Islam.* Edited by John Victor Tolan. New York and London: Routledge, 1996. Pp. 109–28.

_____. *Religious Polemic and the Intellectual History of the Mozarabs, c. 1050–1200.* Leiden: E. J. Brill, 1994.

Burnett, Charles. "Scientific Speculations." In *A History of Twelfth-Centu-*

ry Western Philosophy. Edited by Peter Dronke. Cambridge: Cambridge University Press, 1992. Pp. 151–76.

―――――. "Encounters with Rāzī the Philosopher: Constantine the African, Petrus Alfonsi and Ramón Martí." In *Pensamiento medieval Hispano: Homenaje a Horacio Santiago-Otero*. Vol. 2. Madrid: Consejo superior de investigaciones científicas consejreía de educación y cultura de la junta de Castilla y León Diputación de Zamora, 1998. Pp. 973–92.

―――――. "Las obras de Pedro Alfonso: problemas de autenticidad." In *Estudios sobre Pedro Alfonso de Huesca*. Edited by María Jesús Lacarra. Colección de Estudios Altoaragoneses 41. Huesca: Instituto de Estudios Altoaragoneses, 1996. Pp. 313–48.

―――――. "The Works of Petrus Alfonsi: Questions of Authenticity." *Medium Aevum* 66/1 (1997): 42–79.

―――――. *Introduction of Arabic Learning into England*. The Panizzi Lectures, 1996. London: The British Library, 1997.

Camille, Michael. *The Gothic Idol*. Cambridge and New York: Cambridge University Press, 1989.

Casulleras, Josep. "Las *Tablas astronómicas* de Pedro Alfonso." In *Estudios sobre Pedro Alfonso de Huesca*. Edited by María Jesús Lacarra. Colección de Estudios Altoaragoneses 41. Huesca: Instituto de Estudios Altoaragoneses, 1996. Pp. 349–66.

Chazan, Robert. *European Jewry and the First Crusade*. Berkeley: University of California Press, 1987.

―――――. "The Christian Position in Jacob ben Reuben's *Milhamot Ha-Shem*." In *From Ancient Israel to Modern Judaism: Intellect in Quest of Understanding; Essays in Honor of Marvin Fox*. Edited by Jacob Neusner, Ernest S. Frerichs, and Nahum M. Sarna. Vol. 2. Atlanta, GA: Scholars Press, 1989. Pp. 157–70.

―――――. "The Barcelona Disputation of 1263: Goals, Tactics, Achievements." In *Religionsgespräche im Mittelalter*. Edited by Bernard Lewis and Friedrich Niewöhner. Wiesbaden: Otto Harrassowitz, 1992. Pp. 77–91.

―――――. *Barcelona and Beyond: The Disputation of 1263 and its Aftermath*. Berkeley, Los Angeles, Oxford: University of California Press, 1992.

―――――. "Twelfth-Century Perceptions of the Jews: A Case Study of Bernard of Clairvaux and Peter the Venerable." In *From Witness to Witchcraft: Jews and Judaism in Medieval Christian Thought*. Edited by Jeremy Cohen. Wolfenbütteler Mittelalter-Studien 11. Wiesbaden: Harrassowitz Verlag, 1996. Pp. 187–201.

―――――. "Daniel 9: 24–27: Exegesis and Polemics." In *Contra Iudaeos. Ancient and Medieval Polemics Between Christians and Jews*. Edited by Ora Limor and Guy G. Stroumsa. Tübingen: J. C. B. Mohr, 1996. Pp. 143–59.

―――――. "From the First Crusade to the Second: Evolving Perceptions of the Christian-Jewish Conflict." In *Jews and Christians in Twelfth-Century Europe*. Edited by Michael A. Signer and John Van Engen. Notre Dame Conferences in Medieval Studies 10. Notre Dame, IN: University of Notre Dame Press, 2001. Pp. 46–62.

Cohen, Jeffrey Jerome. "On Saracen Enjoyment: Some Fantasies of Race in Late Medieval France and England." *The Journal of Medieval and Early Modern Studies* 31/1 (2001): 113–46.

Cohen, Jeremy. "The Jews as Killers of Christ from Augustine to the Friars." *Traditio* 39 (1983): 1–27.

_____. "The Mentality of the Medieval Jewish Apostate: Peter Alfonsi, Hermann of Cologne, and Pablo Christiani." In *Jewish Apostasy in the Modern World*. Edited by Todd M. Endelman. New York: Holmes & Meier Publishers, Inc., 1987. Pp. 20–47.

_____. *Living Letters of the Law: Ideas of the Jew in Medieval Christianity*. Berkeley, Los Angeles, London: University of California Press, 1999.

_____. "A 1096 Complex? Constructing the First Crusade in Jewish Historical Memory, Medieval and Modern." In *Jews and Christians in Twelfth-Century Europe*. Edited by Michael A. Signer and John Van Engen. Notre Dame Conferences in Medieval Studies 10. Notre Dame, IN: University of Notre Dame Press, 2001. Pp. 9–26.

Cohen, Martin Samuel. *The Shi'ur Qomah: Liturgy and Theurgy in Pre-Kabbalistic Jewish Mysticism*. New York: University Press of America, 1983.

Cook, Michael. *The Koran: A Very Short Introduction*. Oxford: Oxford University Press, 2000.

Dahan, Gilbert, ed. *Le brûlement du Talmud à Paris 1242–1244*. Paris: Les Éditions du Cerf, 1999.

_____. "L'exégèse de l'histoire de Caïn et Abel du XIIe au XIVe siècle en Occident," RTAM 49 (1982): 21–89; 50 (1983): 5–68.

_____. "L'usage de la *ratio* dans la polémique contre les juifs, XIIe–XIVe siècles." In *Diálogo Filosófico-Religioso entre Christianismo, Judaísmo e Islamismo durante la Edad Média en la Península Ibérica*. Edited by Horacio Santiago-Otero. S.I.E.P.M. 3. Turnholt: Brepols, 1994. Pp. 289–308.

d'Alverny, Marie-Thérèse. "Deux traductions latines du Coran au Moyen Age." *Archives d'histoire doctrinale et littéraire du Moyen Age* 16 (1948): 69–131. Repr. in *La connaissance de l'Islam dans l'Occident médiéval*. Edited by Charles Burnett. Aldershot, Hampshire: Variorum, 1994.

_____. "La connaissance de l'Islam en Occident du IXe au milieu du XIIe siècle." In *Settimane di studio del Centro italiano di studi sull'alto medioevo 12: L'Occidente e l'Islam nell'alto medioevo, Spoleto 2–8 aprile 1964*. Spoleto, 1965. 2: 577–602. Repr. in *La connaissance de l'Islam dans l'Occident médiéval*. Edited by Charles Burnett. Aldershot, Hampshire: Variorum, 1994.

_____. "Pseudo-Aristotle, *De elementis*." In *Pseudo-Aristotle in the Middle Ages: The Theology and Other Texts*. Edited by Jill Kraye, W. F. Ryan, and C. B. Schmitt. London: The Warburg Institute, 1986. Pp. 63–83.

de Bustamante, José Manuel Díaz. "El sistema retorico antiquo en la *Disciplina Clericalis* de Pedro Alfonso." In *Estudios sobre Pedro Alfonso de Huesca*. Edited by María Jesús Lacarra. Colección de Estudios Altoaragoneses 41. Huesca: Instituto de Estudios Altoaragoneses, 1996. Pp. 261–74.

Dolader, Miguel Ángel Motis. "Contexto histórico-jurídico de los judíos del reino de Aragón (siglos XI–XII): pluralidad normativa y preconfiguración de las aljamas." In *Estudios sobre Pedro Alfonso de Huesca*. Edited by María Jesús Lacarra. Colección de Estudios Altoaragoneses 41. Huesca: Instituto de Estudios Altoaragoneses, 1996. Pp. 49–146.

Ducay, María Jesús Lacarra. "La renovación de las artes liberales en Pedro Alfonso: El papel innovador de un judío converso en el siglo XII." In *De Toledo a Huesca: Sociedades medievales en transición a finales del siglo XI (1080–1100)*. Edited by Carlos Laliena Corbera and Juan F. Utrilla Utrilla. Zaragoza: Institución 'Fernando el Católico,' 1998. Pp. 131–39.

Eidelberg, Shlomo, trans. *The Jews and the Crusaders: The Hebrew Chronicles of the First and Second Crusades*. Madison, WI: University of Wisconsin Press, 1977.

Ell, Stephen R. "Blood and Sexuality in Medieval Leprosy." *Janus: Revue internationale de l'histoire des sciences, de la médicine de la pharmacie et de la technique* 71: 1–4 (1984): 153–64.

Elukin, Jonathan M. "The Discovery of the Self: Jews and Conversion in the Twelfth Century." In *Jews and Christians in Twelfth-Century Europe*. Edited by Michael A. Signer and John Van Engen. Notre Dame Conferences in Medieval Studies 10. Notre Dame, IN: University of Notre Dame Press, 2001. Pp. 63–76.

Fahd, Toufy. "De Petrus Alfonsi à Idris Shah." *Revue des études islamiques* 41 (1973): 165–79.

Ferre, Lola. "The Place of Scientific Knowledge in Some Spanish Jewish Authors." In *Micrologus. Natura, scienze e società medievali/Nature, Sciences, and Medieval Societies*. Vol. 9: *Gli Ebrei e le scienze/The Jews and the Sciences*. Sismel: Edizioni de Galluzzo, 2001. Pp. 21–34.

Foa, Anna. "The Witch and the Jew: Two Alikes that Were Not the Same." In *From Witness to Witchcraft: Jews and Judaism in Medieval Christian Thought*. Edited by Jeremy Cohen. Wolfenbütteler Mittelalter-Studien 11. Wiesbaden: Harrassowitz Verlag, 1996. Pp. 361–74.

Fonrobert, Charlotte Elisheva. "Yalta's Ruse: Resistance Against Rabbinic Menstrual Authority in Talmudic Literature." In *Women and Water: Menstruation in Jewish Life and Law*. Edited by Rahel R. Wasserfall. Hanover and London: Brandeis University Press, 1999. Pp. 60–81.

Freudenthal, Gad. "The Place of Science in Medieval Jewish Communities." In *Rashi 1040–1090. Hommage à Ephraïm E. Urbach*. Edited by Gabrielle Sed-Rajna. Paris: Les Éditions du Cerf, 1993. Pp. 599–613.

Friedman, John Block. *The Monstrous Races in Medieval Art and Thought*. Syracuse: Syracuse University Press, 2000.

Friedman, Yvonne. "Anti-Talmudic Invective from Peter the Venerable to Nicolas Donin (1144–1244)." In *Le brûlement du Talmud à Paris 1242–1244*. Edited by Gilbert Dahan. Paris: Les Éditions du Cerf, 1999. Pp. 171–90.

Funkenstein, Amos. *Perceptions of Jewish History*. Berkeley, Los Angeles, Oxford: University of California Press, 1993.

Ginzberg, Louis. *The Legends of the Jews*. Translated by Henrietta Szold. 7 vols. Philadelphia: Jewish Publication Society, 1968.

Goldstein, Bernard R. "Astronomy and the Jewish Community in Early Islam." *Aleph* 1 (2001): 17–57.

Goodich, Michael, ed. *The Other Middle Ages: Witnesses at the Margins of Medieval Society*. Philadelphia, PA: University of Pennsylvania Press, 1998.

Grabois, Aryeh. "The *Hebraica veritas* and Jewish-Christian Intellectual Relations in the Twelfth Century." *Speculum* 50 (1975): 613–35.

Grant, Barbara Hurwitz. "Ambivalence in Medieval Religious Polemics: The Influence of Multiculturalism on the *Dialogues* of Petrus Alfonsi." In *Languages of Power in Islamic Spain*. Edited by Ross Brann. Occasional Publications of the Department of Near Eastern Studies and the Program of Jewish Studies Cornell University 3. Bethesda, MD: CDL Publications, 1997. Pp. 156–77.

Grayzel, Solomon. *The Church and the Jews in the XIIIth Century*. Rev. ed. New York: Hermon Press, 1966.

Gregg, Joan Young. *Devils, Women, and Jews: Reflections of the Other in Medieval Sermon Stories*. Albany: SUNY Press, 1997.

Gudiol, A. Durán, and E. Zaragoza. "Huesca." *Dictionnaire d'histoire et de géographie ecclésiastiques*. Edited by R. Aubert. Vol. 25. Paris: Letouzey et Ané, 1995. Pp. 110–24.

Haverkammp, Alfred. "Baptised Jews in German Lands during the Twelfth Century." In *Jews and Christians in Twelfth-Century Europe*. Edited by Michael A. Signer and John Van Engen. Notre Dame Conferences in Medieval Studies 10. Notre Dame, IN: University of Notre Dame Press, 2001. Pp. 255–310.

Hoffmann, Joseph. *Jesus Outside the Gospels*. New York: Prometheus Books, 1984.

Hunt, Richard William. "The Disputation of Peter of Cornwall Against Symon the Jew." In *Studies in Medieval History Presented to Frederick Maurice Powicke*. Edited by R. W. Hunt, et al. Oxford: Clarendon Press, 1948. Pp. 143–56.

Jódar-Estrella, C. "La interpretación de Is. 7, 14 en el *Diálogo* de Pedro Alfonso y su fundamentación hermenéutica." *Cristianesimo nella storia: richerche storiche esegetiche teologiche* 22/2 (1999): 275–98.

Jolivet, Jean. "Abélard et le philosophe (occident et Islam aux XIIe siècle)." *Revue de l'histoire des religions* 164 (1963): 181–89.

Kedar, Benjamin Z. "Canon Law and the Burning of the Talmud." *Bulletin of Medieval Canon Law* 9 (1979): 78–83.

_____. *Crusade and Mission: European Approaches toward the Muslims*. Princeton, NJ: Princeton University Press, 1984.

Kieckhefer, Richard. *Magic in the Middle Ages*. Cambridge: Cambridge University Press, 1993.

Kniewasser, Manfred. "Die antijüdische Polemik des Petrus Alphonsi (getauft 1106) und des Abtes Petrus Venerabilis von Cluny (d. 1156)." *Kairos: Zeitschrift für Religionswissenschaft und Theologie* 22/1–2 (1980): 34–76.

Koningsveld, P. Sj. van. "Historische betrekkingen tussen moslims en christenen." In *Petrus Alfonsi, een 12de eeuwse schakel tussen islam en christendom in Spanje.* Edited by P. Sj. van Koningsveld. Nijmegen, 1982. Pp. 127–46.

————. "La apologia de Al-Kindi en la Espana del siglo XII. Huellas toledanas de un 'Animal disputax'." In *Estudios sobre Alfonso VI y la Reconquista de Toledo. Actes del II Congreso Internacional de Estudios Mozárabes (Toledo, 20–26 Mayo 1985).* Series historica 5. Toledo: Instituto de Estudios Visigótico-Mozárabes, 1989. Pp. 107–29.

Kritzeck, James. *Peter the Venerable and Islam.* Princeton, NJ: Princeton University Press, 1964.

Langmuir, Gavin I. "The Faith of Christians and Hostility to Jews." In *Christianity and Judaism. Papers Read at the 1991 Summer Meeting and the 1992 Winter Meeting of the Ecclesiastical History Society.* Edited by Diana Wood. Oxford: Blackwell Publishers, 1992. Pp. 77–92.

Lasker, Daniel J. "Jewish Philosophical Polemics in Ashkenaz." In *Contra Iudaeos. Ancient and Medieval Polemics Between Christians and Jews.* Edited by Ora Limor and Guy G. Stroumsa. Tübingen: J. C. B. Mohr, 1996. Pp. 195–213.

————. "Jewish-Christian Polemics at the Turning Point: Jewish Evidence from the Twelfth Century." *Harvard Theological Review* 89/2 (1996): 161–73.

————. "Karaite Attitudes towards Religion and Science." In *Torah et science: perspectives historiques et théoriques. Études offertes à Charles Touati.* Edited by Gad Freudenthal, Jean-Pierre Rothschild, and Gilbert Dahan. Paris: Peeters, 2001. Pp. 119–30.

————. "Karaite Judaism." In *The Encyclopedia of Judaism.* Edited by Jacob Neusner, Alan J. Avery-Peck, and William Scott Green. Vol. 4, supp. 1. Leiden and Boston: E. J. Brill, 2003. Pp. 1808–21.

Lazarus-Yafeh, Hava. *Intertwined Worlds: Medieval Islam and Bible Criticism.* Princeton, NJ: Princeton University Press, 1992.

Lévy, Tony. "Les débuts de la littérature mathématique hébraïque: la géométrie d'Abraham bar Hiyya (XIᵉ–XIIᵉ siècle)." In *Micrologus. Natura, scienze e società medievali/Nature, Sciences, and Medieval Societies.* Vol. 9: *Gli Ebrei e le scienze/The Jews and the Sciences.* Sismel: Edizioni de Galluzzo, 2001. Pp. 35–64.

Limor, Ora. "Christian Sacred Space and the Jew." In *From Witness to Witchcraft: Jews and Judaism in Medieval Christian Thought.* Edited by Jeremy Cohen. Wolfenbütteler Mittelalter-Studien 11. Wiesbaden: Harrassowitz Verlag, 1996. Pp. 55–77.

————. "The Epistle of Rabbi Samuel of Morocco: A Best-Seller in the World of Polemics." In *Contra Iudaeos. Ancient and Medieval Polemics Between Christians and Jews.* Edited by Ora Limor and Guy G. Stroumsa. Tübingen: J. C. B. Mohr, 1996. Pp. 177–94.

Lockshin, Martin I. "Tradition or Context: Two Exegetes Struggle with Peshat." In *From Ancient Israel to Modern Judaism: Intellect in Quest of Understanding; Essays in Honor of Marvin Fox.* Edited by Jacob Neusner,

Ernest S. Frerichs, and Nahum M. Sarna. Vol. 2. Atlanta, GA: Scholars Press, 1989. Pp. 173–86.

Lotter, Friedrich. "Imperial versus Ecclesiastical Jewry Law in the High Middle Ages: Contradictions and Controversies Concerning the Conversion of Jews and their Serfs." In *Proceedings of the Tenth World Congress of Jewish Studies, Jerusalem, August 16–24, 1989.* Edited by David Assaf. 7 vols. Jerusalem: World Union of Jewish Studies, 1990. BII: 53–60.

Maccoby, Hyam, ed. and trans. *Judaism on Trial: Jewish-Christian Disputations in the Middle Ages.* London: Littman Library of Jewish Civilization, 1993.

_____. *Ritual and Morality: The Ritual Purity System and its Place in Judaism.* Cambridge: Cambridge University Press, 1999.

Mercier, Raymond. "Astronomical Tables in the Twelfth Century." In *Adelard of Bath: An English Scientist and Arabist of the Early Twelfth Century.* Edited by Charles Burnett. London: The Warburg Institute, 1987. Pp. 87–118.

Millás Vallicrosa, J. M. "La Aportación astronómica de Pedro Alfonso." *Sefarad* 3 (1943): 65–105.

Miquel, André. *La géographie humaine du monde musulman jusqu'au milieu du 11ᵉ siècle.* 4 vols. Paris: Mouton & Co., 1967–88. Vol. 2, *Géographie arabe et représentation du monde: la terre et l'étranger.*

Monnot, Guy. "Les citations coraniques dans le 'Dialogus' de Pierre Alphonse." In *Cahiers de Fanjeaux, Collection d'histoire religieuse du Languedoc au XIIIᵉ et au début du XIVᵉ siècle.* Vol. 18: *Islam et chrétiens du Midi (XIIᵉ–XIVᵉ S.).* Edited by Edouard Privat. Fanjeaux: Centre d'Études Historiques de Fanjeaux, 1983. Pp. 261–77.

Munoz Sendino, José. "Al-Kindi, Apologia del Cristianismo." *Miscellanea Comillas* 11–12 (1949): 337–460.

Murdoch, John E. *Album of Science: Antiquity and the Middle Ages.* New York: Charles Scribner's Sons, 1984.

Nedelcou, C. "Sur la date de naissance de Pierre Alphonse." *Romania* 35 (1906): 462–63.

Nemoy, Leon. "Al-Qirqisānī's Account of the Jewish Sects and Christianity." *Hebrew Union College Annual* 7 (1930): 317–97.

Neugebauer, Otto. *The Astronomical Tables of al-Khwârizmî. Translated with Commentaries of the Latin Version.* Copenhagen: Munksgaard, 1962.

Pearson, Brook W. R., and Felicity Harley. "Resurrection in Jewish-Christian Apocryphal Gospels and Early Christian Art." In *Christian-Jewish Relations through the Centuries.* Edited by Stanley E. Porter and Brook W. R. Pearson. Sheffield: Sheffield Academic Press, 2000. Pp. 69–92.

Pelikan, Jaroslav. "Hebraica Veritas." In *From Witness to Witchcraft: Jews and Judaism in Medieval Christian Thought.* Edited by Jeremy Cohen. Wolfenbütteler Mittelalter-Studien 11. Wiesbaden: Harrassowitz Verlag, 1996. Pp. 11–28.

Peters, Edward, ed. *The First Crusade: The Chronicle of Fulcher of Chartres and Other Source Materials.* Philadelphia: University of Pennsylvania Press, 1971.

Pichon, Geneviève. "Essai sur la lèpre du haut moyen age." *Le moyen âge* 90: 3–4 (1984): 331–56.

Po-Chia Hsia, Ronnie. "Witchcraft, Magic, and the Jews in Late Medieval and Early Modern Germany." In *From Witness to Witchcraft: Jews and Judaism in Medieval Christian Thought.* Edited by Jeremy Cohen. Wolfenbütteler Mittelalter-Studien 11. Wiesbaden: Harrassowitz Verlag, 1996. Pp. 419–33.

Quillet, H. "Croix (Adoration de la)." In *Dictionnaire de théologie catholique.* Edited by A. Vacant and E. Mangenot. Vol. 3. Paris: Letouzey et Ané, 1908. Pp. 2342–45.

Reinhardt, Klaus, and Horacio Santiago-Otero. "Pedro Alfonso. Obras y Bibliografía." In *Estudios sobre Pedro Alfonso de Huesca.* Edited by María Jesús Lacarra. Colección de Estudios Altoaragoneses 41. Huesca: Instituto de Estudios Altoaragoneses, 1996. Pp. 19–44.

Rembaum, Joel E. "The Talmud and the Popes: Reflections on the Talmud Trials of the 1240's." *Viator* 13 (1982): 203–23.

Resnick, Irven. "Talmud, *Talmudisti*, and Albert the Great." *Viator* 33 (2002): 69–86.

_____. "Humoralism and Adam's Body: Twelfth-Century Debates and Petrus Alfonsi's *Dialogus contra Judaeos.*" *Viator* 36 (2005): 181–95.

Reuter, J. H. L. *Petrus Alfonsi: An Examination of his Works, their Scientific Content and Background.* D. Phil. Oxford University, 1975.

Richards, Jeffrey. *Sex, Dissidence and Damnation: Minority Groups in the Middle Ages.* New York: Barnes and Noble, 1990.

Riley-Smith, Jonathan. *The First Crusade and the Idea of Crusading.* Philadelphia: University of Pennsylvania Press, 1986.

Romano, David. "Mošé Sefardí (= Pedro Alfonso) y la ciencia de origen árabe." In *Estudios sobre Pedro Alfonso de Huesca.* Edited by María Jesús Lacarra. Colección de Estudios Altoaragoneses 41. Huesca: Instituto de Estudios Altoaragoneses, 1996. Pp. 367–80.

Ron, Zvi. "The Priestly Blessing; Hands of the *Kohen.*" *Journal of Jewish Music and Liturgy* 21 (1998–1999): 1–5.

Rosenthal, Erwin I. J. "Anti-Christian Polemic in Medieval Bible Commentaries." *Journal of Jewish Studies* 11 (1960): 116–35.

Rosenthal, Judah M. "The Talmud on Trial. The Disputation at Paris in the Year 1240." *Jewish Quarterly Review*, n.s. 47 (1956): 58–76; 145–69.

Samsó, Julio. "Andalusian Astronomy: Its Main Characteristics and Influence in the Latin West." In his *Islamic Astronomy and Medieval Spain.* Aldershot: Variorum, 1994. Pp. 1–23.

Saperstein, Marc. *Decoding the Rabbis: A Thirteenth-Century Commentary on the Aggadah.* Cambridge, MA: Harvard University Press, 1980.

Schmitz, Rolf. "Jacob ben Rubén y su obra Milhamot ha-Šem." In *Polémica Judeo-Cristiana: Estudios.* Edited by Carlos del Valle Rodríguez. Madrid: Aben Ezra Ediciones, 1992. Pp. 45–58.

Schoonheim, Pieter L. *Aristotle's* Meteorology *in the Arabic-Latin Tradition: A Critical Edition of the Texts with Introduction and Indices.* Leiden, Boston, Cologne: Brill, 2000.

Schreckenberg, Heinz. "Abner v. Burgos." In *Lexikon für Theologie und Kirche*. Vol. 1. Freiburg: Herder, 1993. P. 59.

Schubert, Kurt. "Das christlich-jüdische Religionsgespräch im 12. und 13. Jahrhundert." In *Die Juden in ihrer mittelalterlichen Umwelt*. Edited by Alfred Ebenbauer and Klaus Zatloukal. Cologne: Böhlau, 1991. Pp. 223–50.

Sela, Shlomo. "Abraham ibn Ezra's Special Strategy in the Creation of a Hebrew Scientific Terminology." In *Micrologus. Natura, scienze e società medievali/Nature, Sciences, and Medieval Societies*. Vol. 9, *Gli Ebrei e le scienze/The Jews and the Sciences*. Sismel: Edizioni de Galluzzo, 2001. Pp. 65–87.

Septimus, Bernard. "Petrus Alfonsi on the Cult at Mecca." *Speculum* 56/3 (1981): 517–33.

Shatzmiller, Joseph. "Jewish Converts to Christianity in Medieval Europe, 1200–1500." In *Cross Cultural Convergences in the Crusader Period: Essays Presented to Aryeh Grabois on his Sixty-Fifth Birthday*. Edited by Michael Goodich et. al. New York: 1995. Pp. 297–318.

Simonsohn, Shlomo. *The Apostolic See and the Jews*. 8 vols. Toronto: Pontifical Institute of Mediaeval Studies, 1988–1991.

Smolak, Kurt. "Die Juden als Mittler I: Petrus Alphonsi als Vermittler zwischen Judentum und Christentum und Übermittler orientalisch-arabischer Weisheit." In *Die Juden in ihrer mittelalterlichen Umwelt: Protokolle einer Ring-Vorlesung gehalten im Sommersemester 1989 an der Universität Wien*. Edited by Helmut Birkhan. Vol. 33. Bern, Berlin, Vienna: Peter Lang, 1992. Pp. 79–96.

————. "Petrus Alphonsi als Mittler zwischen lateinisch-christlicher Tradition und orientalisch-arabischer Weisheit." In *Die Juden in ihrer mittelalterlichen Umwelt*. Edited by Alfred Ebenbauer and Klaus Zatloukal. Vienna, Cologne, Weimar: Böhlau Verlag, 1991. Pp. 261–74.

Southern, R. W. *Western Views of Islam in the Middle Ages*. Cambridge, MA: Harvard University Press, 1962.

Stacey, Robert C. "The Conversion of Jews to Christianity in Thirteenth-Century England." *Speculum* 67/2 (1992): 263–83.

Stern, David, and Mark Jay Mirsky, editors and translators. *Rabbinic Fantasies: Imaginative Narratives from Classical Hebrew Literature*. Philadelphia and New York: Jewish Publication Society, 1990.

Stone, Gregory. "Ramon Llull vs. Petrus Alfonsi: Postmodern Liberalism and the Six Liberal Arts." *Medieval Encounters* 3/1 (1997): 70–93.

Stroumsa, Gedaliahu G. "Forms of God: Some Notes on Metatron and Christ." *Harvard Theological Review* 76 (1983): 269–88.

Swartz, Merlin, editor and translator. *A Medieval Critique of Anthropomorphism: Ibn al-Jawzī's* Kitāb Akhbār as-Sifāt. Leiden: Brill, 2002.

Talmage, Frank. "An Hebrew Polemical Treatise. Anti-Cathar and Anti-Orthodox." *Harvard Theological Review* 60 (1967): 323–48.

Taylor, Barry. "La sabiduría de Pedro Alfonso: la *Disciplina Clericalis*." In *Estudios sobre Pedro Alfonso de Huesca*. Edited by María Jesús Lacarra. Colección de Estudios Altoaragoneses 41. Huesca: Instituto de Estudios Altoaragoneses, 1996. Pp. 291–312.

Tena, Pedro Tena. "Una versión incunabula hispana de los *Diálogos contra los Judios* de Pedro Alfonso." *Sefarad: Revista de Estudios Hebraicos* 57/1 (1997): 179–94.

Thorndike, Lynn. *A History of Magic and Experimental Science.* 8 vols. New York: Macmillan and Columbia University Press, 1923–1958.

Timmer, David. "Biblical Exegesis in the Jewish-Christian Controversy in the Early Twelfth-Century." *Church History* 58 (1989): 309–21.

Tolan, John V. "Rhetoric, Polemics and the Art of Hostile Biography: Portraying Muhammad in Thirteenth-Century Christian Spain." In *Pensamiento medieval Hispano: Homenaje a Horacio Santiago-Otero.* Vol. 2. Madrid: Consejo superior de investigaciones científicas consejreía de educación y cultura de la junta de Castilla y León Diputación de Zamora, 1998. Pp. 1497–1511.

————. "La *Epístola a los peripatéticos de Francia* de Pedro Alfonso." In *Estudios sobre Pedro Alfonso de Huesca.* Edited by María Jesús Lacarra. Colección de Estudios Altoaragoneses 41. Huesca: Instituto de Estudios Altoaragoneses, 1996. Pp. 381–402.

————. *Petrus Alfonsi and his Medieval Readers.* Gainesville: University Press of Florida, 1993.

————. *Saracens: Islam in the Medieval European Imagination.* New York: Columbia University Press, 2002.

Trautner-Kromann, Hanne. "Jewish Criticism of the Morals and the Way of Life of the Christians in the Late Middle Ages." In *Proceedings of the Tenth World Congress of Jewish Studies, Jerusalem, August 16–24, 1989.* Edited by David Assaf. 7 vols. Jerusalem: World Union of Jewish Studies, 1990. BII: 69–75.

————. *Shield and Sword: Jewish Polemics Against Christianity and the Christians in France and Spain from 1100–1500.* Tübingen: J. C. B. Mohr, 1993.

Valle Rodríguez, Carlos del. "Jacob ben Ruben de Huesca. Polemista. Su patria y su época." In *Polémica Judeo-Cristiana: Estudios.* Edited by Carlos del Valle Rodríguez. Madrid: Aben Ezra Ediciones, 1992. Pp. 59–65.

————. "Las Guerras del Señor, de Jacob ben Ruben de Huesca." In *La controversia judeocristiana en España (desde los orígenes hasta el siglo XIII). Homenaje a Domingo Muñoz León.* Madrid: Consejo superior de investigaciones científicas instituto de filología, 1998. Pp. 223–33.

————. "El Libro del Néstor el Sacerdote." In *La controversia judeocristiana en España (desde los orígenes hasta el siglo XIII). Homenaje a Domingo Muñoz León.* Madrid: Consejo superior de investigaciones científicas instituto de filología, 1998. Pp. 191–200.

————. "Pedro Alfonso y su Dialogo." In *La controversia judeocristiana en España (desde los orígenes hasta el siglo XIII). Homenaje a Domingo Muñoz León.* Madrid: Consejo superior de investigaciones científicas instituto de filología, 1998. Pp. 201–22.

Vernet, F. "Juifs (Controverses avec les), de 1100 à 1500." In *Dictionnaire de théologie catholique.* Edited by A. Vacant, E. Mangenot, and E. Amann. Vol. 8. Paris: Letouzey et Ané, 1924. P. 1894.

Watt, Jack. "Parisian Theologians and the Jews: Peter Lombard and Peter Cantor." In *The Medieval Church: Universities, Heresy, and the Religious Life. Essays in Honor of Gordon Leff.* Edited by Peter Biller and Barrie Dobson. Woodbridge, Suffolk, UK, and Rochester, NY: Boydell Press for the Ecclesiastical History Society, 1999. Pp. 55–76.

Williams, A. Lukyn. *Adversus Judaeos: A Bird's Eye View of Christian* Apologiae *Until the Renaissance.* Cambridge: University Press, 1935.

Wolf, Kenneth Baxter. "Christian Views of Islam in Early Medieval Spain." In *Medieval Christian Perceptions of Islam.* Edited by John Victor Tolan. New York and London: Routledge, 1996. Pp. 85–108.

Wolfson, Elliot R. "Martyrdom, Eroticism, and Asceticism in Twelfth-Century Ashkenazi Piety." In *Jews and Christians in Twelfth-Century Europe.* Edited by Michael A. Signer and John Van Engen. Notre Dame Conferences in Medieval Studies 10. Notre Dame, IN: University of Notre Dame Press, 2001. Pp. 171–220.

Zias, Joseph. "Lust and Leprosy: Confusion or Correlation?" *Bulletin of the American Schools of Oriental Research* 275 (1989): 27–31.

INTRODUCTION

INTRODUCTION

Petrus Alfonsi's *Dialogus contra Iudaeos*,[1] composed ca. 1109, continues a long history of Christian anti-Jewish polemic.[2] When written, it could draw on nearly one thousand years of literary attacks on Jewish religious life and practice written in Greek, Latin, and Syriac, which collectively constitute what is known as *adversus Iudaeos* literature. Nearly every important Christian theologian seemed compelled to write an attack on Judaism that was also simultaneously a justification of the claims made by Christianity. Indeed, one should not assume that these texts were written primarily in an effort to convert Jews to Christianity, since in most cases they would have been inaccessible, or incomprehensible, to a Jewish audience. Rather, most often they seek to confirm Christian doctrines by explicating those biblical texts—especially prophetic texts—that seemed to support the messianic claims made

1. The title to this work is variously given as *Dialogus* or *Dialogi* (that is, singular or plural) in the manuscript tradition. Since the work contains twelve separate sections or *tituli*, and since these were sometimes copied separately, one can understand why they may have circulated as *Dialogi*. But since we see the twelve *tituli* as forming a single whole, we shall refer to the work throughout in the singular, as the *Dialogus* or *Dialogue Against the Jews*.

2. 1109 is based on a calculation generated by Alfonsi's remark that at the time that he wrote the Jews had already completed 1040 years in exile from the destruction of the Second Temple. Spanish Jews typically understood the destruction to have occurred in 69 C.E., the date accepted by Abraham bar Hayya, one of Alfonsi's Jewish contemporaries. If Alfonsi was using the Christian reckoning rather than the Jewish, which would have accepted either 68 or 70 C.E. as the date of the Temple's destruction, then the work could have been written in 1108 or 1110. For a discussion of this calculation, see Carlos del Valle Rodríguez, "Pedro Alfonso y su Dialogo," in *La controversia judeocristiana en España (desde los orígenes hasta el siglo XIII). Homenaje a Domingo Muñoz León* (Madrid: Consejo superior de investigaciones científicas instituto de filología, 1998), 207. Another piece of evidence supporting 1109 as the date of composition stems from the author's reference to his baptismal sponsor, the Emperor Alfonso. It is usually assumed that this is a reference to the Aragonese Alfonso I the Battler. But Alfonso I was named emperor only upon the death of Alfonso VI, king of Castilla and León, in 1109.

on behalf of Jesus and the Church's proclamation that it, and not the Jews, constituted the New Israel covenanted to God and made heir to his promises. Such an argument, however, depended on an exclusionary dialectic: to prove that Christians were the people of God, it was necessary to prove that Jews were not.

Adversus Iudaeos literature, then, is necessarily a genre rooted in conflict.[3] This conflict was quite specific to the unique relationship between these two communities. Although in the early Church there existed a similar literature that carried the battle standard against pagan cults, by the early fifth century, when the Roman Empire had become officially a Christian and no longer a pagan empire, the classical pagan cults ceased to be a meaningful threat. Once the statue to Victory had been expelled from the Roman Senate and cast into the Tiber River, paganism was no longer a real or symbolic danger. And while the Church continued to battle what it perceived to be the remnants of pagan thought expressed by a variety of Christian heresies, the threat from individual heresies was rarely lasting. With the assistance of the secular arm of government, the Church successfully suppressed or expelled one heretical group after another. At worst, these groups established rival Christian communities beyond the reach of the orthodox world, as did the Nestorians in Persia. But the danger from these previously internal enemies could be controlled although it could never be wholly eliminated.

The Jews, however, enjoyed a unique relationship to western Christendom. This relationship was rooted in part in a familial bond between the two communities: Judaism was in one sense the mother to Christianity. From the Jews, Christians appropriated a sacred literature and made it their own, and from Judaism, Christianity adopted a messianic and apocalyptic eschatology that understood history in terms of a progress (even if not always steady progress) toward the goal of God's final victory over the forces of evil in the world. In this plan the people of Israel occupied a central place. But precisely because Jews and Christians disagreed over the interpretation of their shared sacred texts, and because they disagreed over which of the two

---

3. Still useful for its summaries is A. Lukyn Williams, *Adversus Judaeos: A Bird's Eye View of Christian* Apologiae *Until the Renaissance* (Cambridge: University Press, 1935). For his discussion of Petrus Alfonsi, see 233–40.

communities genuinely represented the people of Israel in the course of the divine plan, they could not recognize one another as truly tied by bonds of either blood or marriage. Yet, too, because they shared so much property in common, they remained locked in a long struggle over ownership. It bears repeating that Christians in antiquity and the Middle Ages did not feel the need to write anti-Buddhist polemics, for example, because Buddhism was hardly a present threat.[4]

The Jews, however, remained a potent, present, internal threat. They could not simply be violently suppressed, like so many pagan cults or Christian heresies. Jews were understood to have a continuing and positive theological role to play in western Christendom. They were, as Jeremy Cohen has so ably demonstrated, "living letters of the law."[5] As Augustine insisted, it was the Jews, as guardians of the Old Testament, who stood proof to the pagan world that Christians had not forged or fabricated their texts that spoke so eloquently to them of the messiah, Jesus. Moreover, it was the Jews, exiled from their land and living in misery in Christian lands, whose historical condition attested to Christian triumph, now and in the future. Finally, it was the Jews (or at least some Jews) who, it had been foretold, would convert at the end time and acknowledge the Christian messiah. Consequently, although undoubtedly the majority of Jews had been rejected by God, as a whole the Jews nevertheless must not be destroyed. As a result, Augustine understands that it is to the Jews that one must apply Ps 59.11: "Slay them not lest my people forget, scatter them by thy power and bring them down, O Lord our shield."[6] They have been conquered, he adds, by the Romans and lost their

4. It bears mention, however, that, since thirteenth-century mendicants missionized among eastern peoples, we do have a record of a religious debate between a Christian, Muslims, and a Buddhist, conducted by the Flemish mendicant William of Rubroek [or Rubruck], whom the French King Louis IX had dispatched to the Mongols. William reached the Mongol capital, Karakorum, in 1254, where the debate took place. For a record of this debate, see Anastaas van den Wyngaert, *Sinica franciscana* (Quaracchi-Firenze: Collegium s. Bonaventurae, 1929–). See especially vol. 1, caps. 32–33, pp. 288–98. For a discussion of this text see R. W. Southern, *Western Views of Islam in the Middle Ages* (Cambridge, MA: Harvard University Press, 1962), 47–52.

5. Jeremy Cohen, *Living Letters of the Law: Ideas of the Jew in Medieval Christianity* (Berkeley, Los Angeles, London: University of California Press, 1999).

6. *De civitate Dei* 18.46, ed. Bernard Dombart and Alphonse Kalb, CC SL 48 (Turnholt: Brepols, 1955), 644.

holy city, to which they are even denied access. But the Jews—like Cain—bear a sign that no one should kill them.[7] They bear the sign or mark of the Law and remain necessary for the nations that believe, for in their misery, Augustine insists, God reveals his mercy for the New Israel and reveals the very truth of Christian claims.[8]

This basis for toleration, even if not altogether benign, continued to operate for most Christian writers after Augustine and was institutionalized in papal policy until the later Middle Ages. Certainly, as Augustine also noted, Jews remained enemies in their hearts, and blind to the truth of the Christian mysteries. Yet they retained a place in the divine economy that demanded their survival.[9] For all of these reasons, Jews were to be tolerated in western Christendom. Indeed, they were the only religious minority that enjoyed this peculiar legal privilege. Although some medieval historians today are inclined to identify medieval Jews as merely one "other" within Christendom (a category to which they may assign Jews, heretics, Muslims, prostitutes, homosexuals, lepers, and still other groups),[10] we need to draw a distinction: of all these groups, the Jews were a unique "other" because only they were *theologically necessary* in medieval society.

7. For the roots of the medieval understanding of this mark of Cain, see Gilbert Dahan, "L'exégèse de l'histoire de Caïn et Abel du XIIᵉ au XIVᵉ siècle en Occident," RTAM 49 (1982): 21–89; 50 (1983): 5–68.

8. See Augustine, *Enarrationes in Psalmos LI–C*, 58, 21, ed. E. Dekkers and J. Fraipont, CC SL 39 (Turnholt: Brepols, 1956), p. 744.

9. Commenting on Augustine's perception of the "new Jewish mission," Bernhard Blumenkranz remarked: "L'économie divine a permis aux Juifs de subsister en vue de porter témoignage aux chrétiens. Ce témoignage, ils le portent doublement: d'abord, par les livres de l'Ancien Testament, qu'ils conservent en leur forme primitive et qu'ils peuvent présenter dès que les chrétiens voient soulevée une contestation de leur authenticité. Mais ce témoignage, ils le portent encore par les conditions mêmes de leur survie: par le fait de leur dispersion, et par le fait de leur dégradation." See his "Augustin et les Juifs—Augustin et le Judaïsme," *Recherches augustiniennes* 1 (1958): 239–40.

10. Evidence of this inclination will be found clearly in the materials included in two good anthologies. See *The Other Middle Ages: Witnesses at the Margins of Medieval Society*, ed. Michael Goodich (Philadelphia, PA: University of Pennsylvania Press, 1998), and Jeffrey Richards, *Sex, Dissidence and Damnation: Minority Groups in the Middle Ages* (New York: Barnes and Noble, 1990). See also Joan Young Gregg, *Devils, Women, and Jews: Reflections of the Other in Medieval Sermon Stories* (Albany: SUNY Press, 1997).

Yet as unwilling witnesses to Christian truth, whose continuing devotion to Judaism challenged Christian claims, Jews were a constant irritant. Christian commitment to toleration of Jews was often strained beyond the breaking point, resulting in violence, as occurred following Pope Urban II's call to the first Crusade in 1095.[11] This military adventure directed against the Islamic presence in the Holy Land was preceded, however, by attacks on Jewish communities of the Rhineland. In response to the alternative offered to them of baptism or death, many Jews chose a martyr's death not only for themselves but for their wives and children as well.[12] In retrospect, it is evident that these attacks presaged changes to the Christian-Jewish relationship.

Perhaps the anti-Jewish violence of the first Crusade helps to explain a remarkable increase in the composition of anti-Jewish polemics, whose total number Simonsohn has estimated to reach six hundred.[13] Although there may have been a brief lull in the production of such literature during the tenth and ear-

---

11. For the background and motives behind the first Crusade, see especially Jonathan Riley-Smith, *The First Crusade and the Idea of Crusading* (Philadelphia: University of Pennsylvania Press, 1986). For Latin chronicles of the first Crusade, see *Belli sacri historia*, in *Museum Italicum seu Collectio veterum scriptorum ex bibliothecis italicis*, ed. Johanne Mabillon and Michaele Germain (Paris: Edmund Martin, John Boudot, and Stephen Martin, 1687); for texts in translation, see *The First Crusade: The Chronicle of Fulcher of Chartres and Other Source Materials*, ed. Edward Peters (Philadelphia: University of Pennsylvania Press, 1971).

12. For the Jewish chronicles of these events, see Robert Chazan, *European Jewry and the First Crusade* (Berkeley: University of California Press, 1987); and, *The Jews and the Crusaders: The Hebrew Chronicles of the First and Second Crusades*, trans. Shlomo Eidelberg (Madison, WI: University of Wisconsin Press, 1977). For interpretations of these records, see Jeremy Cohen, "A 1096 Complex? Constructing the First Crusade in Jewish Historical Memory, Medieval and Modern," in *Jews and Christians in Twelfth-Century Europe*, ed. Michael A. Signer and John Van Engen, Notre Dame Conferences in Medieval Studies 10 (Notre Dame, Indiana: University of Notre Dame Press, 2001): 9–26; and, in the same volume, Robert Chazan, "From the First Crusade to the Second: Evolving Perceptions of the Christian-Jewish Conflict," 46–62. For the symbolic significance of martyrdom, see Elliot R. Wolfson, "Martyrdom, Eroticism, and Asceticism in Twelfth-Century Ashkenazi Piety," op. cit., 171–220.

13. Shlomo Simonsohn estimates that, excluding biblical commentaries which may contain extensive anti-Jewish materials, approximately 600 anti-Jewish polemics were written by Christians, although only about 100 have been edited and printed. See his *The Apostolic See and the Jews* (Toronto: Pontifical Institute of Mediaeval Studies, 1991), 8: 287.

ly eleventh centuries,[14] it appears that more anti-Jewish polemics were written in the twelfth century than in all the earlier Christian centuries combined. Not only did their number increase dramatically, but the tactics employed began to evolve as well. As Amos Funkenstein argued, conservative polemicists from the twelfth and thirteenth centuries continued to follow a traditional pattern that entailed the seemingly endless citation of scriptural proof texts in defense of Christian doctrine. In addition, by the beginning of the twelfth century there appear rationalist polemics, whose goal was to convict Jews of error and defend Christian truths by an almost exclusive appeal to philosophical reason.[15] At the same time, although not always in the same texts, we begin to see accusations directed against the Talmud (or more broadly, against post-biblical Jewish literature) as a source of Jewish error, as well as attempts to locate in this same Jewish post-biblical literature implicit recognition of the truth of Christian claims.[16] Finally, I believe we must add another new strategy to those identified by Funkenstein: arguments were drawn from science—from astronomy, medicine, and physics—to overthrow Jewish claims. The twelfth century, then, appears as a crucial period in the history of *adversus Iudaeos* literature.

Alfonsi's Life and Works

In this history, one figure from the early twelfth century looms large: Petrus Alfonsi.[17] Alfonsi's *Dialogus contra Iudaeos*,

14. David Berger identifies St. Peter Damian's anti-Jewish polemic, written between 1040 and 1041, as having revived the tradition. See his "St. Peter Damian: His Attitudes toward the Jews and the Old Testament," *Yavneh* (1965): 80–112, and especially 80–82. Damian's polemic has been translated as *Letter 1* in the first volume of his *Letters*, trans. Owen Blum, FOTC, MC 1 (Washington, DC: The Catholic University of America Press, 1989).

15. One typical example is Odo of Tournai's *Disputatio*. For the text in translation, see my *Two Theological Treatises of Odo of Tournai: On Original Sin, and a Debate With the Jew, Leo, Concerning the Advent of Christ, the Son of God* (Philadelphia: University of Pennsylvania Press, 1994).

16. See Amos Funkenstein, *Perceptions of Jewish History* (Berkeley, Los Angeles, Oxford: University of California Press, 1993), especially chapter 6, "Polemics, Responses, and Self-Reflection," 169–219.

17. As Charles Burnett notes, the best manuscripts of Petrus Alfonsi's *Disciplina clericalis* and *Epistula ad peripateticos Franciae* identify the author as *Petrus Alfunsus/Anfulsus*, with both names in the nominative case. But in the *Dialogus*

for the first time, employs in a single text *all* of the methods or strategies identified above. In one sense, it can also be viewed as a result of anti-Muslim Christian military expansion, for Alfonsi wrote his polemic—the first systematic anti-Jewish polemic written in Spain[18]—perhaps less than a decade after the Muslim town of Huesca, where he lived, had been conquered by the Christian King Pedro I of Aragon in early 1097.

Under Muslim rule, Huesca had been a chief city of the Muslim kingdom of Saragossa and had an important Jewish community. After the death of Sulaimān of the Banū Hūd dynasty (mid-eleventh century) it once again became briefly the capital of an independent principality, ruled by Lope, one of the sons of Sulaimān ibn Hūd, before it was reunited to the kingdom of Saragossa. As a border city, it was subject to frequent incursions by Christian princes to the north who sought to expand their rule. When the Christian kings of Aragon and Navarre grew stronger in the second half of the eleventh century, its situation became serious. Kings of Aragon viewed Huesca as suitable for a capital and an important haven on the road to Saragossa. Sancho Ramirez, King of Aragon (1063–1094), tore district upon district from Huesca, built fortresses near it, and commanded the approaches to the city, so that it was virtually under constant siege. In response, its Muslim rulers strengthened Huesca's fortifications.

In the last third of the eleventh century, Huesca's population totaled only about 4000. Its Jewish community was located outside the stone wall built as a fortification around the city, but

---

he identifies himself as *Petrus Alfunsi* (gen.) and names Alfonso I as his spiritual father. Alfunsi would seem then to be a patronym: Petrus son of Alfunsus. Only a page later, however, the vocative *Petrus Alfunse* appears, suggesting Alfunsus as a nominative form. "This variation between having both names in the same case and having the second name in the genitive probably reflects a Spanish custom. 'Petrus Alfonsi' has become the standard form of the name in modern scholarship written in English, but *Petrus Alfunsus/Alfunsi* would more accurately represent the Latin forms found in the manuscripts"; Charles Burnett, "The Works of Petrus Alfonsi: Questions of Authenticity," *Medium Aevum* 66/1 (1997), 68, n. 1. For the sake of simplicity, I shall refer to our author as Petrus Alfonsi, or merely Alfonsi.

18. Carlos del Valle remarks, "El *Diálogo* de Pedro Alfonso constituye como tal la primera obra de polémica judeocristiana que se escribe en España con un ataque sistemático del judaísmo." See his "Pedro Alfonso y su Dialogo," 215.

within an earthen rampart that extended for some distance to offer protection. At this time, Huesca's Jewish community represented a significant minority and numbered about 250; but its Jewish population was growing, while the Muslim population was in decline as wealthier Muslim families left for more secure areas. Not only did Jews represent about 6% of the town's population, but they also had extensive holdings in real estate. For generations, most Jews of Huesca had earned a livelihood from agriculture—from working their fields and vineyards. Others were modest craftsmen, such as metalsmiths and workers in textiles. Jewish scholars, like their Muslim counterparts, tended to congregate in larger cities where they could find libraries and patrons to support their studies. But an Arabic source names one wealthy, learned Jew of Huesca from the period just before the Christian conquest, Bassān ben Simeon, with whom the Arabic writer recalls having had friendly literary discussions.[19]

The most famous (or infamous) Jew of Huesca is, however, the Jewish convert to Christianity Petrus Alfonsi, whose intellectual interests and education had likely promoted him to an important position within the Jewish community, first under Muslim rulers and later under their Christian successors.[20] Alfonsi tells us that before his conversion to Christianity in 1106, he was known by the name Moses. As a result, scholars subsequently have referred to him as Moses Sefardi or Moses of Sefarad,[21]

19. For this brief description of Huesca, I have relied principally upon Eliayahu Ashtor, *The Jews of Moslem Spain*, trans. Aaron Klein and Jenny Machlowitz Klein (Philadelphia: Jewish Publication Society, 1979), 2: 269–76. See also A. Durán Gudiol and E. Zaragoza, "Huesca," in *Dictionnaire d'histoire et de géographie ecclésiastiques*, ed. R. Aubert, vol. 25 (Paris: Letouzey et Ané, 1995): 110–24. For a contemporary Muslim account of the state of Jewish scientific learning in the kingdom of Saragossa, see also Sa'id al-Andalusi, *Science in the Medieval World: 'Book of the Categories of Nations,'* trans. Sema'an I. Salem and Alok Kumar (Austin: University of Texas Press, 1991), 79–82.

20. For the demographics and cultural characteristics of Jews in Aragon about the time of the Christian conquest, see also Miguel Ángel Motis Dolader, "Contexto histórico-jurídico de los judíos del reino de Aragón (siglos XI–XII): pluralidad normativa y preconfiguración de las aljamas," in *Estudios sobre Pedro Alfonso de Huesca*, ed. María Jesús Lacarra, Colección de Estudios Altoaragoneses 41 (Huesca: Instituto de Estudios Altoaragoneses, 1996), 49–146.

21. *Sefarad* is the Hebrew usually employed to refer to Spain. Thus, Jews of Spanish origin typically are called *sefardim*.

although this tradition seems to have no echo in medieval texts. One can assert unequivocally that Alfonsi received a typical Jewish Andalusian education, with training in Arabic, Hebrew, Jewish religious texts, and secular studies. These secular studies included astronomy,[22] mathematics, and medicine—interests that his Iberian Jewish contemporaries, Abraham ibn Ezra and Abraham bar Hayya, shared.[23] In addition, in his *Dialogue*, written in Latin, Alfonsi defends his mastery of Jewish religious texts and points out that, while still a Jew, he had preached in the synagogues on their proper interpretation, lest some Jews apostatize.[24] But one cannot substantiate the Dominican Raymund

22. For a general introduction to astronomical studies in Andalusia, although without special reference to Petrus Alfonsi, see Julio Samsó, "Andalusian Astronomy: Its Main Characteristics and Influence in the Latin West," in his *Islamic Astronomy and Medieval Spain* (Aldershot: Variorum, 1994), 1–23.

23. Abraham bar Hayya (ca. 1065–ca. 1136) resided in Barcelona and composed a number of important works on geometry, astronomy, and astrology. He also worked with Plato of Tivoli to translate texts of Greek or Arabic science into Latin. For a good introduction to his works, see his *The Meditation of a Sad Soul*, trans. Geoffrey Wigoder (London: Routledge & Kegan Paul, 1969), 1–7. Abraham ibn Ezra (b. 1089/92), may have come from Huesca. In addition to his important role as a biblical exegete, he made significant contributions to mathematics and the sciences. See also Tony Lévy, "Les débuts de la littérature mathématique hébraïque: la géométrie d'Abraham bar Hiyya (XIᵉ–XIIᵉ siècle)," 35–64; and Shlomo Sela, "Abraham ibn Ezra's Special Strategy in the Creation of a Hebrew Scientific Terminology," in *Micrologus. Natura, scienze e società medievali/ Nature, Sciences, and Medieval Societies*, vol. 9, *Gli Ebrei e le scienze/The Jews and the Sciences* (Sismel: Edizioni de Galluzzo, 2001), 65–87.

24. Apostasy was, of course, a grave concern for European Jewish communities. For a general discussion, see Joseph Shatzmiller, "Jewish Converts to Christianity in Medieval Europe, 1200–1500," in *Cross Cultural Convergences in the Crusader Period: Essays Presented to Aryeh Grabois on his Sixty-Fifth Birthday*, ed. Michael Goodich et. al. (New York: Peter Lang Publishing, Inc., 1995), 297–318. See also Jonathan M. Elukin, "The Discovery of the Self: Jews and Conversion in the Twelfth Century," in *Jews and Christians in Twelfth-Century Europe*, ed. Michael A. Signer and John Van Engen, Notre Dame Conferences in Medieval Studies 10 (Notre Dame, Indiana: University of Notre Dame Press, 2001), 63–76. In this same volume, see Alfred Haverkammp, "Baptised Jews in German Lands during the Twelfth Century," 255–310. After Petrus Alfonsi, perhaps the best known twelfth-century Jewish convert to Christianity was Hermann Judaeus, whose autobiographical account can be found in translation in Hermann of Cologne, *A Short Account of His Own Conversion*, in *Conversion and Text: The Cases of Augustine of Hippo, Herman-Judah, and Constantine Tsatsos*, trans. Karl F. Morrison (Charlottesville, VA: University of Virginia Press, 1992), 76–113. If one can correlate the risk of Jewish apostasy with the appearance of Jewish anti-Christian polemics in Europe, then certainly this risk must have been perceived as more serious

Martini's claim, appearing late in the thirteenth century, that Alfonsi was a rabbi, nor is there good evidence for Raymund Martini's claim that after his conversion he entered holy orders.[25]

Nor do we know where he was born, or precisely when. Biographers had once assumed that he was born in 1062, on the basis of a passage in the *Dialogue Against the Jews* where Alfonsi seemingly writes that he was baptized in 1106, 44 years after his birth.[26] But at the beginning of the twentieth century Nedelcou argued convincingly that this is a textual corruption, and that the text should read, "I believed in the blessed apostles and the holy Catholic Church. This occurred on the nativity of the Lord, in the year 1106, the year 1144 [of the Spanish era], in the month of June."[27] Thus he was not baptized 44 years after his birth, but in the year 1144 of the Spanish era. Consequently, Alfonsi provides no information on which to establish his date of birth.[28] One can say only that he must already have been an adult in 1106 at the time of his baptism.

The motive behind his conversion is equally obscure. In one

---

beginning with the twelfth century. See Hanne Trautner-Kromann, *Shield and Sword: Jewish Polemics Against Christianity and the Christians in France and Spain from 1100–1500* (Tübingen: J. C. B. Mohr, 1993); and eadem, "Jewish Criticism of the Morals and the Way of Life of the Christians in the Late Middle Ages," in *Proceedings of the Tenth World Congress of Jewish Studies, Jerusalem, August 16–24, 1989*, ed. David Assaf (Jerusalem: World Union of Jewish Studies, 1990), BII: 69–75.

25. Raymund Martini, *Pugio fidei* 2.3.4 (Leipzig, 1687; repr. Farnsborough, 1967).

26. See *infra*, p. 40.

27. See C. Nedelcou, "Sur la date de naissance de Pierre Alphonse," *Romania* 35 (1906): 462–63. 1062 still appears in some modern treatments, however, as the date of Alfonsi's birth; see, e.g., Kurt Smolak's "Die Juden als Mittler I: Petrus Alphonsi als Vermittler zwischen Judentum und Christentum und Übermittler orientalisch-arabischer Weisheit," in *Die Juden in ihrer mittelalterlichen Umwelt: Protokolle einer Ring-Vorlesung gehalten im Sommersemester 1989 an der Universität Wien*, ed. Helmut Birkhan (Bern, Berlin, Vienna: Peter Lang Publishing, Inc., 1992), 33: 79–80. This article is essentially a reprint of his "Petrus Alphonsi als Mittler zwischen lateinisch-christlicher Tradition und orientalisch-arabischer Weisheit," in *Die Juden in ihrer mittelalterlichen Umwelt*, ed. Alfred Ebenbauer and Klaus Zatloukal (Vienna, Cologne, Weimar: Böhlau Verlag, 1991): 261–74.

28. Dolader also examines the controversy over the date of Alfonsi's birth, for which 1062, 1075, and 1076 have been suggested. See his "Contexto histórico-jurídico de los judíos del reino de Aragón (siglos XI–XII)," p. 50, n. 5.

sense, his *Dialogue* constitutes an elaborate attempt to justify his conversion, after having himself counseled other Jews to avoid apostasy. To do so, he composed a lengthy dialogue in which he appears both as interrogator and respondent. As interrogator, he appears in the *Dialogue* using his Christian name, Petrus; as respondent, he uses his Jewish name, Moses. Thus he explains: "I have divided the entire book into a dialogue, so that the reader's mind may more quickly achieve an understanding. To defend the arguments of the Christians, I have used the name which I have as a Christian, whereas for refuting the arguments of the adversary, I have used the name Moses, the name which I had before baptism." Both because the king served as his godfather, and because he was baptized on the feast day of the apostles Peter and Paul, Moses adopted Petrus Alfonsi as his Christian name.

Although fraught with possibilities for psychological self-examination, in fact the *Dialogue* will disappoint any reader expecting the author to reveal the doubts and vacillation of a tortured soul, of the sort that Saint Augustine displays in his *Confessions*. He reveals no second thoughts, no period of agonized deliberation. He appears fully confident of the truth of Christianity and the errors of Judaism, which he claims to prove using both reason and scriptural authority. He depicts himself as a Jew who made a deliberate, calculated, and voluntary conversion that seems to have been well considered, rather than the result of a sudden mystical transformation.[29] The only clues he provides concerning his motive appear in response to criticisms he attributes to his former co-religionists, who proposed that he had converted because he had badly misunderstood the Mosaic law and the prophetic books, or that he had abandoned his ancestral tradition at the baptismal font to promote his career, perhaps as a physician, at the court of the Christian king, Alfonso I.

It is impossible to know whether these complaints put in the

29. For some attempt to divine Alfonsi's motive, see Jeremy Cohen, "The Mentality of the Medieval Jewish Apostate: Peter Alfonsi, Hermann of Cologne, and Pablo Christiani," in *Jewish Apostasy in the Modern World*, ed. Todd M. Endelman (New York: Holmes & Meier Publishers, Inc., 1987), 20–47.

mouths of Jews actually express the opinions of some of Alfonsi's contemporaries, or whether in fact they do not more properly reflect the expectations of the Christian society which he had joined. On the one hand, Christians clearly understood that in the eyes of the Jews, it was the Christian who misunderstood the Law and the writings of the prophets; on the other hand, Christians insisted that Jews failed to obtain the inner meaning of these texts but were content to read them only superficially and according to the letter. In fact, this Christian perception was somewhat disingenuous: Jews also accepted that passages in Scripture were fraught with levels of meaning, and could be interpreted literally as well as mystically and allegorically. Nevertheless, to subvert christological exegeses, twelfth-century Jewish biblical commentators tended to place most emphasis on the *peshat* or simple sense.[30] This was the result of a deliberate choice, however, rather than a reflection of Jewish intellectual shortcomings. But most twelfth-century Christians thought Jews were unable to rise above the literal interpretation of the text. This conviction conformed to other beliefs that they held, for example, that Jews had become blind to deeper, spiritual meanings because of their carnality, materiality, and venality.[31] When Moses asks for an explanation of the Ascension, after a few brief remarks Alfonsi adds: "To be sure, if I were to treat this with some believer, I would say no more. Whereas because you are without faith, and understand only what is so obvious as to be nearly palpable, I will respond to you a little more explicitly,

30. See Erwin I. J. Rosenthal, "Anti-Christian Polemic in Medieval Bible Commentaries," *Journal of Jewish Studies* 11 (1960): 116–35. For a discussion of Rashbam (R. Samuel ben Meir) and Abraham ibn Ezra as examples of *peshat* exegetes—one from northern France and the other from Spain in the twelfth century—see Martin I. Lockshin, "Tradition or Context: Two Exegetes Struggle with Peshat," in *From Ancient Israel to Modern Judaism: Intellect in Quest of Understanding; Essays in Honor of Marvin Fox*, ed. Jacob Neusner, Ernest S. Frerichs, and Nahum M. Sarna (Atlanta, GA: Scholars Press, 1989), 2: 173–86.

31. See Anna Sapir Abulafia, "Jewish Carnality in Twelfth-Century Renaissance Thought," in *Christianity and Judaism. Papers Read at the 1991 Summer Meeting and the 1992 Winter Meeting of the Ecclesiastical History Society*, ed. Diana Wood (Oxford: Blackwell Publishers, 1992): 59–75. For the increasingly politicized nature of anti-Jewish polemics in the twelfth century (with a focus on Rupert of Deutz), see also David Timmer, "Biblical Exegesis in the Jewish-Christian Controversy in the Early Twelfth-Century," *Church History* 58 (1989): 309–21.

both for this reason and because I desire that thereby you will believe something of the good."[32] The Jew's faithlessness, then, weighs down his reason and prevents it from rising above "what is so obvious as to be nearly palpable."

Carnality and materiality imply not only an alleged intellectual incapacity of Jews to reach the level of a spiritual understanding, but also an overpowering concern for things of this world and its rewards.[33] Alfonsi himself ridicules Jews for holding that in the messianic age they will be returned to the earthly rather than the spiritual Jerusalem, or that after the resurrection they will enjoy once again conditions of physicality. When Alfonsi suggests, then, that it was Jews who suspected that he had converted in order to advance his career, one cannot help but wonder whether this is not in reality a reflection of a certain Christian expectation regarding Jews: that if they convert to Christianity, it may only be for material gain, owing to their essential carnality. This also accords with what we noted above, namely, that the audience for this Latin work was Christian. Alfonsi could likely never really justify his conversion to other Jews. Rather, he may have hoped to establish his *bona fides*—his "good faith," but also his credentials as a good Christian—before an audience that might look upon his conversion with guarded enthusiasm, if not outright suspicion. Christian communities at the beginning of the twelfth century certainly had knowledge of Jews who, having converted during the first Crusade (perhaps under compulsion or from fear of violence), later abandoned Christianity and returned to Judaism once the threat disappeared. Although ecclesiastics might protest that their baptism was binding, secular rulers often permitted this "apostasy." Thus in 1097 Henry IV allowed the Jews of Regensburg who had been converted by force to return to Judaism, as did England's William Rufus for the Jews of Rouen.[34] But "force" and "compulsion" in baptism were still

32. See *infra*, p. 241.

33. At times, the emphasis on the Jews' alleged intellectual inability to grasp higher truths leads one to wonder whether Christian polemicists ever really believed that their arguments could result in the Jew's conversion. For a discussion, see Anna Sapir Abulafia, "Twelfth-Century Christian Expectations of Jewish Conversion: A Case Study of Peter of Blois," *Aschkenas* 8/1 (1998): 45–70.

34. For the tensions between secular and ecclesiastical rulers on this point,

poorly defined canonical categories, and one can easily imagine the paradox that suspicion of Jewish converts was growing
at the very moment when the number of literary polemics, os-
tensibly written to promote their conversion, had dramatically increased. Even though Alfonsi's conversion was apparently
voluntary, his Christian contemporaries may well have experienced disappointment previously over a Jew who contested the
voluntary character of his conversion in order to return to his
ancestral religion. In such a climate, Alfonsi may have felt it ad-
visable to emphasize not only that he freely had chosen Christianity, but also that his choice did not conceal some baser, economic motive.

In fact, in the Middle Ages people changed religion for many
of the same reasons as people do today. When not compelled
by violence, they converted from genuine religious conviction,
possibly because of a romantic liaison with a member of another religious community, or perhaps because of some disagreement with members of their own community, or at some times
for social or economic advancement.[35] Nevertheless, Alfonsi in-

---

see Friedrich Lotter, "Imperial versus Ecclesiastical Jewry Law in the High Middle Ages: Contradictions and Controversies Concerning the Conversion of Jews
and their Serfs," *Proceedings of the Tenth World Congress of Jewish Studies, Jerusalem,
August 16–24, 1989*, ed. David Assaf (Jerusalem: World Union of Jewish Studies,
1990), BII: 53–60.

35. Despite Shatzmiller's remark that "unlike modern times converts, who,
in many instances, were driven by ambitious careerism, medieval converts—with
few exceptions—had very little to gain in this respect. In fact, they had much to
lose, Jews and Muslims alike, by changing religion: feudal law and civil authorities would conceive of their acts as a rebellion. The king who thus lost one of
his 'serfs' and the income he had generated in the past, would now retaliate
and confiscate the converts [*sic*] property"; "Jewish Converts to Christianity in
Medieval Europe, 1200–1500," 311. For thirteenth-century England, at least,
this seems not to have been the case, as it was largely the crown and secular authority that provided institutional support for new converts. See Robert C. Stacey, "The Conversion of Jews to Christianity in Thirteenth-Century England,"
Speculum 67/2 (1992): 263–83. Despite Funkenstein's agreement that the economic position of the Jewish convert often worsened after conversion (see *Perceptions of Jewish History*, 184), it is not clear that this was the case in early twelfth-
century Aragon. Nor should one ignore the repeated papal appeals to church-
men to support financially Jewish converts, so that they would not return to
their former Judaism because of poverty. See Solomon Grayzel, *The Church and
the Jews in the XIIIth Century*, nos. 6, 8, rev. ed. (New York: Hermon Press, 1966),
95, 97–99.

sists that his conversion was instead a simple response to his discovery of religious truth. Moreover, his *Dialogue* also contains an extensive anti-Muslim polemic, which seeks to explain not only why he abandoned Judaism but also why he did not choose to enter the community of Islam. He could easily have done so for, as is clearly evident, he was quite familiar with Islam and certainly was well acquainted with Arabic texts. Indeed, Moses asks: "I wonder why, when you abandoned your paternal faith, you chose the faith of the Christians rather than the faith of the Saracens, with whom you were always associated and raised." Responding to this question, Alfonsi seizes an opportunity not only to demonstrate the superiority of Christianity to Islam, but also to support the integrity of his conversion. Had he become a Christian only to advance his career, why had he not previously converted to Islam for the same reason? Truth alone, he insists, compelled his choice.

After completing his *Dialogue* (and before 1120) the author moved to England, where he may have become a personal physician to King Henry I.[36] He does not tell us *why* he left Spain, but one may conjecture that he perceived new career opportunities in England, or that his *Dialogue* had offended and alienated the Jewish community in Huesca, making his continued presence there uncomfortable. It is quite certain that in England he introduced the new Arabic science—particularly, astronomy and astrology—to a Christian intellectual community still ignorant of it.[37] In England he became a mentor to the astronomer Walcher of Malvern (d. 1135). Walcher's interest in astronomical observation apparently antedated his encounter with Petrus Alfonsi, since in lunar tables he composed between 1107 and 1112 Walcher describes one eclipse that he viewed in Italy in 1091, and another that he observed scientifically, with the aid of an astrolabe, in England in 1092.[38] According to his testimo-

36. Thus is Petrus Alfonsi identified in a fourteenth-century manuscript of his *Dialogus*, Cambridge University MS Ii.6.11, fol. 95.

37. Like Alfonsi, many Jews in Spain were drawn into the Muslim intellectual world by an interest in astrology and astronomy. See Bernard R. Goldstein, "Astronomy and the Jewish Community in Early Islam," *Aleph* 1 (2001): 17–57.

38. Lynn Thorndike, *A History of Magic and Experimental Science* (New York: Macmillan and Columbia University Press, 1923), 2: 68–69.

ny, in *De dracone* (ca. 1120) he translated or reported upon astronomical doctrines he had learned from Petrus Alfonsi.[39] This text examines the times when the orbit of the moon may cross that of the sun—that is, times when an eclipse may occur—and endeavors to create a model that has predictive value. Similarly, Petrus Alfonsi's influence has been discerned in Adelard of Bath's *De opere astrolapsus* as well as in Adelard's introduction to the astronomical tables of al-Khwârizmî.[40]

De dracone is a reminder that although Petrus Alfonsi is remembered principally as a polemicist for his *Dialogue* and as a storyteller for the fables and *exempla* in his popular *Disciplina clericalis*,[41] he saw himself primarily as a scientist, physician, and natural philosopher.[42] The science of the Arab world was widely stud-

39. This text, which Walcher entitled *Sententiae Petri Ebraei . . . de dracone* is perhaps best described as a *reportatio* of a conversation with Petrus Alfonsi, which Walcher "translated," perhaps from the vernacular, into Latin. For the Latin text of *De dracone*, see J. M. Millás Vallicrosa, "La aportación astronómica de Pedro Alfonso," *Sefarad* 3 (1943), Appendix I, 87–97; for a discussion of the text, see in the same work 67–75. Also see especially John Tolan, *Petrus Alfonsi and his Medieval Readers* (Gainesville: University Press of Florida, 1993), 61–66.

40. See Marie-Thérèse d'Alverny, "Pseudo-Aristotle, *De elementis*," in *Pseudo-Aristotle in the Middle Ages: The* Theology *and Other Texts*, ed. Jill Kraye, W. F. Ryan, and C. B. Schmitt (London: The Warburg Institute, 1986), 65; J. H. L. Reuter, *Petrus Alfonsi: An Examination of his Works, their Scientific Content and Background* (D. Phil. diss., Oxford University, 1975), 155–58; Charles Burnett, "The Works of Petrus Alfonsi," 53–54.

41. There is a vast literature on this text, also written after his conversion. For a good introduction, see John Tolan, *Petrus Alfonsi*, 73–94. For modern English translations, see Joseph Ramon Jones and John Esten Keller, trans., *The Scholar's Guide: A Translation of the Twelfth Century* Disciplina clericalis *of Pedro Alfonso* (Toronto: Pontifical Institute of Mediaeval Studies, 1969); and *The* Disciplina Clericalis *of Petrus Alfonsi*, [German] trans. and ed. Eberhard Hermes, trans. into English P. R. Quarrie (London: Routledge Kegan & Paul, 1977). Several recent discussions will be found, too, in the anthology *Estudios sobre Pedro Alfonso de Huesca*, ed. María Jesús Lacarra, Colección de Estudios Altoaragoneses 41 (Huesca: Instituto de Estudios Altoaragoneses, 1996): e.g., José Aragüés Aldaz, "*Fallacia dicta*: narración, palabra y experiencia en la *Disciplina Clericalis*," 235–60; José Manuel Díaz de Bustamante, "El sistema retorico antiquo en la *Disciplina Clericalis* de Pedro Alfonso," 261–74; and Barry Taylor, "La sabiduría de Pedro Alfonso: la *Disciplina Clericalis*," 291–312. Toufy Fahd has remarked that Alfonsi's *Disciplina* was an important "vulgarization" of oriental culture, making it available to a popular audience, that promoted the myth of the Wisdom of the Orient. See his "De Petrus Alfonsi à Idris Shah," *Revue des études islamiques* 41 (1973): 173.

42. Kniewasser remarks, "Seine [Alfonsi's] Beschäftigung mit den Wissen-

ied by Jewish communities in Spain,[43] and it was often through
these—rather than through Iberian Muslim communities—that
it was introduced to the Latin West. The sciences were not as yet
truly experimental disciplines, although authors like Petrus Alfonsi often invoke experience and observation,[44] but they were
certainly attempting to discover a rational order in nature. As
an advocate for the scientific wisdom of the Arab world, Alfonsi
keenly felt the backward nature of the scientific disciplines in
the Latin West. These were, in his eyes, still dependent on the
errors, myths, and fables found in ancient authorities like Macrobius's fifth-century commentary on Cicero's *Somnium Scipionis.*

In yet another work, his *Epistola ad peripateticos,* written some-
time after 1116 and possibly in France, Alfonsi attempts to
persuade French scholars of the importance of astronomy in
general and the superiority of the astronomical doctrines of
the Arabs in particular.[45] In it, he incorporates sections taken
directly from his introduction to the astronomical tables of al-
Khwârizmî[46] (the *Zîj al-Sindhind*), which he had translated.[47] In

schaften liegt in den Übersetzungen astronomischer Werke der Araber ins
Lateinische vor, in astronomischen Traktaten, die auch medizinische Passa-
gen enthalten sowie in den astronomischen Abschnitten und in der Darlegung
eines philosophischen Systems in den 'Dialogen'"; Manfred Kniewasser, "Die
antijüdische Polemik des Petrus Alphonsi (getauft 1106) und des Abtes Petrus
Venerabilis von Cluny (d. 1156)," *Kairos: Zeitschrift für Religionswissenschaft und
Theologie* 22/1–2 (1980): 37.

43. For a brief discussion, see Lola Ferre, "The Place of Scientific Knowledge
in Some Spanish Jewish Authors," in *Micrologus. Natura, scienze e società medievali/
Nature, Sciences, and Medieval Societies,* vol. 9, *Gli Ebrei e le scienze/The Jews and the
Sciences* (Sismel: Edizioni de Galluzzo, 2001), 21–34.

44. See Charles Burnett, "Scientific Speculations," in *A History of Twelfth-
Century Western Philosophy,* ed. Peter Dronke (Cambridge: Cambridge University
Press, 1992), 151–76.

45. For remarks on this work, see John Tolan, *Peter Alfonsi,* 66–72; for the
Latin text and translation, see his Appendix I, 163–81. Also, see John Tolan,
"La *Epístola a los peripatéticos de Francia* de Pedro Alfonso," in *Estudios sobre Pedro
Alfonso de Huesca,* 381–402. Gad Freudenthal has remarked that of all the sciences, it was principally astronomy that interested medieval European Jewish
communities. See his "The Place of Science in Medieval Jewish Communities,"
in *Rashi 1040–1090. Hommage à Ephraïm E. Urbach,* ed. Gabrielle Sed-Rajna (Paris: Les Éditions du Cerf, 1993), 599–613.

46. See Otto Neugebauer, *The Astronomical Tables of al-Khwârizmî. Translated
with Commentaries of the Latin Version* (Copenhagen: Munksgaard, 1962).

47. See Josep Casulleras, "Las *Tablas astronómicas* de Pedro Alfonso," in *Es-*

the *Epistola ad peripateticos*, Alfonsi urges on the French a rad-
ically different catalogue of the liberal arts, which again illustrates his emphasis upon science in the intellectual life.[48]

Traditionally, the seven liberal arts had been divided into two
rubrics: *trivium* and *quadrivium*. The *trivium* included grammar,
rhetoric, and dialectic (or logic), whereas the *quadrivium* con-
sisted of arithmetic, geometry, music, and astronomy. In general
these arts were those that were understood to be freed from the
mutability of matter, and therefore capable of producing true
knowledge. Alfonsi, however, proposed a different list. First, in
the *Epistola* Alfonsi insists that "grammar . . . cannot be counted
among the seven liberal arts, since it is neither knowledge subject to proof nor is it in every language the same. . . ." Dialectic,
so highly prized and developed in the French schools, remains
"first in order of all arts."[49] But neither grammar nor rhetoric, although useful, can be judged to provide true or scientific knowledge. Of the remaining arts, Alfonsi accepts arithmetic, geometry, music, medicine (*phisica*), and astronomy. Medicine is of
course useful for preserving or restoring the health of the body.
Yet although medicine is necessary for health, for Alfonsi it can
only be known through astronomy, since astronomy alone can
predict the permutations of the seasons. On the basis of these
changes, disease can be anticipated and its treatment sought. It
is astronomy, too, that enables the physician to determine the
proper times for bloodletting, cauterizing, incisions, and other
procedures. As a result, in this work Alfonsi reduces the seven

---

tudios sobre Pedro Alfonso de Huesca, 349–66. Charles Burnett suggests that it may
have again been Walcher who helped Petrus Alfonsi to make a Latin version of
these tables, and that the latter may also have collaborated with Adelard of Bath
for the completion of his own tables. See his *The Introduction of Arabic Learning
into England*, The Panizzi Lectures, 1996 (London: The British Library, 1997),
39–40. For a discussion of the *Zîj*, or astronomical handbook of al-Khwârizmî,
see also Raymond Mercier's discussion, "Astronomical Tables in the Twelfth
Century," in *Adelard of Bath: An English Scientist and Arabist of the Early Twelfth Century*, ed. Charles Burnett (London: The Warburg Institute, 1987), 87–118 (especially 95–97 for Petrus Alfonsi's *Zîj*).

48. For Alfonsi's scientific contributions, especially those drawn from Jewish
and Muslim culture, see David Romano, "Mošé Sefardí (= Pedro Alfonso) y la
ciencia de origen árabe," in *Estudios sobre Pedro Alfonso de Huesca*, 367–80.

49. John Tolan, *Peter Alfonsi*, 173.

liberal arts to six, but to a group of six that gives a place for the first time to medicine, even if it is subordinated to astronomy.[50] In doing so, he gives far more attention to astronomy and medicine than his Latin contemporaries, reflecting perhaps the intellectual interests of the Iberian Jewish community.[51] As a polemicist, however, Alfonsi will use his knowledge of astronomy to attack rabbinic tradition.

Another text sometimes associated with Alfonsi is the *Liber ysagogarum Alchorismi in artem astronomicam*, an introduction in five books to the *quadrivium*. This attribution has, however, more recently been discounted.[52] Two others are sometimes identified as Alfonsi's as well: *De humano proficuo* and *De elementis*.[53] Both are now lost, but have been attributed to Alfonsi on the basis of an entry in the fourteenth-century *Catalogus scriptorum ecclesiae* of Henry of Kirkstead. There *De humano proficuo* is identified as comprising the last part of a larger book of *Three Dialogues. De humano proficuo* is also cited in Peter of Cornwall's late twelfth-century *Liber disputationum contra Symeon Judaeum*,[54] which includes Alfonsi's *Dialogue* among its sources, lending some support to claims for his authorship. Kirkstead's catalogue, however,

---

50. Gregory Stone gives a coherent account of Alfonsi's reconfiguration of the arts, even if his remark that "Alfonsi is a French Enlightenment-style liberal . . ." seems unjustified. See his "Ramon Llull vs. Petrus Alfonsi: Postmodern Liberalism and the Six Liberal Arts," *Medieval Encounters* 3/1 (1997), 75. In his *Disciplina clericalis*, however, Alfonsi restores a seventh to the liberal arts, which seems to be grammar for those who are not philosophers, or necromancy or *res naturales* for those who are. On this, see J. H. L. Reuter, *Petrus Alfonsi*, 176–82.

51. See María Jesús Lacarra Ducay, "La renovación de las artes liberales en Pedro Alfonso: El papel innovador de un judío converso en el siglo XII," in *De Toledo a Huesca: Sociedades medievales en transición a finales del siglo XI (1080–1100)*, ed. Carlos Laliena Corbera and Juan F. Utrilla (Zaragoza: Institución 'Fernando el Católico,' 1998), 131–39.

52. See Charles Burnett, "The Works of Petrus Alfonsi: Questions of Authenticity," 50–51.

53. For an examination of Petrus Alfonsi's works and their editions, see especially Klaus Reinhardt and Horacio Santiago-Otero, "Pedro Alfonso. Obras y Bibliografía," in *Estudios sobre Pedro Alfonso de Huesca*, 19–44. For *De humano proficuo* and *De elementis*, see 30–32. See also John Tolan, *Petrus Alfonsi*, 205–11.

54. For this text, see Richard William Hunt, "The Disputation of Peter of Cornwall Against Symon the Jew," in *Studies in Medieval History Presented to Frederick Maurice Powicke*, ed. R. W. Hunt et al. (Oxford: Clarendon Press, 1948), 143–56.

also lists a *De elementis* with Marius Salernitanus as author. More recently a *De elementis* has been discovered in a manuscript in the British Library[55] attributed to a certain Marius. At the end of the work, the author writes that he has written another book, entitled *De humano proficuo*. This entails several possibilities, but leaves unresolved the issue of Alfonsi's authorship.[56]

After his composition of the *Epistola ad peripateticos*, it seems Alfonsi is again in England. Yet he must have returned to Iberia by April 1121, when his signature witnesses a bill of sale by which a French knight who had served under Alfonso I obtained an estate in Saragossa that previously had belonged to a Muslim. After this his movements are unknown, as is the date of his death. In recent years, having corrected the mistaken notion that he was baptized 44 years after his birth, discussion has raised again the possibility that Petrus Alfonsi and another Peter, Peter of Toledo, are one and the same. This hypothesis has been most actively promoted by P. Sj. van Koningsveld. Peter of Toledo was a Jewish convert translating Arabic materials in Toledo in the third and fourth decades of the twelfth century. If Alfonsi had been born 44 years before his baptism (i.e., in 1062), it would seem unlikely that he could still be active as a scholar and translator eighty years later. But if one only supposes that Alfonsi was an adult at the time of his baptism—perhaps in his twenties—then he certainly could be active in his sixties.

Peter of Toledo is best remembered as the translator of the anti-Muslim polemic of pseudo-al-Kindi, the *Risālah* (*Apology*), completed in 1142. The work consists of two letters. The first purports to have been written by a Muslim closely related to the caliph Al-Ma'mūn, who ruled from 813 to 833; the second is a much longer reply to the first, and was allegedly written by a Christian in the caliph's service. The caliph is said to have heard of the letters and had them read to him. The Muslim writer is identified as al-Hāshimi; the Christian, as al-Kindi, although it

---

55. See British Library, MS Cotton Galba E. iv.

56. Although Marie-Thérèse d'Alverny remarked, "The attribution of the *Liber Marii* to Peter Alfonsi, author of *De humano proficuo . . .* is based on quite solid ground"; "Pseudo-Aristotle, *De elementis*," 73. For a good discussion of the complexity of the problem, see Charles Burnett, "The Works of Petrus Alfonsi: Questions of Authenticity," 60–61.

is likely that the two authors are fictional. Al-Birūni (d. 1048) attests that the work was current in his day, suggesting that it may be from the tenth century.[57] It is this work that Peter of Toledo translated in 1142 at the urging of the Cluniac abbot Peter the Venerable, who provided him with the assistance of Peter of Poitiers.[58] The text used as the basis for the translation seems to have been in Judeo-Arabic, which can be inferred from the presence of various corruptions or name changes resulting from the transition from Arabic to Hebrew script. The fact that Peter of Toledo worked from a Judeo-Arabic text supports the conclusion that he, too, was a converted Jew.[59]

On the one hand, the identification of Peter of Toledo and Petrus Alfonsi as one and the same receives some additional support from Alfonsi's utilization of Ps.-al-Kindi's *Risālah*.[60] On the other, this putative identification creates other difficulties. Not only does it demand that we accept that Alfonsi was active as a translator in Spain in the 1140s, but it also places in doubt Alfonsi's ability to write effectively in Latin, since Peter of Poitiers was assigned as a secretary to Peter of Toledo because the latter did not know Latin as well as Arabic and Hebrew. But if Petrus Alfonsi required assistance in Latin composition in the 1140s,

57. For a good discussion, see James Kritzeck, *Peter the Venerable and Islam* (Princeton, NJ: Princeton University Press, 1964), 101–7.

58. For the Latin text, see Jose Munoz Sendino, "Al-Kindi, Apologia del Cristianismo," in *Miscellanea Comillas* 11–12 (1949): 337–460. The text itself begins on 377, following the translator's long introduction, and is based on two manuscripts: Oxford MS 184, Corpus Christi College, fols. 272–353; and Paris, MS Lat. 6.064, Bibl. Nat., fols. 83–105. Kritzeck has noted, however, that this edition did not take into account the Arsenal MS, which provides better readings and includes passages Sendino's edition omits.

59. See P. Sj. van Koningsveld, "La apologia de Al-Kindi en la Espana del siglo XII. Huellas toledanos de un 'Animal disputax,'" in *Estudios sobre Alfonso VI y la Reconquista de Toledo. Actes del II Congreso Internacional de Estudios Mozárabes (Toledo, 20–26 Mayo 1985),* series historica 5 (Toledo: Instituto de Estudios Visigótico-Mozárabes, 1989), 119.

60. Ps.-al-Kindi's *Risālah* informed anti-Muslim polemic in medieval Spain for centuries. For some discussion, see John V. Tolan, "Rhetoric, Polemics and the Art of Hostile Biography: Portraying Muhammad in Thirteenth-Century Christian Spain," in *Pensamiento medieval Hispano: Homenaje a Horacio Santiago-Otero* (Madrid: Consejo superior de investigaciones científicas consejería de educación y cultura de la junta de Castilla y León Diputación de Zamora, 1998), 2: 1497–1511.

then what likelihood is there that he wrote his *Dialogue* and other works in Latin unaided in the first and second decades of the twelfth century?[61] Such problems render the attempt to link the two figures highly speculative.

Nevertheless, it is clear that Alfonsi extensively utilized Ps.-al-Kindi's *Risālah* when he composed the fifth book or *titulus* of his *Dialogue*,[62] which contains his polemic against Islam. This portion of the *Dialogue* is important for conveying to the West far more reliable information about Islam than it had known previously.[63] For the medieval West, as Benjamin Kedar remarked, the *Dialogue* "probably served as the single most important source of information about Islam."[64] Christendom's encounter with Islam certainly expanded as a result of the first Crusade, which culminated in the Latin conquest of Jerusalem. Although western Christians knew something of Mohammad and were acquainted with the Arab tribes, or Saracens, that had for centuries threatened the Byzantine empire, their knowledge of Islam and its religious claims was woefully poor. In Spain, Christians had been subject to Muslim rule since the eighth century, but as Kenneth Baxter Wolf notes, "the earliest impressions that the Muslims

61. Charles Burnett has raised the possibility that Alfonsi had one or more associates who aided him with his Latin compositions. See his "The Works of Petrus Alfonsi: Questions of Authenticity." This paper revised his earlier "Las obras de Pedro Alfonso: problemas de autenticidad," in *Estudios sobre Pedro Alfonso de Huesca*, ed. María Jesús Lacarra, Colección de Estudios Altoaragoneses 41 (Huesca: Instituto de Estudios Altoaragoneses, 1996): 313–48.

62. For Alfonsi's debt to Ps.-al-Kindi, see P. Sj. van Koningsveld, "Historische betrekkingen tussen moslims en christenen," in *Petrus Alfonsi, een 12de eeuwse schakel tussen islam en christendom in Spanje*, ed. P. Sj. van Koningsveld (Nijmegen, 1982), 127–46; Guy Monnot, "Les citations coraniques dans le 'Dialogus' de Pierre Alphonse," *Cahiers de Fanjeaux, Collection d'histoire religieuse du Languedoc au XIIIᵉ et au début du XIVᵉ siècle*, no. 18, *Islam et chrétiens du Midi (XIIᵉ–XIVᵉ S.)*, ed. Edouard Privat (Fanjeaux: Centre d'Études Historiques de Fanjeaux, 1983): 271–72; and J. H. L. Reuter, *Petrus Alfonsi*, 84–89.

63. See Marie-Thérèse d'Alverny, "La connaissance de l'Islam en Occident du IXᵉ au milieu du XIIᵉ siècle," in *Settimane di studio del Centro italiano di studi sull'alto medioevo 12, L'Occidente e l'Islam nell'alto medioevo, Spoleto 2–8 aprile 1964* (Spoleto, 1965), 2: 577–602, reprinted in *La connaissance de l'Islam dans l'Occident médiéval*, ed. Charles Burnett (Aldershot, Hampshire: Variorum, 1994), V.

64. Benjamin Z. Kedar, *Crusade and Mission: European Approaches toward the Muslims* (Princeton, NJ: Princeton University Press, 1984), 92.

made on Spanish Christians were military and political ones."[65]
Islam did not principally impress itself on many western Christian
observers, then, as a *religious* culture, and as a result depictions of
Muslim religious belief were usually quite scant and misleading.
One need only turn for confirmation to the *Song of Roland*, which
depicts Islam as a perversion of Christian truth and incorrectly
identifies Mohammad as one person in an Islamic divine trinity.
In the first half of the twelfth century, however, European Christians were struggling to address their ignorance of essential Muslim teaching.[66] At the forefront of this effort was Peter the Venerable, who commissioned Herman of Carinthia and Robert of
Ketton to translate Arabic texts, including the Qur'an, which became available in 1143 in Robert of Ketton's Latin translation.[67]
Peter the Venerable correctly perceived that such translations
were absolutely necessary to any Christian effort to convert Muslims, or even merely to defend Christian teaching before Muslim
detractors. He himself made use of this Latin Qur'an in his *Contra Saracenos*[68] (ca. 1150) which, along with his *Contra Judaeorum*[69]
and *Contra Petrobrusianos*[70] (ca. 1139), defines Peter the Venerable as a polemicist whose concern extends not only to Jews and
Christian heretics (the Petrobrusians) but also to Islam. Nevertheless, Peter the Venerable's *Contra Saracenos* survives in but a

65. Kenneth Baxter Wolf, "Christian Views of Islam in Early Medieval Spain,"
in *Medieval Christian Perceptions of Islam*, ed. John Victor Tolan (New York and
London: Routledge, 1996), 86. For Tolan's own treatment, see his *Saracens: Islam in the Medieval European Imagination* (New York: Columbia University Press,
2002) and especially 147–55 for a discussion of Petrus Alfonsi's contribution to
the tradition of anti-Muslim polemic.

66. For the information available to western Christians on Islam from 1085–
1110, see Kedar, *Crusade and Mission*, 85–92.

67. See Marie-Thérèse d'Alverny, "Deux traductions latines du Coran au
Moyen Age," *Archives d'histoire doctrinale et littéraire du Moyen Age* 16 (1948): 69–
131, reprinted in *La connaissance de l'Islam dans l'Occident médiéval*, ed. Charles
Burnett (Aldershot, Hampshire: Variorum, 1994), I.

68. For the Latin text of the *Liber contra sectam sive haeresim Saracenorum*, see
James Kritzeck, *Peter the Venerable and Islam*, 220–91.

69. For a critical edition, see Peter the Venerable, *Adversus Judeorum inveteratam duritiem*, ed. Yvonne Friedman, CC CM 58 (Turnholt: Brepols, 1985).
Friedman discusses Peter the Venerable's dependence on Petrus Alfonsi for his
knowledge of the Talmud especially on pp. xiv–xvii.

70. For a critical edition, see *Contra petrobrusianos haereticos*, ed. James Fearns,
CC CM 10 (Turnholt: Brepols, 1968).

single manuscript copy, in contrast to the eighty extant manuscripts containing Alfonsi's *Dialogue*. Based on this statistic, there seems little doubt that Alfonsi's work was the more significant source for information concerning Islamic religion. To be sure, prior to his effort in the early twelfth century, there was little available on the religion of Islam in Latin. In the ninth century Paul Alvarus wrote in Spain against both Judaism and Islam, but his knowledge of Judaism was far superior to his knowledge of Islam.[71] Whereas medieval anti-Jewish polemicists could exploit a Christian literary tradition that was more than one thousand years old, no such treasury of information about Muslims and Islam existed. In the twelfth century, Christian authors had to break new ground.

In this effort, Petrus Alfonsi's anti-Muslim polemic in his *Dialogue* played a vital part. R. W. Southern described Petrus Alfonsi's account of Islam as "by far the best informed and most rational . . . in the twelfth century, and one of the best in the whole of the Middle Ages."[72] As J. H. L. Reuter noted, "[Alfonsi's] appraisal [of Islam] is far better informed and much wider in scope than any other available in the West in the early twelfth century."[73] Although Alfonsi attacked Mohammad for personal depravity and immorality, and rejected every claim that he was a prophet of the Lord, nevertheless it has been argued that he "undemonized" contemporary Islam.[74] Certainly he attributes to his interlocutor, Moses, the conviction that Islam is grounded in reason, whereas in contrast Alfonsi himself attacks Judaism (or Jews themselves) as irrational.[75] This notion

71. For his polemic against Islam, see his *Indiculus luminosus*, composed in 854 C.E. (PL 121: 513–56). A critical edition can be found in the *Corpus Scriptorum Muzarabicorum*, ed. Joannes Gil (Madrid: Consejo superior de investigaciones científicas, 1973), 1: 270–315.

72. R. W. Southern, *Western Views of Islam in the Middle Ages*, 35, n. 2.

73. J. H. L. Reuter, *Petrus Alfonsi*, 89–90.

74. See Benjamin Z. Kedar, *Crusade and Mission*, 92; and Barbara Hurwitz Grant, "Ambivalence in Medieval Religious Polemics: The Influence of Multiculturalism on the *Dialogues* of Petrus Alfonsi," in *Languages of Power in Islamic Spain*, ed. Ross Brann, Occasional Publications of the Department of Near Eastern Studies and the Program of Jewish Studies Cornell University 3 (Bethesda, MD: CDL Publications, 1997): 156–77.

75. Funkenstein's claim that for Alfonsi "Islam is even further from reason than Judaism" (*Perceptions of Jewish History*, 188) seems quite mistaken.

that Islam is a rational religion can be found in the work of several later twelfth-century Christian writers, perhaps because of Alfonsi's influence.[76] Peter the Venerable himself relied upon Alfonsi's treatment of Islam, just as he did for his understanding of Judaism.[77] Indeed, both Robert of Ketton and Herman of Carinthia seem to have been acquainted with Alfonsi's *Dialogue*, and they may have been responsible for making it available to Peter the Venerable during his sojourn in Spain.[78] Alfonsi's anti-Muslim polemic was not the only one to emerge from Andalus in the twelfth century, but the number of extant manuscripts strongly implies that it was the most widely read.[79] Indeed, it was even made available separately in Spanish translation in an early printed text from the late fifteenth century.[80]

Popularity and Importance

If we can infer from the number of manuscript copies something about a work's popularity, then probably the fourteenth-century *Epistle of Rabbi Samuel of Morocco* deserves the award for

76. For examples and bibliography, see *infra*, pp. 146–47, n. 1.

77. For the view that Peter the Venerable, too, held Islam in higher esteem than Judaism, see Robert Chazan, "Twelfth-Century Perceptions of the Jews: A Case Study of Bernard of Clairvaux and Peter the Venerable," in *From Witness to Witchcraft: Jews and Judaism in Medieval Christian Thought*, ed. Jeremy Cohen, Wolfenbütteler Mittelalter-Studien 11 (Wiesbaden: Harrassowitz Verlag, 1996), 187–201.

78. See Manfred Kniewasser, "Die antijüdische Polemik des Petrus Alphonsi (getauft 1106) und des Abtes Petrus Venerabilis von Cluny (d. 1156)," 63–64.

79. Thomas Burman discusses several other examples of Andalusian anti-Muslim polemic which have been preserved in manuscripts containing the Muslim responses. One of these, the "Tathlîth al-wahdânîyah," he attributes to a Jewish *converso* and dates to between 1120–1200. See his "'Tathlîth al-wahdânîyah' and the Twelfth-Century Andalusian-Christian Approach to Islam," in *Medieval Christian Perceptions of Islam*, ed. John Victor Tolan (New York and London: Routledge, 1996), 109–28. For a fuller discussion of other twelfth-century Andalusian anti-Muslim polemics, see Burman's *Religious Polemic and the Intellectual History of the Mozarabs, c. 1050–1200* (Leiden: E. J. Brill, 1994), especially chapter 2 (pp. 33–94). On pp. 240–385 of this volume, the author provides the Latin text and English translation for the polemic *Liber denudationis* (composed between 1085 and 1132).

80. Pedro Tena Tena has discovered the fifth *titulus* of the *Dialogus* printed in the *Viaje de la Terra Santa* of Bernard of Breidenbach (Saragossa, 1498). See his "Una versión incunabula hispana de los *Diálogos contra los Judíos* de Pedro Alfonso," *Sefarad: Revista de Estudios Hebraicos* 57/1 (1997): 179–94. For the Spanish text see 184–94.

"best-seller" among Latin anti-Jewish polemical works.[81] This work, translated into numerous languages, exists in some 300 manuscripts. Alfonsi's *Dialogue*, by contrast, survives in only 80 manuscript copies, although this is still quite a large number.[82] Still, Alfonsi's text left its imprint on the *Epistle of Rabbi Samuel of Morocco*,[83] just as it left an indelible impression on other medieval religious polemics.[84] We have already noted its influence on two twelfth-century polemics: Peter of Cornwall's *Liber disputationum contra Symeon Judaeum* and Peter the Venerable's *Contra Judaeorum*. In the thirteenth century, it was also summarized by Vincent of Beauvais, who included a long extract from the *Dialogue* in his popular encyclopedia, the *Speculum historiale*.[85] It was exploited by Raymund Martini in his monumental *Pugio fidei*, and utilized by Abner de Burgos (Alphonse of Valladolid; ca. 1270–1347) in his *Mostrador de Justicia*.[86] It was also likely used by Pablo Christiani at the public disputation at Barcelona (1263

81. The *Liber de adventu messiae praeterito* was allegedly translated into Latin in the fourteenth century from an eleventh-century Arabic work attributed to Rabbi Samuel of Morocco, although probably it is a Latin forgery from the hand of the Spanish Dominican, Alphonsus Buenhombre (d. 1353). The text can be found in PL 149: 333–68. It was translated into English by Thomas Calvert. See his *The Blessed Jew of Morocco or A Blackmoor Made White* (York: T Broad, 1648).

82. Klaus Reinhardt and Horacio Santiago-Otero list eighty manuscripts still extant, plus ten that can be identified but have been destroyed. See their "Pedro Alfonso. Obras y Bibliografía," 19–22.

83. See Ora Limor, "The Epistle of Rabbi Samuel of Morocco: A Best-Seller in the World of Polemics," in *Contra Iudaeos. Ancient and Medieval Polemics Between Christians and Jews*, ed. Ora Limor and Guy G. Stroumsa (Tübingen: J. C. B. Mohr, 1996), 184–85, n. 32.

84. Note Carlos del Valle Rodríguez's remark, "El *Diálogo* de Pedro Alfonso ocupa un singularísimo puesta en la historia del debate judeo-cristiano. Constituye ciertamente una de esas obras que dejan huella indeleble en la posteridad, que determinan en la polémica todo un modo nuevo y original de abordar y tratar los temas"; "Pedro Alfonso y su Dialogo," 203.

85. Vincent of Beauvais, *Speculum historiale* 25.118–145 (Douai: Bellerus, 1624; repr. Graz: Akademische Druck- u. Verlagsanstalt, 1965), 1043–55.

86. Abner de Burgos converted to Christianity from Judaism ca. 1295 and proposed to convert Jews by demonstrating the truth of Christianity using the Bible, Talmud, and kabbalistic midrash. For bibliography, see F. Vernet, "Juifs (Controverses avec les), de 1100 à 1500," in *Dictionnaire de théologie catholique*, ed. A. Vacant, E. Mangenot, and E. Amann (Paris: Letouzey et Ané, 1924), 8: 1894; and Heinz Schreckenberg, "Abner v. Burgos," *Lexikon für Theologie und Kirche* (Freiburg: Herder, 1993), 1: 59.

C.E.)[87] and later by Jerome de Santa Fe for the disputation at Tortosa (1413–1414 C.E.).[88]

The *Dialogue* was unique for its time because, as already noted, it employed all of the various polemical techniques identified by Amos Funkenstein. It employed arguments based on philosophical reason, the conclusions of medieval science, and a long tradition of Christian biblical exegesis. But more important still, it was the first polemical work written in Spain, or anywhere in Europe for that matter, that turned systematically to Jewish post-biblical literature in general, and the Talmud in particular, in order to demonstrate the inferiority of Judaism and the truth of Christian teaching. In so doing, Alfonsi would transform Christian polemical tradition, marking his treatise as the most important such work to be written in a thousand years.

The Talmud consists of several genres of material: legal debate *(halakha);* folklore or legend *(aggadah);* and exegesis and explication *(midrash)*. Petrus Alfonsi will invoke the aggadic material in particular in order to argue that Judaism requires one to believe things about God or creation that contradict reason and science. For example, he cites several passages from the Talmud that anthropomorphize the divine nature as instances of Jewish foolishness or stupidity. He was not the first Christian polemicist to condemn this feature of Jewish mystical tradition. The Carolingian Bishop Agobard of Lyons had also included in his catalogue of Jewish errors the complaint, "They [the Jews] say that their God is corporeal and that he is differentiated throughout the limbs according to corporeal dimensions; on the one hand, some say that he hears, others that he sees, whereas others say that he speaks as we do. . . ."[89] Nevertheless, Agobard made no ef-

87. Hebrew and Latin accounts of the Barcelona disputation can be found in translation in *Judaism on Trial: Jewish-Christian Disputations in the Middle Ages,* ed. and trans. Hyam Maccoby (London: Littman Library of Jewish Civilization, 1993). On the outcome of the disputation, see Robert Chazan, "The Barcelona Disputation of 1263: Goals, Tactics, Achievements," in *Religionsgespräche im Mittelalter,* ed. Bernard Lewis and Friedrich Niewöhner (Wiesbaden: Otto Harrassowitz, 1992), 77–91.

88. For the Christian account of this debate, see Maccoby's *Judaism on Trial,* 187–215; a brief translation of the Hebrew account, taken from Solomon ibn Verga's *Shevet Yehuda,* is found on 168–86.

89. "Dicunt denique Deum suum esse corporeum et corporeis liniamentis

fort to refute such claims by reason and science, nor did he have the detailed knowledge of Alfonsi. Moreover, Alfonsi reflects an already heated debate within Jewish communities. A growing corpus of literature, produced both outside and within rabbinic Jewish communities, would portray various aggadic utterances as trivial, foolish, irrational, or absurd. The attack may have been spearheaded by the Karaites, a sectarian Jewish community.[90] Like Alfonsi, the Iraqi Karaite Ya'qūb al-Qirqisānī, a tenth-century sectarian Jew, complained of talmudic statements that "attribute to Him [human] likeness and corporeality, and describe Him with the most shameful descriptions; (they [i.e., rabbinic Jews] assert) that He is composed of limbs and has a (definite) measure. They measure each limb of His in parasangs.[91] This is to be found in a book entitled 'Shi'ūr qōmāh,'[92] . . . This, as well as other tales and acts, etc., mentioned by them in the Talmud and their other writings does not suit (even) one of the (earthly) creatures, much less the Creator."[93] His colleague and contemporary, Salmon ben Yeruham (b. ca. 910), also mocks

---

per membra distinctum, et alia quidem parte illum audire ut nos, alia videre, alia vero loqui . . . ," Agobard of Lyons, *De judaicis superstitionibus*, cap. 10, in *Agobardi Lugdunensis opera omnia*, ed. L. Van Acker, CC CM 52 (Turnholt: Brepols, 1981), 205. The text was written ca. 825. For his knowledge of Jewish traditions, see Bat-Sheva Albert, "*Adversus Iudaeos* in the Carolingian Empire," in *Contra Iudaeos. Ancient and Medieval Polemics Between Christians and Jews*, ed. Ora Limor and Guy G. Stroumsa (Tübingen: J. C. B. Mohr, 1996), 119–42. For Agobard's role in the development of Christian-Jewish polemics, see also Jeremy Cohen, *Living Letters of the Law: Ideas of the Jew in Medieval Christianity* (Berkeley and Los Angeles: University of California Press, 1999), chapter 4.

90. For the Karaites, see Daniel Lasker, "Karaite Judaism," in *The Encyclopedia of Judaism*, ed. Jacob Neusner, Alan J. Avery-Peck, and William Scott Green (Leiden and Boston: E. J. Brill, 2003), vol. 4, supp. 1, pp. 1808–21.

91. A parasang equals three miles.

92. For Shi'ūr qōmāh, the "measure of the stature [of God]," see Martin Samuel Cohen, *The Shi'ur Qomah: Liturgy and Theurgy in Pre-Kabbalistic Jewish Mysticism* (New York: University Press of America, 1983). Cohen has translated text and commentary on pp. 187–265, based on Oxford MS. 1791 (fols. 58–70). For an attempt to provide an early date, concurrent with the development of the Talmud, see Brook W. R. Pearson and Felicity Harley, "Resurrection in Jewish-Christian Apocryphal Gospels and Early Christian Art," in *Christian-Jewish Relations through the Centuries*, ed. Stanley E. Porter and Brook W. R. Pearson (Sheffield: Sheffield Academic Press, 2000), 69–92.

93. From Qirqisānī's *Book of Lights and Watch-Towers*, cap. 3, translated in Leon Nemoy, "Al-Qirqisānī's Account of the Jewish Sects and Christianity," *Hebrew Union College Annual* 7 (1930), 331. For Qirqisānī's commitment to the use

stood such anthropomorphisms as metaphors,[98] this may not
have been the case. Meir Bar-Ilan has pointed out that twelfth-
century European rabbinic culture continued to embrace an
anthropomorphic conception of divinity.[99] Christian polemicists, however, were quick to pick up this weapon with which to
attack Jewish tradition and beliefs. Although some Jews might
contend—as Nachmanides did at the Barcelona disputation
in 1263—that they are not compelled to accept as true *all* of
the aggadic legends or stories contained within the Talmud,[100]
many more Jews were unwilling to impugn the authority of the
sages. Their authority and, consequently, the authority of the
Talmud were very much at stake. In fact, Alfonsi himself never
employs the term "Talmud," preferring instead the expression
the "teaching of your sages" (*doctrina doctorum vestrorum*). But in
the Christian world, *doctrina* carried with it an irrefutable sense
of religious authority and likely reflects Alfonsi's view that one
did not have the option of picking and choosing through the
aggadot. Either the Talmud was *doctrina* in its entirety, or it was
not.[101] Consequently, although Alfonsi does not attack the legal
decisions (*halakha*) in the Talmud, this need not imply that he
was unfamiliar with such materials. Rather, he may simply have
perceived that it was a much easier strategy to criticize the *aggadot*—already subject to criticism even in certain circles in the

98. As, for example, did Saadia Gaon. See *The Book of Beliefs and Opinions*,
2.5, trans. Samuel Rosenblatt (New Haven: Yale University Press, 1976), 107.

99. According to Meir Bar-Ilan, "in twelfth-century Provence (even) learned
rabbis did not see anything wrong in believing in an anthropomorphic God."
See his "The Hand of God: A Chapter in Rabbinic Anthropomorphism," in
Rashi 1040–1090. Hommage à Ephraïm E. Urbach, ed. Gabrielle Sed-Rajna (Paris:
Les Éditions du Cerf, 1993), 335.

100. For Nachmanides's view at the Barcelona disputation on the authority
of *aggadah*, see the valuable summary by Robert Chazan, *Barcelona and Beyond:
The Disputation of 1263 and its Aftermath* (Berkeley, Los Angeles, Oxford: University of California Press, 1992), 142–57. For translation of the Hebrew and Latin
accounts of the disputation, see Maccoby's *Judaism on Trial: Jewish-Christian Disputations in the Middle Ages*, 97–150.

101. Peter the Venerable seems to hold the same view. See Yvonne Friedman's introduction to his *Adversus Judeorum inveteratam duritiem*, pp. xvi–xvii.
Moreover, the equation of Talmud and *doctrina* fully entered into later ecclesiastical discussions. Thus, in a letter to the clergy of France (June 9, 1239), Pope
Gregory IX excoriates the Jews' "'Talmud,' that is 'Teaching' . . ." ("Talmud, id
est Doctrina"). For the text, see Solomon Grayzel, *The Church and the Jews in the
XIIIth Century*, 240–41, n. 96.

Jewish world—and that, if these two genres could be depicted as equally authoritative, then a successful attack upon the one was also a successful attack upon the other.

With increasing frequency, attacks on the Talmud would become an integral part of polemical literature from this point on.[102] It may go too far to suggest a direct link between Alfonsi's criticism and the repeated attempts in various Christian lands, beginning in the thirteenth century, to burn the Talmud as a source of error and blasphemy.[103] Yet certainly Alfonsi, and Peter the Venerable after him, helped create an atmosphere in the Christian world that was increasingly hostile to the Talmud.[104] For their part, Jews from rabbinic communities in Europe sought to defend and preserve the Talmud as essential to their religious understanding and practice, but Christian opinion increasingly opposed it.

Although we know of no direct Jewish response to Alfonsi's *Dialogue*, some scholars have seen it as underlying the composition of Jacob ben Reuben's *Milhamot ha-Shem* (*Wars of the Lord*) in 1170.[105] Written as a dialogue between a Jew and a Christian in

102. See Kurt Schubert, "Das christlich-jüdische Religionsgespräch im 12. und 13. Jahrhundert," in *Die Juden in ihrer mittelalterlichen Umwelt*, ed. Alfred Ebenbauer and Klaus Zatloukal (Cologne: Böhlau, 1991), 223–50. For a discussion of Jewish efforts to defend the Talmud before its Christian detractors, see especially 232–37.

103. The best-known attempt to burn the Talmud occurred in Paris in 1242–44, and a number of Parisian masters were involved in this effort. See Alexander of Hales (*Summa Theologica* 2, 2, Inq. 3, tr. 8, sect. 1, q. 1, tit. 2, membrum 1, cap. 1, ad obj. 2), who noted that the Talmud should be burned because of the blasphemies it contains against Jesus and his mother, Mary. For discussion of the burning in Paris, see especially the collection of essays, *Le brûlement du Talmud à Paris 1242–1244*, ed. Gilbert Dahan (Paris: Les Éditions du Cerf, 1999); Joel E. Rembaum, "The Talmud and the Popes: Reflections on the Talmud Trials of the 1240's," *Viator* 13 (1982): 203–23; Benjamin Z. Kedar, "Canon Law and the Burning of the Talmud," *Bulletin of Medieval Canon Law* 9 (1979): 78–83; Judah M. Rosenthal, "The Talmud on Trial. The Disputation at Paris in the Year 1240," *Jewish Quarterly Review*, n.s. 47 (1956): 58–76, 145–69; and my own "Talmud, *Talmudisti*, and Albert the Great," *Viator* 33 (2002): 69–86.

104. For Peter the Venerable's contribution to the burning of the Talmud, see Yvonne Friedman, "Anti-Talmudic Invective from Peter the Venerable to Nicolas Donin (1144–1244)," in *Le brûlement du Talmud à Paris 1242–1244*, ed. Gilbert Dahan (Paris: Les Éditions du Cerf, 1999), 171–90.

105. For the text, see Jacob ben Reuben, *Milhamot ha-Shem*, ed. Judah Rosenthal (Jerusalem: Mosad ha-Rav Kuk, 1963).

twelve books or chapters, like Alfonsi's own work, *Milhamot ha-Shem* was one of the first Hebrew anti-Christian polemics in Europe, written to dissuade Jews from following the path of apostasy. Indeed, the fact that Jacob ben Reuben was also an Iberian Jew and probably from Huesca seems to increase the likelihood that he would have been familiar with Alfonsi's polemic.[106] Just as Alfonsi turned to reason and Scripture for his attack, so too did Jacob ben Reuben. In response to the new emphasis on *ratio* (reason) in Christian anti-Jewish polemics, Jacob ben Reuben insisted that it was not Judaism but Christianity that sinned against reason, particularly by its dogmas of the Trinity and Incarnation.[107] Moreover, certainly Jacob ben Reuben and possibly Alfonsi as well were acquainted with an older Jewish anti-Christian polemic, perhaps from the middle of the ninth century, *The Polemic of Nestor the Priest*.[108] This Judeo-Arabic work from

106. Carlos del Valle remarks, "Aunque el *Sefer Milhamot ha-Šem* no puede considerarse ciertamente como una refutación del *Dialogus* de Pedro Alfonsi ni en argumentos concretos ni en metodología, sí es, en el fondo, una réplica global a la tesis última del converso cristiana." See his "Jacob ben Ruben de Huesca. Polemista. Su patria y su época," *Polémica Judeo-Cristiana: Estudios,* ed. Carlos del Valle Rodriguez (Madrid: Aben Ezra Ediciones, 1992), 63. See also Carlos del Valle, "Las Guerras del Señor, de Jacob ben Ruben de Huesca," in *La controversia judeocristiana en España (desde los orígenes hasta el siglo XIII). Homenaje a Domingo Muñoz León* (Madrid: Consejo superior de investigaciones científicas instituto de filología, 1998), 233. For the claim that Jacob ben Reuben wrote his work not in Huesca but in Gascogne, see Rolf Schmitz, "Jacob ben Rubén y su obra Milhamot ha-Šem," in *Polémica Judeo-Cristiana: Estudios,* 45–58. For other sources for *Milhamot ha-Shem,* see also David Berger, "Gilbert Crispin, Alan of Lille, and Jacob ben Reuben," *Speculum* 49 (1974): 34–47; and Robert Chazan, "The Christian Position in Jacob ben Reuben's *Milhamot Ha-Shem*," in *From Ancient Israel to Modern Judaism: Intellect in Quest of Understanding; Essays in Honor of Marvin Fox,* ed. Jacob Neusner, Ernest S. Frerichs, and Nahum M. Sarna (Atlanta, GA: Scholars Press, 1989), 2: 157–70.

107. For this approach in several twelfth-century Jewish anti-Christian polemics, see Daniel Lasker, "Jewish-Christian Polemics at the Turning Point: Jewish Evidence from the Twelfth Century," *Harvard Theological Review* 89/2 (1996): 161–73. Elsewhere, Lasker suggests that a defense of the rationality of Judaism was especially prominent among Spanish Jewish polemicists. See his "Jewish Philosophical Polemics in Ashkenaz," in *Contra Iudaeos. Ancient and Medieval Polemics Between Christians and Jews,* ed. Ora Limor and Guy G. Stroumsa (Tübingen: J. C. B. Mohr, 1996), 195–213.

108. The text and translation can be found in the two volumes of *The Polemic of Nestor the Priest,* trans. Daniel J. Lasker and Sarah Stroumsa (Jerusalem: Ben-Zvi Institute for the Study of Jewish Communities in the East, 1996).

the Muslim world, but circulating in Spain in Hebrew translation by the middle of the twelfth century, attacked the irratio-
nality of Christian teaching with rather crude and vulgar arguments. It has been suggested that Petrus Alfonsi knew this work,
and sought to respond to it in his *Dialogue*, just as later Jacob ben
Reuben cited it in his own *Milhamot ha-Shem*.[109] If this is so, then
Alfonsi wrote his *Dialogue* not merely as an attempted self-justi-
fication, but as part of a growing polemical antiphon of Jewish-
Christian debate.

This translation seeks to make available to a wider audience,
then, one of the most important texts from the *adversus Iudaeos*
tradition. A Latin edition of Petrus Alfonsi's *Dialogue* was first
published in Cologne in 1536 by J. Gymnicum.[110] This text,
which fell far short of a critical edition, was reprinted in 1618
in Cologne,[111] again at Lyon in 1677,[112] and once more in the
nineteenth-century *Patrologiae cursus completus, Series Latina*.[113] In
1982, however, Klaus-Peter Mieth prepared an edition based on
the examination of a larger number of manuscripts for his doc-
toral dissertation.[114] In 1996, his Latin text was reprinted with a
Spanish translation by Esperanza Ducay.[115] Unfortunately, this

109. Again, Carlos del Valle remarks, "No tengo duda alguna de que Pedro
Alfonso conoció el 'Relato' (*Qissa*), ya sea en el original árabe, o en la versión
hebrea, y su obra, el 'Diálogo', responde a ella. . . . Hay, pues, en el 'Diálogo'
una respuesta frontal y directa a las tesis defendidas en el 'Libro de Néstor el
Sacerdote.'" See his "Pedro Alfonso y su Dialogo," 222. In the same volume, see
his "El Libro del Néstor el Sacerdote," 191–200.
110. For a detailed discussion of the printed editions, see Klaus-Peter Mieth,
*Der Dialog des Petrus Alfonsi: seine Überlieferung im Druck und in den Handschriften
Textedition* (Inaug. diss.: Freien Universität Berlin, 1982), pp. xiii–xix.
111. See *Magna bibliotheca veterum patrum*, ed. M. de la Bigne (Cologne:
Agrippinae, 1618), vol. 12/1: 358–404.
112. See *Maxima bibliotheca veterum patrum* (Lyon, 1677), 21: 172–221.
113. Ed. J.-P. Migne, PL 157 (Paris, 1854): 535–672.
114. Klaus-Peter Mieth, *Der Dialog des Petrus Alfonsi*. Mieth examined a group
of thirteen manuscripts in Paris, as well as two manuscripts found in Berlin.
From this larger group, he selected a smaller group of four manuscripts and the
first Cologne edition, whose variants will be found in the apparatus. These are
designated as follows: B¹= Berlin Dt. Staatsbibl. MS. Phill. 1721 (12th C.); B²=Dt.
Staatsbibl. MS. Ham 21 (14th C.); P¹= Bibl. Nat. lat. 10,624 (12th C.); P²= Bibl.
Nat. lat. 10,722 (12th C.); and K=the first Cologne edition. B¹ served as his base-
line manuscript.
115. *Diálogo contra los Judíos*, trans. Esperanza Ducay (Huesca: Instituto de
Estudios Altoaragoneses, 1996).

1996 publication introduced numerous typographical errors to Mieth's 1982 edition. Consequently, for my translation I have returned to Mieth's 1982 text, although I have sometimes benefited from notes and explanation accompanying the 1996 publication. Since the 1996 printed edition is more easily accessible, in my notes I will indicate when Mieth's 1982 text has been followed by designating it "A" and the 1996 text "B."

Scriptural passages have been translated following the Douai version of the Latin Vulgate, except where Alfonsi's citation departs from the Vulgate. I have attempted to note such departures in the footnotes. The numeration of the psalms conforms to that of the Vulgate.

DIALOGUE AGAINST
THE JEWS

PROEMIUM AND PROLOGUE

HE PROEMIUM OF Petrus Alfonsi, an illustrious man and [converted to] a Catholic Christian from a Jew, begins.

To the one and first eternal omnipotent creator of all things who is without beginning and without end, knowing all, who accomplishes all that he wills, who placed humankind, endowed with reason and wisdom, above every animal, so that with these two powers he may desire with understanding things that are just and flee from those that are contrary to salvation, [to him be] honor and glory, and may his marvelous name be blessed forever and ever. Amen.

PROEMIUM ENDS.

The prologue by the same person begins, on his dialogue.

The author of the following work said: The Omnipotent One has inspired us with his spirit and led me on the correct path, first removing the white spot from the eyes[1] and then the weighty veil of a corrupt soul. Then the halls of the prophets lay open for us and their secret places were revealed, and we applied the mind to perceiving their true understanding and we tarried over interpreting it.

Thus we considered both what ought to be understood and what ought to be believed thereby, namely, that God is one in a trinity of persons, which do not precede one another in time whatsoever, nor are they separated from one another by any division, which [persons] Christians name Father, Son, and Holy Spirit; and that the blessed Mary, conceiving by the Holy Spirit, gave birth to Christ without mixing with a man, generating an animate body that was the dwelling place of the incomprehen-

---

1. For the phrase *albuginem . . . in oculo,* see Lv 21.20 (Vulg.).

sible deity. Therefore, there is one Christ, complete with three substances, namely, body, soul, and deity, and this very same one is both God and man. And [we believe] that the Jews crucified him by their disposition and will, so that just as he was the Creator, he would also become the Redeemer of the entire holy Church (namely, of the faithful both preceding and following after), and he died in the body and was buried, and on the third day was resurrected from the dead. Then he ascended into heaven and he is there at the same time with the Father; he will come again on the day of judgment, to judge the living and the dead, just as the prophets have spoken and have predicted for the future.

Therefore, when I had arrived at so exalted a degree of this faith, by the impulse of divine mercy, I took off the cloak[2] of falsehood and was stripped bare of the tunic[3] of iniquity and was baptized in the see of the city of Huesca in the name of the Father and the Son and the Holy Spirit, having been purified by the hands of Stephen,[4] the glorious and legitimate bishop of the same city.

At the moment of baptism, in addition to those things that have already been mentioned, I believed in the blessed apostles and the holy Catholic Church.

This occurred in the year 1106, the year 1144 of the [Spanish] era from the nativity of the Lord, in the month of June, on the feast day of the apostles Peter and Paul.[5]

Thus I took upon myself the name of the apostle, that is, Peter, out of reverence for and as a remembrance of this same day. Moreover, my spiritual father [godfather] was Alfonsus,[6] the glorious emperor of Spain, who received me at the sacred font. This is why I took for myself the name Petrus Alfonsi, appending his name to the name of mine that I have already mentioned.

2. "Cloak": *pallium,* also a mantle worn by members of the ecclesiastical hierarchy.

3. *Tunica:* a long outer vestment worn by subdeacons when assisting the priest at solemn functions.

4. Bishop of Huesca, 1099–1130.

5. The feast day of Sts. Peter and Paul falls on 29 June.

6. I.e., Alfonso I, the Battler, King of Aragon from 1104 to 1134.

And when it became known to the Jews who had known me previously, and had considered me well-trained in the books of the prophets and the sayings of the sages, and to have even a portion, although not great, of all the liberal arts, that I had accepted the law and faith of the Christians and was one of them, some of them thought that I only did this because I had abandoned all sense of shame, to such an extent that I had condemned both God and the law. Others, besides, claimed that I had done this because I had not understood the words of the prophets and the law appropriately. Still others accused me of vainglory and falsely claimed that I had done this for worldly honor, because I perceived that the Christians' nation [*gens*] dominated all others.[7]

Therefore I have composed this little book so that all may know my intention and hear my argument, in which I set forth the destruction of the belief of all the other nations, after which I concluded that the Christian law is superior to all others. Moreover, last, I have set down all the objections of any adversary of the Christian law and, having set them down, have destroyed them with reason and authority according to my understanding.

I have arranged the entire book as a dialogue, so that the reader's mind may more quickly achieve an understanding. To defend the arguments of the Christians, I have used the name that I now have as a Christian, whereas in the arguments of the adversary refuting them, I have used the name Moses, which I had before baptism. I have divided the book into twelve headings [*tituli*],[8] so that the reader may find whatever he desires in them more quickly.

7. Indeed, some eleventh-century Jews in Muslim states did convert to Islam to advance their political careers, as John Tolan points out. See his *Petrus Alphonsi and his Medieval Readers* (Gainesville: University of Florida Press, 1993), 6. The same certainly occurred in Christendom.

8. *Titulus*, which we have translated as "heading," is an unusual term with multiple meanings. By the early twelfth century, it is used to designate a division or section of a written work. Charles Burnett points out that although it is rarely used in scientific works, it does appear in a tenth-century work on the astrolabe, *Horologium regis Ptolomei*, probably by Lupitus of Barcelona, which he believes may have served as Alfonsi's model. See his "The Works of Petrus Alfonsi: Questions of Authenticity," 43.

The first heading shows that the Jews understand the words of the prophets according to the flesh and explain them falsely.

The second leads to knowledge of the cause of the present captivity of the Jews, and how long it has to last.

The third is for refuting the silly belief of the Jews over the resurrection of their dead, whom they believe both will be resurrected and will inhabit the earth again.

The fourth is to demonstrate that the Jews observe but a little bit of the entire law of Moses, and that this little bit is not pleasing to God.

The fifth is for the purpose of destroying the law[9] of the Saracens and refuting the stupidity of their opinions.

The sixth is on the Trinity.

The seventh concerns how the Virgin Mary, conceiving by the Holy Spirit, gave birth without intercourse with [her] husband.

The eighth, how the Word of God was incarnate in the body of Christ and how Christ was God and man at one and the same time.

The ninth, that Christ came in that time when it was predicted by the prophets that he would come, and that whatever they predicted concerning him was revealed in him and his works.

The tenth, that Christ was crucified and killed by the Jews by their free will.

The eleventh, concerning the Resurrection and ascent of Christ to heaven, and his Second Coming.

The twelfth, that the law of Christians is not contrary to the Mosaic law.

I beseech those who are about to read this little book, that if they find that it contains some imperfect or superfluous statement, they forgive this venial error, since no one is without fault [*vitium*].

HERE ENDS THE PROLOGUE. THE BOOK BEGINS.

From the tender age of youth a certain one, a most perfect friend, named Moses, stuck by me, who had been my companion and fellow student from the very earliest age. When word

9. "Law": *lex*, but a term that can also refer to customary religious practice.

reached him that I had chosen the Christian faith, having abandoned the law of my fathers, he came to me in haste, after having abandoned the place of his residence. Wearing the expression of an indignant man on his face as he approached and upbraiding me, he greeted me not as a friend but as if I were a stranger, and thus he began [saying]:

Alas, Petrus Alfonsi,[10] a great deal of time has passed since I have wanted, desperately, to come to you, to see you, to speak with you, and to be with you, but my desire lacked effect until just now, when, by the grace of God, I see you with a happy expression on your face. Now, then, I beg you to reveal to me [your] intention and why you abandoned the old law, or reveal the reason that you chose a new law.

For I knew well that earlier you used to excel in the writings of the prophets and the sayings of our sages, and that from your youth you were more zealous for the law than all your contemporaries; that if there were any adversary, you opposed him with a shield of defense; that you preached to the Jews in the synagogues, lest any withdraw from the faith; that you taught your companions; [and] that you led the learned to greater things. See, then, I do not know nor do I see why you have changed and become estranged from the path of rectitude, which, to my mind, I think was done in error.

PETRUS: I said to him: It is the practice of the Jewish people and of untutored people, that if they observe one do anything whatsoever contrary to their own practice, even if it remains correct and most just, nevertheless in their estimation and judgment he will be subject to the name and crime of injustice. You, however, who have been reared in the cradle of philosophy, suckled on the breasts of philosophy,[11] with what impudence can you cast blame on me, before you have been able to determine whether the things I have done are just or unjust?

MOSES: Two contrary arguments come to mind: the one, that I consider that you are a prudent man who could not have with-

10. The vocative *Petre Alfunse* is employed, indicating an appropriate nominative form of Petrus Alfunsus. See n. 17 on pp. 8–9.

11. Cf. Boethius, *Philosophiae consolatio* 1.2.2, ed. Ludovicus Bieler, CC SL 94 (Turnholt: Brepols, 1984), 4.

drawn from the law which you held unless you knew that the one you have received truly is better; and the other, that the law which I hold and which you abandoned, I consider to be better. This is why I think that what you have done is an error, and I do not know to which side I should lean.

For this reason I beg you to dispel from my mind the anxiety of this doubt, and let us both run back and forth by turns on the field of argument, until I arrive at an investigation of this matter and may be able to learn whether your action is just or unjust.

PETRUS: Human nature has this characteristic: that while the soul is confounded by some matter, it lacks the eye for judgment in discerning truth and falsehood. Now then, unless you remove every confusion from your heart, so that in the manner of wise men we may praise together what is just and scornfully reject what is unjust without contention, we will cast our words into an abyss, and no end will be established for our task.

MOSES: I accept this agreement willingly, and I ask that you accept the same for your part.

PETRUS: Certainly, I agree happily.

MOSES: I implore this as well, if you please: that if you introduce some authority from the Scriptures, you choose to do this according to the Hebrew truth [*Hebraica veritas*].[12] Because if you do otherwise, you know that I will not accept it. But also, if I adduce some [authority] for you according to the way we have it, I want you not to contradict it in any way but to receive it and to acknowledge it as true.

PETRUS: And certainly I do not refuse this, for I desire greatly to slay you with your own sword.

MOSES: Moreover, if something should enter in at some point which seems to be irrelevant to a discussion of laws, do not let

---

12. On the *Hebraica veritas*, see especially Aryeh Grabois, "The *Hebraica veritas* and Jewish-Christian Intellectual Relations in the Twelfth Century," *Speculum* 50 (1975): 613–35; and Jaroslav Pelikan, "Hebraica Veritas," in *From Witness to Witchcraft: Jews and Judaism in Medieval Christian Thought*, ed. Jeremy Cohen, Wolfenbütteler Mittelalter-Studien 11 (Wiesbaden: Harrassowitz Verlag, 1996), 11–28. In one sense, *Hebraica veritas* may refer to the reading of the text of Scripture found in Hebrew codices; in another, it may refer to the interpretation given a passage by Jewish exegetes. Despite Alfonsi's apparent willingness to argue according to the *Hebraica veritas*, often he fails to do what he promises.

it annoy you, I beg you, but strive to respond to the questioner from the other arts, when a convenient place arises. Also I want you to agree that sometimes it will be appropriate to question me, sometimes to respond to me, and sometimes to oppose me with an alternate argument just as the discussion will allow me to do.

PETRUS: I agree. Now, let it be granted to you to ask about whatever you wish to know and with whatever intention you like.

MOSES: Do you agree that Moses, the son of Amram,[13] was a true prophet of the Israelite people and that he was truly sent by God, and that whatever he prophesied in the name of God, he articulated and spoke faithfully?

PETRUS: Certainly I concede this.

MOSES: Do you concede also that all the prophets after Moses came to confirm his law, not to contradict it in some way?

PETRUS: This, too, I concede.

MOSES: You do not deny that the law which the Jews presently hold and which they assert was written by Moses, remains the same in all respects, just as Moses wrote it?

PETRUS: How, I ask you, will I be able to deny this, especially since the same law previously was translated from the words of the same Moses by our sages, in whom we have confidence, and is considered by us to be Scripture, except that when appropriate in certain places the words are changed, although nevertheless the meaning is the same?[14]

MOSES: Why, then, do I see that you have transgressed and deviated from its paths?

PETRUS: This is not the case; rather, now I preserve its complete faith, just as I ought, and I proceed along its very straight paths with a straight step.

13. Cf. Ex 6.20.
14. This remark seems to recall Jerome's defense of his Vulgate translation. To those who criticized him for abandoning the LXX when he translated the book of Job, Jerome replied that his translation actually restored the text by following the Hebrew, Aramaic, or Syriac texts, either literally or according to their sense of meaning. See the excerpt from Augustine's *Epistle* 71, in *Selecta veterum Scriptorum Testimonia de Hieronymanis versionibus Latinis SS. Bibliorum*, PL 28: 139B.

MOSES: Is one given to understand from your words that you apprehend the correct sense from the words of the law and the prophets, whereas the Jews, worshipers of the same law, stand outside its correct intention, whence they seem to understand it badly, in your judgment?

PETRUS: You have apprehended the meaning of my words well.

MOSES: Make me understand, then, how it seems to you that the Jews have erred in the explanation of the law, which you understand better.

PETRUS: Since I see that they attend to the surface [meaning] and the letter of the law alone, and do not explicate it spiritually but rather carnally, this is why they are especially beguiled by error.

MOSES: I do not understand well enough what you mean by these words, so I urge you to speak more clearly.

PETRUS: Are you not mindful of your teachers who wrote your teaching,[15] on which your entire law relies, according to you, how they claim that God has a form and a body, and they attribute such things to his ineffable majesty as it is wicked to believe and absurd to hear, seeing that they are not based on reason? And that they advanced such opinions concerning him which appear to be nothing other than the words of little boys making jokes in school, or women telling old wives' tales in the streets. Again, explaining the law according to the capacity of your intellect, you hope that you are about to escape from captivity, in a manner that cannot happen. Again, in the escape from captivity, you hope that God will perform an unwonted miracle, so that he will raise your dead, who will begin to dwell on the earth in the manner they did previously. Likewise, I note that while living in captivity you observe very little of all the laws' precepts, even according to your own explanation. Moreover, that which you do [observe] you believe is pleasing and acceptable to God, but you never confess that he will hold you blameworthy for what you omit, and you seem to have fulfilled

15. "Teaching": *doctrina*, an allusion to post-biblical Jewish tradition generally and the Talmud in particular. See Introduction, p. 32.

for yourselves everything which clearly holds the chief place of error. Again, there are several other errors that they have committed on the basis of unsound explanations of the law.

MOSES: You inveigh too severely against our disgrace, and you want to denigrate the Jewish nation. And indeed the words are few and light, but in them there is a great and weighty judgment. And if we want to conclude the whole argument under one judgment and to compass many things under one heading, when we ought to shed light on individual things instead, we introduce darkness by mixing everything together indiscriminately. So, if it seems good to you, let us assign individual headings to individual issues, so that once each has been delimited we may advance in an orderly manner from one argument of the debate to another.

PETRUS: Let what you have said well be done, and let what you worthily advise be fulfilled. Therefore, once their headings have been affixed to individual issues, ask what you wanted [to know] earlier, since I am prepared to answer.

FIRST *TITULUS*

OSES: LET US construct this first heading, then, so as to contain the arguments with which you have inveighed against us and against our sages, namely, that we attribute form and body to God and that we add such things to his nature as the truth of reason abhors. Therefore, let us discuss this matter carefully, until, by reason and argument, we arrive at its investigation.[1]

PETRUS: I praise what has been said.

MOSES: In the first place, then, I want you to show me where our sages have said that God has a form and a body and how they have spoken about this matter.[2]

PETRUS: If you want to know where it is written: [it is] in the first part of your teaching, whose name is *Benedictions*.[3] Then, if you want to know how: they have said that God has a head and arms and wears a little box tied by a band on the hair;[4] that the

1. For Alfonsi's understanding of reason and argument (*ratio*) here and throughout the *Dialogus*, see especially Gilbert Dahan, "L'usage de la *ratio* dans la polémique contre les juifs, XIIᵉ–XIVᵉ siècles," in *Diálogo Filosófico-Religioso entre Christianismo, Judaísmo e Islamismo durante la Edad Média en la Península Ibérica*, ed. Horacio Santiago-Otero, S.I.E.P.M. 3 (Turnholt: Brepols, 1994): 289–308.

2. In Christian texts, the view that *contemporary* Jews *(moderni Iudaei)* erred as a result of anthropomorphic conceptions of deity had clearly become a commonplace by the end of the twelfth century, thanks, in part, to this work. See, for example, Alexander Nequam, *Speculum speculationum*, 1.18.8, ed. Rodney M. Thomson, Auctores Britannici medii aevi 11 (Oxford: Oxford University Press, 1988).

3. That is, tractate *Berachot* of the Talmud.

4. The reference here is clearly to phylacteries or *tefillin*. It may be worth noting that the term the author uses to identify the box, *pyxis*, is often used in Christian texts to designate the vessel in which the consecrated host has been reserved. Although it is tempting to translate these rather cumbersome expressions referring to the boxes and bands or thongs simply by the word *tefillin* (or phylacteries), I have avoided doing so simply because the author does not use this term, which certainly would have been familiar from Mt 23.5 (Vulg.)—"dilatant enim phylacteria sua" ("they make their phylacteries broad").

See B.T. *Ber.* 6a (which quotes this same passage from Isaiah, which follows

knot of this same band is made fast from the rear part of the head under the skull; that within the box there are four parchments that contain praises of the Jews; that on the upper part of the left arm, moreover, he wears another box bound in a similar fashion by a band, and that there is a parchment there that contains all the praises which are said to be written in the four previously mentioned. Do you admit that all these things are thought to be written in this manner in the place I have mentioned?

MOSES: I am unable to deny what is so evident.

PETRUS: I ask you, what authority do they have for this matter?

MOSES: They derive authority for the box which he wears on the hair and for the knot of the band from the place where the Lord says to Moses: "You will see my back; my face will not be seen."[5] For then Moses sees the knot of the band.[6] It is necessary that the knot be of some box of his. Moreover, for the one which he wears on the arm they claim authority from Isaiah, who says: "The Lord swore on his right side and in the arm of his strength."[7] He wants the left arm to be understood by "the arm of strength," in which the power of the box is contained.

PETRUS: You have reminded me. For I recall that I have already read this passage, but this authority contains no defense for you. In fact, since the law proclaims that God said to Moses, "You will see my back," and because it is clear that God cannot deceive, so we should not doubt that this occurred later, although Scripture is silent on the matter. Nevertheless, the law never mentions that Moses saw something *on* his back. How, then, do you say that he saw the knot of the band, which can

---

below) for the claim that God dons *tefillin* and for the passages contained in them. In Jewish practice, adult males typically wear *tefillin* at weekday morning services. The *tefillin* consist of two leather boxes attached by leather thongs or straps: one is attached to the left arm and hand (or the right arm and hand if the wearer is left-handed); the other is attached to the forehead, with the straps extending behind the head. The boxes contain parchment(s) on which are written four scriptural passages: Ex 13.1–10; 13.11–16; Dt 6.4–9; 11.13–21.

5. Ex 33.23.

6. R. Hama ben Bizana taught that R. Simon the Pious claimed that Ex 33.23 teaches that Moses saw the knot of the *tefillah* on God's neck. See B.T. *Ber.* 7a.

7. Is 62.8.

hardly be said without laughter? Likewise, since not only the nape of the neck but any part of the body whatsoever can properly be understood by "back" [*posteriora*], you do not prove what you assert—that he saw the neck—by reason or by the authority of the law, but only by wishful thinking [*sola . . . voluntate*].

MOSES: Our sages say that the neck ought to be understood by "back."

PETRUS: It is pleasing to proceed along the chain of your foolish explanation, which lacks the aid of both reason and Scripture. Let me concede that God has a neck—which really both seems to be and is something wicked for a wise man [to say]. Nevertheless, it could have happened that Moses saw nothing on him except the neck. Or if we should invent that he saw something else, he could have seen a cap or the knot of the band of his crown, which you say that the angel named Metatron [*Mitraton*] places on God's head each day.[8]

MOSES: Certainly our sages contend that it was the knot of the band that Moses saw and this is why they affirm that God showed Moses his neck, so that he would see the knot of the band.

PETRUS: Let us concede that it is as you state, to your destruction. For should we say falsely that Moses saw the knot of the band, how has this demonstrated that God wears the box on the front part of the head, since he did not see his face at all?[9]

MOSES: Since Moses saw the knotted band, our sages understood that the box that it binds was on God's head.

8. For the angel Metatron, see the useful article ("Metatron") by Gershom Scholem in the *Encyclopedia Judaica* 11: 1443–46. See B.T. *Hagiga*, 13b, for this activity of crowning God, attributed to Sandlfon, a "brother" of Metatron. The tenth-century Karaite Ya'qūb al-Qirqisānī, however, criticizes rabbanites because "they say in the 'Book of Ishmael' [Hēkālōt de Rabbi Yishmā'ēl] that every morning Metatron ties phylacteries upon the head of the Creator . . ." See Qirqisānī's *Book of Lights and Watch-Towers,* cap. 4, trans. Leon Nemoy, "Al-Qirqisānī's Account of the Jewish Sects and Christianity," p. 351. For a possible etymology of the name, as the "measure" and hypostatic image of God, from early Gnostic Jewish-Christian sources, see Gedaliahu G. Stroumsa, "Forms of God: Some Notes on Metatron and Christ," *Harvard Theological Review* 76 (1983): 269–88.

9. The *tefillah* worn on the head consists of a leather box worn on the forehead, bound with a leather thong knotted behind the neck. Alfonsi is asking this: even if Moses saw a knot behind God's neck, how could he be certain that the knot and its thong were connected to the leather box, since he did not see God from the front as well?

PETRUS: This is by no means a well-founded understanding, since even if we say that God wears something, nevertheless the band could have bound a cymbal or some sort of bell or a precious gem or something of this sort. Truly, so that I may remove all your foolish responses, let me concede that this is as you wish and as you say. But having conceded this, how, I beg you, was Moses able to understand that parchments are contained inside, when you say that he did not know what is thought to have been written on them? But beyond all these things, what is even more deserving of astonishment is the fact that you believe that nothing else is written on that parchment but the verses which Moses produced on his own (when he was dying, a long time afterwards) for teaching the Israelite people, praising them,[10] and [what] Solomon composed, after the course of many years, for their praise, while adoring God.[11] There is no reason why one ought to believe that it is written on God's head.

MOSES: What Moses did not see with eyes of the flesh he knew from the revelation of the Holy Spirit. I have no argument, I confess, for the writings of the parchments, however.

PETRUS: Glory to God, already little by little you abstain from a foolish response. Again, if we concede that Moses saw some of these things, that he knew some with the Holy Spirit revealing them, since Moses himself left behind no record of it, nor did any of the prophets after him produce one, how did he reveal the mystery of such a secret matter to your sages?

MOSES: Through the tradition of the ancients, it came finally to the attention of our sages.[12]

PETRUS: Your argument wanders to the refuge of an irrational conclusion, since you will be able to ground every falsehood on the tradition of the ancients. Nevertheless, it is unworthy of support because you ascribe to your sages what perhaps they themselves reject, since they themselves attest that they have not

10. According to B.T. *Ber.* 6a, within the boxes of God's *tefillin* are passages from 1 Chr 17.21, praising the nation of Israel. The boxes on the head and arm contain Dt 4.7–8; Dt 33.29; Dt 4.34; and Dt 26.19. Moses proclaims Dt 33.29 shortly before his death.

11. "Solomon": an error for David, if 1 Chr 17.21 is meant.

12. What is meant here is the oral tradition of rabbinic Judaism, which is understood to have been passed down from Moses to Joshua, the elders, and ultimately to the rabbis themselves, as an unwritten doctrine.

received this through Moses by the report of the ancients, but that they themselves invented such things in the course of explaining the verses.

MOSES: I did not answer taking into consideration what is correct, but seeking an opportunity for flight.

PETRUS: Let us avoid foolish notions, holding to the truth, since we both decided this at the beginning of the argument.

MOSES: I deem that worthy.

PETRUS: Tell me, I beg you, do you know how much this tale is denigrated by reason, even apart from the fact that it was asserted a little while ago without an authority?

MOSES: I see the destruction of authority in both.[13] Now, then, I demand of you that you show this through an argument of nature.

PETRUS: You [Jews] contend that God has a head, arms, and the entire form of the body. If this is the case, then it is necessary that you confess that God consists of the dimensions of length, breadth, and height. If he is truly encompassed by these three dimensions, he is bounded by the six parts of a body,[14] so that he would appear in his own place, which is unsuitable. Moreover, I propose to you two things for the band[15] which you say he has on his head. For either the band comes from him, or from something else. If truly it comes from him, then God is divided from himself.[16] If from something else, then it is either a creator or a creature. If a creator, then there are two creators. If it is a creature, then some creature is greater than a certain part of the creator, which is unsuitable. Again, I ask whether he wears what he wears on his head or his arm by some necessity or without necessity. If he wears it of necessity, then the creator requires a creature, which is something unsuitable. If he wears it without necessity, then God wears on himself something super-

13. Moses seems to acknowledge that an assertion that invokes the authority of tradition but in fact lacks such authority, and which also offends reason, ultimately undermines authoritative tradition itself.

14. That is, each dimension—length, height, and breadth—will have two limits or boundaries. Thus there will be six parts or sides to the body.

15. "Band": *corrigia*, or, again, the phylacteries.

16. That is, if it is a "part" of God, then God is divided into parts or "divided from himself."

fluous, and this is unsuitable. Now, then, clearly you can understand what you demanded be shown to you by reason, namely,
how worthless what you believe about the band really is.

MOSES: I accept that.

PETRUS: Again, your sages report in a book of teachings, that
God exists only in the west, confirming this by the authority of
Ezra, who said: "The army of heaven beseeches you,"[17] which
they explain in this way: when all the stars set in the west, then
the army of heaven beseeches God. And since this entreaty of
the stars occurs in the west, that is why they claim that God is
in the west.[18] What I describe is their opinion. Who would not
perceive how unworthy this is of God, no matter how estranged
they may be from knowledge of God, just by knowing something
about the shape of the world?

MOSES: I would like you to show me, if you please, how one
concludes from this expression that they did not know the
shape of the world.

PETRUS: Since we only call "east" that place where the first
star appears, and only "west" that place where it is removed from
our view.

MOSES: Now I entreat you to show me the fixed place of east
and west and to discuss in detail [*subtiliter*] a knowledge of this
matter.

PETRUS: Since you have asked for this matter to be demonstrated to you in detail, it is fitting, too, that you examine it with
a subtle eye. Consider it in this way. Stand in any place you like,
and extend from this place a straight line in the direction of the
east. When it has reached a place[19] beyond which you cannot

17. Neh 9.6. Vulg. reads, "exercitus coeli te adorat" ("the army of heaven
worships you").

18. On the notion that the divine spirit or presence *(Shekhinah)* dwells in the
west, see B.T. *Baba Batra* 25a. Although it is clear there that the *Shekhinah* is om-
nipresent, R. Shesheth would not pray toward the east, since the *minim* (sectar-
ians or heretics) pray toward the east. In this way, perhaps, there arose the notion that the *Shekhinah* dwells only in the west.

19. Reading *locum* (A) for *lucum* (B). This expression may be compared to
that brought forth by Peter Damian (d. 1072), Cardinal Bishop of Ostia, who
insists that "Christ is truly the East," bringing to bear Zec 6.12 for support. See
Peter Damian, *Die Briefe des Petrus Damiani*, 136, 1, ed. Kurt Reindel, MGH,
Die Briefe der Deutschen Kaiserzeit, vol. 3 (Munich: Monumenta Germaniae

extend your [line of] sight,[20] know that this very place is east
of you. In the same way, if you extend a straight line to the west
from that place where you are standing, when it reaches such a
place that it imposes a limit on your sight, reckon this place as
west of you.

MOSES: I would like you to show it to me from the hour of
the absolute rise and the hour of the absolute setting.

PETRUS: Extend the aforementioned line from the rising
[*nascente*] star to the very position of the star and fix the line in
the center of that star, so that one half appears over the earth
and another half is still hidden, and you call that hour the rising of this star. When, therefore, the sun begins to rise in such
a fashion over the earth, according to the astronomers that
hour is the true rise of the day. In the same way, if you fix the
aforementioned line from the setting star to the direction of
the west, directing the end of the line to the center of the star,
so that half stands over the earth and half [stands] under the
earth, you say that this hour is its setting. And when the sun sets
in such a way, this hour is the true setting of the day and the beginning of night according to the astronomers.

MOSES: This conclusion proceeds from your argument: that
although the eastern part of the orb is the same for all, nevertheless the location of the east is not the same for all. Likewise,
although the western [part] of the orb is the same for all, nevertheless the location of the west is not the same for all. Nor is the
hour of sunrise the same for us as it is for everyone else, nor is
the hour of sunset the same for us as it is for other people, but
rather the location of the west and of the east and the hour of
sunrise and sunset vary according to the difference in longitude
of places of the earth.[21]

Historica, 1983–93), 463. For translation, see *The Letters of Peter Damian*, FOTC,
MC 6, *Letters 121–150*, trans. Owen Blum and Irven M. Resnick (Washington,
DC: The Catholic University of America Press, 2004).

20. I.e., the horizon.

21. This argument also demonstrated, of course, that the earth must be
round, and not flat. A similar demonstration that the earth is round will be
found in a roughly contemporary text, Pseudo-Bede's *De mundi celestis terrestrisque constitutione*, where it is said that "the earth is said to be round. . . . For we
have different sunrises and sunsets and middays in accordance with the revolu-
tion of the firmament and the sphericity of the earth. For when it is midday to

PETRUS: I am happy that you grasp the truth of the matter.

MOSES: Still, I beg you, speak more plainly and reveal so subtle a matter with some kind of analogy.

PETRUS: Let us place the sun, then, in the first degree of Aries and in the first minute of the [first] degree, and let us say that it began to rise in this way over the city Aren,[22] which is situated in the first of the seven *climata* of the earth,[23] being 90 degrees to the east and just as many to the west, being also 90 degrees to the north pole and just as many to the south. When the sun begins to rise over this city, I ask, what time will it be in that city which is 30 degrees to the west of the city of Aren?

MOSES: According to what I have found written in the books of the astronomers, there remain still two hours of the previous night.[24]

---

the people of the East, it is sunrise to the people in the middle; and when it is sunset to the people of the East, it is sunrise to the people in the West." For the text, see *De mundi celestis terrestrisque constitutione: A Treatise on the Universe and the Soul,* ed. and trans. Charles Burnett (London: Warburg Institute, 1985), 20–21.

22. The central Indian city of Udidjayn—see the *Encyclopedia of Islam,* ed. H. A. R. Gibb, vol. 10 (Leiden: Brill, 1999), 778b—but treated as an ideal rather than real city (sometimes Arim or Arin), which Muslim geographers located at the center of the world. One finds the city over the center of the equator in an illustration from a twelfth- or thirteenth-century manuscript of a treatise entitled *De recta imaginatione sphere,* usually ascribed to the ninth-century Thabit ibn Qurra. See John E. Murdoch, *Album of Science: Antiquity and the Middle Ages* (New York: Charles Scribner's Sons, 1984), 142, ill. 130. For a discussion of Aren, see also André Miquel, *La géographie humaine du monde musulman jusqu'au milieu du 11ᵉ siècle,* vol. 2, *Géographie arabe et représentation du monde: la terre et l'étranger* (Paris: Mouton & Co., 1967–88), 486–87.

23. *Climata:* These are the bands into which ancient and medieval geographers had divided the known world. For early medieval authors, most popular was the Macrobian map showing five *climata,* based on the zones described in Macrobius's *Commentary on the Dream of Scipio.* Of these five, three were uninhabitable. Later authors often expanded the number of *climata* to seven or eight (see Pseudo-Bede, *De mundi celestis terrestrisque constitutione,* p. 21). The number seven was adopted by Albert the Great, for example, for the division of the northern hemisphere. For a good discussion of medieval geography and cosmography as revealed in different types of maps, and their placement of the "monstrous races," see John Block Friedman, *The Monstrous Races in Medieval Art and Thought* (Syracuse: Syracuse University Press, 2000), 37–58.

24. Since, according to the medieval geocentric cosmology, it takes the sun twenty-four hours to travel 360 degrees, returning to its place on the next day, if we divide 360 by twenty-four, it is clear that in one hour the sun travels 15 degrees across the sky. Consequently, when it has moved thirty degrees, two hours will have passed.

PETRUS: Therefore, when the sun has set on the city of Aren, what hour will it be in the aforementioned city?

MOSES: Similarly, two hours of the day remain.

PETRUS: When, however, the sun begins to rise over the city [*urbs*], how many hours will there be in the city [*civitas*] of Aren?

MOSES: Two hours have passed, and the third hour is beginning.

PETRUS: And when the sun has begun to set on the city, what time is it in the city of Aren?

MOSES: Two hours of night will have already been completed.

PETRUS: If then you should draw a thread straight from the city of Aren and you direct one end of it to the east and the other to the west, and you do the same thing in the other city, drawing out from it a straight line, one end of which extends to the east and the other to the west, I ask you, will the ends of each line be able to come together from either direction at the same time?

MOSES: Hardly, but the more distant the cities are from one another, the more distant the ends of the lines will be on either side at the same time, that is, by thirty degrees.

PETRUS: Now it is entirely clear to you that the positions of East and West and the hours for sunrise and sunset are not the same for all, but vary according to the different longitudes of the earth.

MOSES: I understand this well at last.

PETRUS: Again, when the sun rises over the city of Aren, if you extend a line at the same hour at the other city which we have mentioned, to the west of this same city from the east of this same city, what point in the heaven will the extreme point of each end touch?

MOSES: That end point that stretches to the east will reach the first minute of the first degree of Pisces,[25] whereas the one that is extended to the west strikes the first minute of the first degree of Virgo.

25. "Minute," *punctus*, and "degree," *gradus*, used in their astronomical sense.

PETRUS: Again, if with the sun setting over the city of Aren, we should draw out a line at the other city in the way we have mentioned, as far as both sides of heaven, which part of heaven will each end touch?

MOSES: The one that extends to the east runs as far as the first minute of the first degree of Virgo, but the one extending to the west runs to the first minute of the first degree of Pisces.

PETRUS: Again, if as the sun is rising over the city, we should draw a line at the city of Aren to its east and to its west, extending it as far as heaven itself, which part of heaven will each end touch?

MOSES: The one that touches the east will strike the first division of the first degree of Taurus, whereas the one touching the west will run from the first minute of the first degree of Scorpio.

PETRUS: If, however, when the sun is setting over that city, we should draw the same line at the city of Aren in the manner described to the cardines of heaven, which parts of this same heaven will each end touch?

MOSES: The eastern end will touch the beginning of the first degree of Scorpio, whereas the western end will touch the beginning of the first degree of Taurus.

PETRUS: Now, then, you can recognize that the degree of the sign which is in the east as the sun is appearing over the city of Aren is not the same as the one which appears to the other city at the same time. Similarly the degree that is in the west when the sun is setting in Aren is not the same as the one which appears over the other city at the same time, and thus it will touch on all cities in proportion to the distance between them in longitude.

MOSES: I understand all these things clearly.

PETRUS: Nor is that division of the heaven, which appears today at sunrise in the east in some place on earth, the same as that one which will appear tomorrow at the same place on the same earth, at the same time.

MOSES: And this is clearly shown.

PETRUS: This variation of the degrees in heaven occurs daily, just as each day the sun itself varies through the same degrees.

MOSES: I am unable to deny what reason demonstrates.

PETRUS: Seeing that this is just as we say, it follows according to a necessary reason that in the expanse of the entire earth the places of the sunrise and sunset are not equal, nor are the hours at which the sun rises and sets the same. Therefore it follows of necessity that when the stars are setting for some, they are rising for others at the same hour, and in the entire sphere of the heaven there is no fixed place for sunrise and sunset, but rather it changes daily through various degrees. Then how much less should one believe that sunrise and sunset occur for celestial creatures, for whom no [period of] darkness ever intervenes. Rather, the perpetual clarity of an unfailing light illuminates them, just as David the prophet says: "But darkness will not be dark to you, and night will be illuminated just as is the day, for its darkness and its light are just the same."[26] And Daniel says: "He reveals deep and hidden things and knows what is placed in darkness, and light will always be with him."[27] Since, then, there can be no change of position[28] upwards or downwards in heaven, it is most clearly evident to anyone that neither is there an east or west in heaven. Since this has been proved, the foolishness is evident of those who say that God's location is in the west, where the stars supplicate God.

MOSES: Although I am unable to refute such clear arguments, I would like you to show me, if you please, how the longitudes of the distances of cities from each other can be known or proved, so that we may know better the differences of the hours that appear at the same time over them.

PETRUS: Let us then place the sun in the first minute of Aries, and let an eclipse of the sun begin to occur at the city of Aren at the first minute of the seventh hour of the day, so that at the same hour the first degree of Cancer will be in the east of Aren. Now, if you want to know at what hour this eclipse began to occur in the other city that we mentioned, if you look closely you will find that it began there in the first minute of the fifth hour, and it will appear that at that same moment the

26. Ps 138.12.
27. Dn 2.22.
28. Reading *localis* (A) for *locatis* (B).

first minute of Gemini is in the east of that city. Thus, beyond any doubt it is clear that there are thirty degrees of longitude between these two cities. In this way astronomers discover how much longitude there is between two cities.

MOSES: Removing a veil of great blindness from my breast, you have poured into it the light of the clearest truth, which is why God gives you a worthy repayment as a reward. But since I remember that you said previously that the city of Aren is situated in the middle hemisphere of heaven, so that it is equidistant from all the parts, and that it is positioned in the first of the seven *climata*, I would like you to make me understand this, showing clearly a description of its position, so that I can imagine myself to be in that city. For since you say that Aren is positioned in the middle of the earth, you seem to say that the surface of the earth itself is flat. Whereas in the argument already advanced concerning East and West, you had indicated that the earth is a round sphere. Every round thing, however, lacks a beginning and an end [*finis*], but wherever you seek out a beginning or a boundary [*terminus*], without doubt you will find a middle there as well.

PETRUS: Consider, then, that Aren is in such a position on the earthly sphere that it is equidistant from both the north and the south pole,[29] and that each day the first two minutes of Aries and Libra pass through its middle. Therefore, there will be 90 degrees to each pole, and in this way Aren[30] will be in the first part of the first climate with respect to the earth's latitude, and in the middle of this same climate with respect to longitude.

MOSES: One gathers from your words[31] that the entire habitable part of the earth exists in only one part. I would like to know, then, which this would be.

PETRUS: From the middle of the earth to the northern part.

MOSES: I want this to be shown to me with a geometric illustration, seeing that I do not doubt but that different peoples have thought different things concerning this matter, based on

29. I.e., it is at the equator.
30. Reading with Migne's edition *ita Aren* rather than the text's *terra Aren* (A and B). Mieth's apparatus shows that *eritque ita* is found in all but MS B[1].
31. Reading *verbis* (A) for *vervis* (B).

the writings of [their] books. Moreover, they divide the earth
by a partition into five zones, of which they say that the middle
one is burned by the sun's heat and therefore is uninhabitable,
whereas they prove that the two extreme [zones] are likewise
uninhabitable because of the extreme nature of the cold, since
they are so distant from the sun, while they claim that the two
middle [zones] alone are habitable, because they are tempered
by its heat and from their cold.[32]

PETRUS This opinion does not stand up to the evidence of
observation [*visus*]. From observation we prove that Aren is situated in the middle of the earth, and a straight line drawn from
the beginning of Aries to the beginning of Libra passes over the
city, and that the air is very temperate, so that the temperature
is almost always the same in spring, summer, autumn, and winter. There all sorts of things grow that are fragrant, beautifully
colored, and sweet to taste. There men's bodies are neither fat
nor thin, but well-fitted with modest vigor. The temperate nature of the seasons makes men's bodies and hearts harmonious,
since they reign with ineffable wisdom and material justice.[33]
How could anyone presume to say of this place, over which the
sun passes in a direct line, that it is uninhabitable? Rather, the
entire inhabitable area of the earth extends from this place to
the north of the globe, an area that the ancients divided into
seven parts, which they called the seven climates, according to
the number of the seven planets. The first begins on the me-
dian line[34] where the city of Aren was founded, the seventh is

32. Moses notes that many say that there are five zones; that the middle
(equatorial) is uninhabitable because of heat, and the polar zones because of
cold, leaving only two inhabitable zones. This tradition of five zones was accepted by Macrobius, Pliny, Isidore, and Bede, but was not the view of Ptolemy or
Arab geographers. Petrus Alfonsi, immediately below, will articulate a notion of
three zones. The two extremes are uninhabitable, but the middle zone is then
divided into seven "climates" (*climata*), of which all are, in principle, habitable.

33. My thanks to Charles Burnett, for drawing my attention to Adelard of
Bath's similar description of the first climate in his *De opere astrolapsus*. Adelard
identifies this climate as the "home of philosophers," where "all seeds spring up
spontaneously and the inhabitants always do the right thing . . . and live happily . . . [where] the first man was born." The translation is Burnett's, and will
be found in his *The Introduction of Arabic Learning into England*, The Panizzi Lectures, 1996 (London: The British Library, 1997), 44–45.

34. I.e., the equator.

at the extreme north of the world, and the remaining climates
occupy the space in between. And no place is uninhabitable except where either the dryness of many deserts with their pau-
city of water or the mountains' ruggedness does not permit the
work of plowing or reaping. The following figure demonstrates
to the eye all of the things already described.[35]

MOSES: Thanks be to God, that you have satisfied my desire
by showing me, visibly, the truth of the matter. Therefore, I beg
you to show me why that part of the earth which is to the south
of Aren is not inhabited, like that one which is nearer the north,
so that Aren would be in the middle of the habitable region; or,
why that part which is on the other side is not habitable, and
why that one which is lying near to the north is uninhabitable.

PETRUS: Because the orbit of the sun [*circuli solis*] is eccentric to the earth's orbit, on the northern side.[36] Hence, when the
sun descends to the six signs of the southern region, which are
from Libra to Aries, since it is nearer to the earth then, burning
it by its proximity with its heat, it renders the earth unfruitful
for all things and altogether sterile, and this is why it is uninhabitable. Therefore, from the first climate as far as the northern
region, a habitable space remains that is divided into seven climates. Whatever is from the seventh climate, however, remains
devoid of all heat, since the sun descends from there to the six
signs of the southern part, and there abounds there an excess of
clouds, snow, and cold, so that no animal has a dwelling there.
Moreover, the illustration[37] that is available to the eyes clearly
demonstrates the manner in which the center of the sun's orbit
is eccentric to the earth's orbit on the northern side.

MOSES: I give thanks; you have demonstrated for me with a
brief but excellent argument what I did not know before, and I
see that the response is adequate for those who think somewhat
differently about the division of the earth.

PETRUS: Having completed our present discourse, by the will
of God, let us return to the discussion.

MOSES: I think that is worthwhile.

35. See illustrations on pp. 62 and 63.
36. I.e., the northern hemisphere.
37. "Illustration": *descriptio*. See illustration on p. 65.

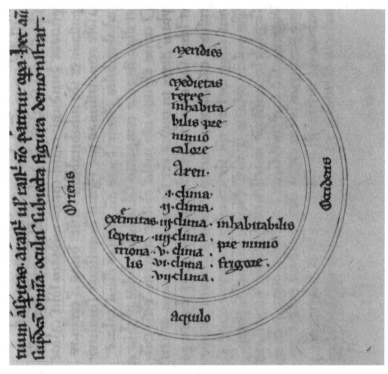

Alfonsi's map of the world. Along the outside circle are the 4 compass points, with south [*meridies*] at the top. At the center of the inner circle is the city Aren. Below Aren are the seven climates [*climata*]. Above the city Aren is a note that the middle of the earth is uninhabitable because of extreme heat. Source: British Library Additional MS 15404, fol. 41.

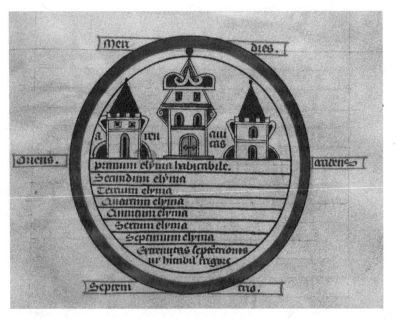

Alfonsi's map of the world. Outside the circle are the 4 compass points, with south [*meridies*] at the top. Inside the circle is the city Aren. Below Aren are the seven climates [*climata*]. Again, the extreme north is shown to be uninhabitable because of excessive cold. Source: Bodleian Library, MS. Laud Misc. 356, fol. 120r.

PETRUS: Your sages affirm in the third book of [their] teaching that God exists in a place bounded on six sides, asserting this on the basis of the testimony of Daniel, who says: "When I went forth, there appeared the prince of the Greeks coming."[38] On the basis of this, they imagine that God is in such a place that has an entrance and exit. But if this is so, clearly it reveals then that he exists in a place bounded on six sides. If he is circumscribed in an actual place that is bounded, then there is some place that is emptied of God. But if this is the case, then how will he know what there is in another place, where he does not himself exist, or how will he act in it?

MOSES: Certainly he can possess such wisdom and will that he may know through wisdom what is somewhere else, and act upon it through the will.

PETRUS: I want you to answer me, whether this wisdom and will are always in him and with him, or whether they are apart from him and thus sometimes exist without him. For if you say that they are in him and not apart from him, then the same thing results for them as for him—since they will not be in every place, then how can they know or act on what is somewhere else? If, however, you say that they exist and fill every place outside of him, then they are distinct from him. For they know something which he himself does not know, and they work by themselves what he himself does not work. Therefore, these are capable of creating by themselves, and the world does not need God.

MOSES: These can be in him and radiate to every place while knowing and operating, as the sun, although it exists in one place, nevertheless continually diffuses its rays both while heating and bringing light.

PETRUS: If this is so, then it follows that that wisdom and will do not exist everywhere equally. For whatever is diffused in this way does not have the same power at the end as it has at its beginning, which hardly befits God. Since, however, you dare to impose a limit on God, would that you believe that he is simple[39] and not ascribe corporeal accidents to him.

38. Dn 10.20.
39. I.e., not composite.

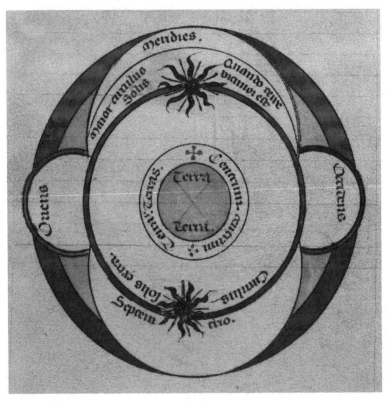

Alfonsi's map of the world. Outside the circle are the 4 compass points, with south [*meridies*] at the top. The central circle contains the earth. The circle surrounding it depicts the movement of the sun. Source: Bodleian Library, MS. Laud Misc. 356, fol. 120r.

MOSES: How do you say that we believe this?

PETRUS: Indeed, you say that every day, once a day, he grows angry, bringing forth the testimony of David, who says: "He is angry every day."[40] You affirm that he is angry at the first hour of the day, saying that the cause of his anger is that at that hour the kings of iniquity arose and placed the diadem on themselves and worshiped the sun.[41] Do you not see how absurd this remark is and how foolish they are who have uttered it, since they do not actually know the definition of anger; if they did know it, they would not think this about God.

MOSES: What do you think anger is, then?

PETRUS: Anger is, after some word that is unpleasant has been heard, when red choler [*cholera rubea*], that is, bile, boils over and is diffused over the liver and mixes with blood.[42] From this a man heats up and becomes pale in the face. This does not suit God in any way, unless he is composed of the four elements.[43] God, however, is not subject to such features.

MOSES: I am unable to contradict the truth.

PETRUS: Nor is it less abhorrent that they say that he grows angry over a thing for which he cannot avenge himself. That if he could, his anger would actually be calmed. Moreover, they

40. Ps 7.12.

41. A claim attributed to R. Meir. See B.T. *Ber.* 7a.

42. A person with a complexion dominated by red bile typically is understood to be prone to anger. See Bede, *De temporum ratione liber*, c. 35, ed. Ch. W. Jones and Th. Mommsen, CC SL 123B (Turnholt: Brepols, 1977), 392. Yet I have not found a source for this seemingly uncommon definition of anger. By contrast, Alfonsi's older contemporary, the Cassinese monk and physician Constantine the African, defines anger or wrath as a "bubbling" of the blood that is within the heart, and the sudden exit of natural heat: "Ira est ebullitio sanguinis in corde existentis, et motus caloris naturalis subito extra corpus vindicandum exeuntis"; *Constantini Africani de communibus medico cognitu necessariis locis*, 5, 37, in Constantine the African, *Theorices* (Basel: Henri cum Petrum, 1536). Alfonsi takes up the definition of anger again in the tenth *titulus*, when discussing Adam's fall and subsequent loss of a balanced humoral complexion. See *infra*, p. 225.

43. The diverse humoral complexions derive from the mixture of the four elements of earth, air, fire, and water, which are the simplest components of any body. A choleric complexion is warm and dry, with more of fire and earth in its composition. See Constantine the African, *Pantegni*, 1, 6, in *L'Arte universale della medicina (Pantegni)*, trans. Marco T. Malato and Umberto de Martini (Rome: Istituto di storia della medicina dell'università di Roma, 1961); Michael Scot, *Liber phisionomiae*, cap. 33.

say that no one ever knew the minute of that hour when he becomes angry except Balaam, the son of Beor.[44] But with this claim you contradict your own words since, on the one hand Moses calls him a soothsayer,[45] whereas you call him wicked, [and] on the other hand you indicate that he has more foresight than Moses about God, because he knew the minute of the hour which was unknown to Moses. And although this may be said with great admiration, nevertheless it pales in comparison to an even greater foolishness, when you say that the rooster, an irrational animal, knows the minute of the exact hour each day. Do you concede that they have said all these things?

MOSES: Even should I wish to, I cannot deny it.

PETRUS: Nor is it enough for them to say this about God, but they also say that he cries once each day, every day, and they say that two tears coming from his eyes fall into the great sea,[46] and they assert that these tears are that brightness [*fulgur*] that seems to fall from the stars at night.[47] This argument, however, shows that God is composed of the four elements. For tears only occur from an abundance of moisture descending from the head. If, then, this is so, then the elements are the matter of God. For all matter is prior to and simpler than form. Therefore, these tears, too, are prior to and simpler than God, which is a wicked thing to believe. Therefore, if God is such as you say he is, since he enjoys neither food nor drink, and yet daily he emits tears from himself, then it is necessary that he suffer decrease, unless perhaps he continually imbibes of the waters

44. For this claim about Balaam, see B.T. *Ber.* 7a.

45. Nm 22.5.

46. Cf. B.T. *Ber.* 59a.

47. I have been unable to find a source that indicates that God's tears are the source of lightning or this heavenly brightness. Ginzberg records a tradition that lightning emanated from God's mouth. See Louis Ginzberg, *The Legends of the Jews*, trans. Henrietta Szold, vol. 3 (Philadelphia: Jewish Publication Society, 1968), 95. Alfonsi may be referring to shooting stars, or perhaps to one ancient view of the origin of lightning, which holds that it is a reflection of the sun, moon, or stars from moisture-bearing clouds, or a kind of fire trapped in them. Cf. Aristotle, *Meteor.* 2.9 (369b12–16; 370a11ff.). Aristotle's text was widely read in the Middle Ages, in Latin, Hebrew, and Arabic translations. For discussion and texts, see Pieter L. Schoonheim, *Aristotle's* Meteorology *in the Arabic-Latin Tradition: A Critical Edition of the Texts with Introduction and Indices* (Leiden, Boston, Cologne: Brill, 2000).

that are above the heavens. One understands, then, from their words, that they do not know what that brightness is.[48]

MOSES: I would like to know what you think about this brightness.

PETRUS: A certain very dry, smoky vapor arises from the earth, from which it passes through the place of the clouds, arriving at a place where there is not much heat, since it is remote from the movement of the firmament. Hence, when it arrives and when a great deal of it gathers in one place, it is gradually burned by the heat of that place (even though it is slight), and once burned it evaporates, and this is what we see traverse the air.

MOSES: Since without interruption I am made more learned by you, I properly give thanks without cease.

PETRUS: They also say that the cause of this weeping, which they unworthily ascribe to God, is the Jews' captivity. Moreover, they assert that, on account of grief, he roars like a lion three times a day and that in so doing he strikes the heavens with his feet in the manner of someone treading in a [wine] press,[49] [and] that like a dove he makes a cooing sound, and moves his head from side to side and says, with a voice like one grieving: "Woe is me, woe is me! that I have reduced my house to a desert, and burned my temple, and removed my children to the gentiles. Alas for the father who has removed his children, and alas for the children who have been removed from the table of their father."[50] Moreover, they say that one of your sages heard this voice in a certain place of ruins. In addition, they say that he rubs the feet together as if they were itching, and just like one who is grieving he claps the hands together, and that he prays daily that his mercy would rise above his anger and that he would come upon his people in mercy. Tell me, O Moses, when God prays, I ask whom does he worship—himself, or another? If another, then the one he worships is more powerful than he. If he worships himself, either he has power over that for which he prays, or he is impotent. If he is impotent, he worships himself in vain. Whereas if he has power, either he wills

48. Cf. B.T. *Ber.* 59a.
49. Cf. Jer 25.30.
50. Cf. B.T. *Ber.* 3a.

that for which he prays, or he does not will it. If he does not will it, then he prays for nothing. If, however, he wills it, then it is not necessary to pray. You see then, O Moses, how this people is altogether estranged from divine knowledge. Therefore, if it is true that God cries for you, that he roars like a lion, strikes the heaven with [his] feet, laments like a dove, moves his head, calls out "woe is me" on account of too much grief, and that in addition he rubs [his] feet together and claps [his] hands together and prays each day to have mercy on you, what then prevents you from being freed from your captivity? Does this delay stem from you or from him? For if it is from him, then you show that his power is inadequate to fulfill his will, since you affirm that he weeps like a child from being unable to complete something he wills. If, then, he is impotent now, tell me whether he will have the power in the future or not? If he will never have it, then both his grief and yours will be without end and your prayer empty and your hope null. Whereas if he will have the power, either he has not had it yet but will have it at a certain and predetermined time at which, when he has it, he will free you from captivity. Or he has already had it, but he lost it by the intervention of some accidents, and then when these have been removed, once again he will recover the power and lead you forth from captivity. If, however, he will have it at a certain time, it remains for you to say what it is that prevents him from having it now, namely, whether you impute this to his youthfulness,[51] or the weakness of his members, or to an obstacle of any type whatsoever from which he cannot be defended. But it is wicked to believe this of God. For we read in the sacred Scriptures, to which you entrust faith together with us, that God performed miracles in ancient times greater than would be required to free you from captivity, as when he struck Egypt with the ten plagues[52] and led you out from there with a strong hand, and divided the Red Sea, in which he drowned Pharaoh and his army,[53] and also fed you in the desert with manna and quail from heaven,[54] and fixed the waters of the Jordan in one place,

---

51. "Youthfulness": lit., the brevity of his years.
52. Cf. Ex 7.17–11.7.   53. Cf. Ex 14.21–28.
54. Cf. Ps 77.24–30; Ex 16.15–35; Nm 11.31–33.

resembling a mountain,[55] and fixed [in one place] the sun and the moon in response to Joshua's prayers[56] and caused 175,000 to be slain from the army of Sennacherib in one night.[57] In the days of Ezekiel, he commanded the sun to go back 10 degrees[58] and freed Daniel from the lion's den.[59] He freed Ananias, Misael, and Azariah from fire[60] and freed you from the Babylonian captivity,[61] and performed many other miracles too many to enumerate. Therefore you cannot say that he was not powerful in ancient days. If, however, you concede that he was powerful, as is proper, but say that he was made impotent by the intervention of other accidents, after whose departure you believe that he will recover his power, then it is necessary that you confess one of two things: either that accidents existed outside of him or in him, as an illness that befalls a human being checks the effectiveness of his will until he convalesces, or that these are imposed on him by another, as captivity imposed on anyone by the king deprives him of the power of his own will, until, when freedom arrives, it withdraws. If you say that they were outside of him and in him, then you say that God has a body, which is susceptible to contraries, which it is not fit to think about God. Whereas if you say that they are imposed upon him by another, you demonstrate that that one who imposed them is more powerful than God, which is not less inappropriate. If, however, you say that you yourselves are the cause of your captivity, it is as if you consider yourselves better off in captivity in some way than you were previously in freedom. It is clear to anyone that this is a deception, because captivity is never comparable to freedom. If, however, you delay your freedom, not with that intention, but with the intention that he free you by willing it, you oppose his will through pertinacity, with the inevitable result that, because he cast you into captivity, from contrariness you will remain in this captivity longer than he wills. Therefore, he ought

55. Cf. Jos 3.16.
56. Cf. Jos 10.13.
57. Cf. 2 Kgs 19.35; Sir 48.24. Note that the 175,000 is surely a scribal error for 185,000; at the beginning of the third *titulus*, Alfonsi has the correct number.

58. Cf. 2 Kgs 20.10–11; Sir 48.26.   59. Cf. Dn 6.20–24.
60. Cf. Dn 3.88.   61. Cf. 1 Esd 7.

to satisfy your will and not burden himself continually with so much grief, or it would be fitting for him to spare you and not to make you so sorrowful. But this cannot stand at all since daily you pray to him to snatch you from captivity. Therefore, I beg you, Moses, to remove such twists and turns from your breast.

MOSES: None of those things that you enumerated prevents our captivity [from ending], but we confess that God always was and always is omnipotent. Nor do we deny that we want to escape captivity, but [we confess] that God has affixed a certain limit to our captivity, and until that time approaches which he established, swore, and confirmed, we say that we cannot be freed in any way.

PETRUS: With this claim you attribute a lack of knowledge to God, since you say that he established and swore in such a way that later he repented of what he swore and confirmed, an indication of which is that he is continually afflicted on your behalf in so many ways. But if he had known this in advance, he would not have established it earlier. Therefore, according to you, he was foolish. Since you agree on this, you ought certainly to indulge him and to cease to disturb him with continual prayers. For the more often you pray, the more you renew his grief; and since you do not disturb him more when ceasing from prayer, you allow him to be consoled so much more. But tell me, I beg you, O Moses, tell me, I ask you, should anyone give credence to sages of this sort and adopt a faith from their treatises?

MOSES: Since they confirm their sayings with the authority of the prophets, why do you inveigh against them so severely and why do you say nothing against the prophets? Do you not know that the prophets said that God has a head, eyes, nostrils, hands, arms, and all the outlines of a body? They have even said that he grows angry on particular days and that he roars like a lion, and many other things, which are proved with their authority.

PETRUS: The sayings of the prophets are obscure, and they are not sufficiently clear to all. For this reason, when we find things such as this in the prophets, which, when accepted literally, cause us to depart from the path of reason, we interpret them as allegories, so that we may return to the narrow path

of reason.[62] Now, necessity compels us to do this, since reason
cannot support the text otherwise. Your sages, however, have
not known God as was necessary, and for this reason, explicating the sayings of the prophets in a superficial way, they erred
against him. Therefore, on account of this instance and on account of many others like this, I said above that I understand
the sayings of the prophets as a sound sense requires.

MOSES: Now I want a passage to be shown to me which must
be understood allegorically because, explicated literally, [rea-
son] cannot support it, so that it is clear that what you say is
true.

PETRUS: I will show you what you seek. For Moses said to
Pharaoh, "The locust will cover the eye of the whole earth."[63]
Now does the earth have an eye? Likewise, concerning the sons
of Korah: "the earth opening its mouth will devour them."[64]
Now, then, does the earth have a mouth? Again, in the book of
Judges Gaal says to Zebul: "Look, a people is descending from
the navel of the earth."[65] But does the earth have a navel? And
again, Isaiah says: "From the wing of the earth we heard praises."[66] Does the earth have a wing? And David, too, says: "The
fields will exult and all that is in them."[67] And again he says:
"The rivers will clap their hands, the mountains will exult."[68]
Now then, can the fields rejoice, or do the rivers have hands, or
can the mountains exult? Solomon says, too: "The birds of heav-

62. Jewish authors also interpreted such biblical passages allegorically. Thus,
toward the end of the twelfth century, Joseph Kimhi notes that "Scripture says,
eyes of God, ears of God, mouth of God, hand of God, face of God, foot of God. All of this
is expressed metaphorically so that people might know something about Him
by conceiving of Him as a human being . . ."; *Book of the Covenant,* trans. Frank
Talmage (Toronto: Pontifical Institute of Mediaeval Studies, 1972), 42.

63. Ex 10.4. The Vulg. reads, "will cover the surface of the earth" (*operiat su-
perficiem terrae*).

64. Nm 16.30.

65. Jgs 9.37.

66. Is 24.16. Alfonsi is apparently aware that the Hebrew word for "end" or
"ends" of the earth, כנף, can also mean "wing" (a bird's wing). Therefore, in
translating this Isaian passage here, he provides the *Hebraica veritas* and departs
from the Vulg.—which he reproduces below when he cites this text again in the
second *titulus*—in order to give a more literal translation from the Hebrew.

67. Ps 95.12.

68. Ps 97.8.

en will carry your word, and one that has feathers will announce the judgment."[69] Now, can either a bird speak a word, or can one that has feathers announce anything? Also, Habakkuk the prophet says: "The rock will cry out from the wall, and the timber, which is between the joints of the building, will answer."[70] Can either a rock cry out or can timber answer?

MOSES: I confess that what you say is true, that in many places the allegorical sense would be necessary; nevertheless, I do not know why you say that what the prophets have said about the corporeal outlines of God, if it is explicated according to the letter, is absurd.

PETRUS: The corporeal outlines that you ascribe to God only befit a corporeal substance and imaginary thing. It is improper, however, to believe that God is of this sort. Therefore, it is unsuitable to explicate the things that have been said about him, as if of a body, according to the letter alone. For if anyone thinks this, he shows himself to be opposed equally to reason and to Scripture.

MOSES: I would like you to show me why someone who understands it in this way is opposed to Scripture.

PETRUS: Because if we say that God has any image or likeness, then we oppose many authoritative statements of the prophets. For Moses said to the children of Israel: "Carefully guard your souls. You saw no likeness on the day that the Lord spoke to you at Horeb out of the midst of the fire, lest perhaps, being deceived, you make for yourselves a graven likeness or image of a man or a woman, a likeness of all of the beasts which are upon the earth, or of the birds flying under heaven, or of the reptiles which move upon the ground, or of the fish which dwell underneath in the waters."[71] And when he prohibited them, so that they not make God resemble composite bodies, then, being anxious, he added this, lest they make him conform to simple bodies: "Lest perhaps having raised your eyes to heaven you see the sun and the moon and all the stars of heaven and, being deceived by error, you adore and worship them, which the Lord your God created for the nations that are under heaven."[72] You

69. Eccl 10.20.	70. Hab 2.11.
71. Dt 4.15–18.	72. Dt 4.19.

should not think that when Moses commanded these things for the people, he was afraid that they would worship the shapes or images of the aforementioned bodies, since they did not doubt even then that they are creatures. Instead, he feared this: that they would believe that God has an image among one of these, and this is why they would worship some sort of likeness made to represent him.

MOSES: This judgment is certainly subtle, and it is not transparent to every understanding; wherefore, some things yet are necessary to make it clearer for me.

PETRUS: The prophet Isaiah says: "To whom have you likened me and made me equal, says the Holy One?"[73] And again, "To what have you made a likeness of God, or what image will you propose for him?"[74] And again, "To whom have you likened and equated and compared me and made me similar?"[75] Also, David's words prove that God is not in a place, and as a result they imply that he does not have a body. For he says: "Whither shall I go from your spirit, and whither shall I flee from your face? If I ascend to heaven you are there; if I descend to hell, you are present. If I take up my wings at dawn and dwell in the most distant parts of the sea, even there your hand will lead me and your right hand shall hold me."[76] Solomon perceives the same thing when he says: "Should one think that God will dwell upon the earth? For if heaven and the heaven of heavens cannot hold you, how much less can this house which I have built?"[77] And elsewhere, "In every place, the eyes of the Lord contemplate goods and evils."[78] And Jeremiah [says]: "Shall a man be concealed in hidden places, that I shall not see him, says the Lord? Do I not fill both heaven and earth, says the Lord?"[79] Now you can observe clearly that if we explicate the Scriptures in a superficial way, saying that God has a body and all the members of a body, then we contradict all the testimonies introduced above by whose authority we wish to prove this.

MOSES: Because I see how much my understanding is op-

73. Is 40.25.
74. Is 40.18.
75. Is 46.5.
76. Ps 138.7.
77. 2 Chr 6.18.
78. Prv 15.3.
79. Jer 23.24.

posed to the Scriptures, and the extent to which it departs from reason, I desire to hear the second thing promised.

PETRUS: When we will lie down in the palace of great Reason, let us strew the ground of this same palace with some flowers of opinions, so that afterward we will sit there more delightfully when we argue. Some of these opinions will be steps for us to prove that God is, and to know what he is. For first we ought to prove that God exists, and then afterward to show that there is nothing else like him. For a certain portion of men deny that God exists, and assert that the world has existed from eternity and without a creator. This necessity compels us first to show that a God exists, who created the world.

MOSES: Why did you not undertake this at all in what went before, when speaking of the Scriptures, to show first that God exists?

PETRUS: Those who conform their faith to the Scriptures do not deny that God exists. And this is why it was not necessary to prove this to those who believe in Scripture, but only to those who do not believe in anything that was written.

MOSES: Since you do not want to prove through the Scriptures that God exists, and since he is himself incomprehensible to every corporeal sense, it will help me a great deal to hear how this can be proved by philosophical reason.

PETRUS: If I show that the world and all that is in it were created, then necessarily I conclude that there is a God, who is understood to be the creator.

MOSES: And how can you prove this?

PETRUS: One is said to think of existence in three modes. Now, one way is when it is perceived by some corporeal sense; another, when it is known only by a necessary reason; and another, when it is discovered through an analogy to other things. What is perceived by some [corporeal] sense cannot be proved by any other evidence, just as one who has been blind from birth cannot distinguish the variety of colors in any other way than by hearing alone, and hearing does not satisfy his mind on the whole, and so, too, for the other corporeal senses. Whereas that which is known by necessary reason is something of this sort, as when we say that some body cannot stand still at the same moment as it is moved, and likewise that a body cannot be in different places at the same time, or that it cannot be predicated truthfully of anything both that it is and is not. That, however, which is perceived by analogy is of this sort: that if you hear a voice somewhere, you understand that there is something making the voice there, even though you do not see it, or when you see smoke somewhere, you know that there is fire, too, even if you do not see it.[80] Likewise, if we see some vessel that has been made, we know with certainty that someone was its maker, even if we do not see him. And so we have to prove first that the world was created, in order to establish that someone was its creator. And when we have proven that there is a creator for the world, we will show with reason that, as a result, the creator himself has no likeness.

MOSES: It is appropriate for me to bless your words,[81] from which I believe that I receive such great fruit. Therefore, fulfill the promise, and now bestrew the palace with the flowers which you mentioned.

PETRUS: Almost all philosophers agree on this: that the origin of things is the Perfect Wisdom, the very Bright Light, the Substance of Substances, the reason for all things. After this comes the world of the universal soul, and after that is matter. These two, however, namely, the universal soul and matter, are simple and the first of all created things, and the origin and cause of the whole composite thing, out of which the firmament is made, gradually, with all the forms and images which it contains.[82]

MOSES: Your words lead one to understand that the firmament is a composite, along with all the things that are in it. I have found it written in many places, however, that whatever is below the orbit of the moon is a composite, whereas whatever is above it is simple.

PETRUS: Indeed, the firmament, with all that it contains, is,

80. "Analogy": i.e., a reasoned inference.

81. Reading *benedicere* (A) for *venedicere* (B).

82. See Marie-Thérèse d'Alverny's "Pseudo-Aristotle, *De elementis*," for the claim that Alfonsi's emanationist scheme here follows the pseudo-Aristotelian text.

in the truth of the matter, composite, but it is said to be simple
in respect to those things which lie below the orbit of the moon.
For this is the way it is for all things, that something is said to be
composite with respect to that from which it is made, but simple
with respect to that which comes to be from it. For example, a
thread is a composite compared to the flax, whereas to the web
which comes to be from it, it is simple. In the same way, whatever is above the moon is something simple compared to those
things that are below the moon, because they are made from
that simple one, whereas, compared to matter, it is composite,[83]
since it is made from it.

MOSES: I want to understand very clearly how the firmament
is said to be composite, since it is one substance.

PETRUS: Every body is composite. Every composite, however,
is so either substantially or partially [*partiale*]; substantially, as
when one substance is joined to another, and partially, when
parts of one substance are joined together. Now a substance is
joined to a substance when a body is composed of bone, flesh,
and veins joined together, just as a door is composed of wood
and iron. Thus every thing that is completed by the union of diverse substances is said to be substantially composite. The composition of a partial composite, however, is more subtle. This
is clear from the fact that every body that has length, breadth,
and height, is not joined to a different body, but is composed
from parts of its own substance alone, as many parts of silver
are joined together until they produce something weighty and
solid. This composite, however, is simpler than the one above,
whereas that one is said to be completely simple which is devoid
of a composition of either sort. And because the firmament is
a body consisting of three dimensions, indeed it is truly a composite, yet nevertheless it is partially composite.

MOSES: I would like to know the reason why every body that
consists of length, breadth, and height is composite.

PETRUS: Every body whose nature is subject to motion [*mobi-*

83. The "it" in this clause can only refer to the simple superlunary substance.
Alfonsi's point is that even a superlunary substance, which appears to be simple
when compared with some sublunary substance, appears composite when compared to the [prime] matter from which it is composed.

lis] into some part is moved into the same part only through its nature. Moreover, it is known that that part, to which it is moved by nature, is its natural place. And since this is so, it would be impossible for it to have any dimension[84] to another part that would be contrary to its natural place. But if it was found to have some dimension to another part, one of these two is the cause why that should happen: namely, either that it is externally composite, like a wall that is joined by the superimposition of rocks, or internally composite, as the parts of a tree projecting from the ground spread themselves on this side and that and receive some dimension. Moreover, both of them give it to be understood that whatever has some dimension to another part, which is contrary to the natural part of its motion, is a composite. Therefore, the firmament also, although it is one substance, is composite.

MOSES: Now reason has instructed that the firmament is a composite, with all that it possesses. I do not know, however, how the universal soul and matter can be found in it, or how these would be simple.

PETRUS: Since it has been proved that the firmament is a composite, necessarily one must conclude that there is some matter from which it is composed, like a bed, whose matter is wood, or a knife, whose matter is iron. Moreover, it is necessary for this matter to be simpler than the firmament, in the same way that wood is simpler than a bed and iron is simpler than a knife. And since every material is simpler than whatever is made from it, and it does not contain in itself the form or image of its composite, it is clear that the matter of the firmament has no corporeal form in itself and for this reason it is altogether simple. But if we say that some composite exists in it, then it is necessary that there be some matter that is even simpler, from which [matter] the composite exists. But then when we speak of that matter as composite, we will confess that it has another matter still more simple, and so on to infinity. But to avoid this, it is necessary that we confess that that matter is simple. See, it

84. "Impossibile est, ullam dimensionem habeat ad aliam partem . . ." This is a strange use of the noun *dimensio*, which here seems to imply spatial extension.

has been proved adequately that there is matter in the firmament and that it is simple. We will, however, find the soul to be like this in the same [firmament], namely, because those forms with which matter itself is informed were not made for the sake of the completion of the body alone. For forms are spoken of in two ways. For some only reveal the boundary of body, like triangularity or rotundity or some other shape in a rock, which are able to do nothing but effect the shape of the body itself. Other [forms] both inform body and seem to be made fit for a certain use, at nature's urging, like the form of the ear for hearing, [the form] of the eye for seeing, and as the individual forms of the other members are suited to their own function. In the same way, the form of the knife is appropriate for cutting, that of the saw for sawing, and that of a mattock for digging. And since matter received various new forms into itself which it never had before, it follows that it had them not from itself, but from a union with something else which is even more powerful and simpler, which produced the diverse forms and images in itself, especially since there was no necessity for such forms or images to occur in it. This has occurred more from the desire of the soul, which willed to be mixed with a thing of a sort with which it had never been mixed, so that its power would be evident in it. Therefore, after it is mixed and connected with that thing, the matter is informed with new forms from the new mixture. Since, according to the philosophers, it is not doubted that the firmament is composite, along with all that it contains, it is necessary for one to believe that it has a beginning. For every composite has some beginning. In this way, it is clear that the world is created. Moreover, it is necessary for every composite to have a compositor, for nothing can compose itself, and in the same way it is necessary that every thing that is created have a creator. For nothing can create itself. Therefore, it is necessary that there exist a creator of the world, who is called God.

MOSES: An opponent can respond, saying that the power of the universal soul is the compositor, which power is called, namely, Nature. Which soul when joined to matter, I say, composed the firmament and all the things that are in it, and there is no other compositor or creator of things.

PETRUS: What you say cannot stand. Because we see that the various forms with which matter is informed are fitted for various uses, it follows that nature itself, by whose admixture and power the forms were made, has a power that is not entirely unrestrained, but rather one that is restricted in some way. But it is necessary for this restricted nature to have some restrictor who is, nevertheless, restricted by nothing else.

MOSES: I respond that the soul itself is that restrictor, which has restrained its power just as it pleased it to do.

PETRUS: Such works cannot belong to the soul, but to such a maker who is perfected through himself by [his own] wisdom. The soul, however, does not have perfect wisdom.

MOSES: With what argument can you show that the soul does not have perfect wisdom?

PETRUS: Because once the soul is mixed with matter, and matter is incorporated to soul, afterward the soul is never without the vicissitude of pains and desires. Indeed, no desire arises unless pain has preceded it, so that no one ever takes delight in drinking, unless earlier he had suffered from thirst, no one takes delight in a meal unless pain had preceded it in hunger, or even takes delight in rest, unless previously he had suffered from labor, and it is even this way in all things that affect us [*affectus*]. Reason, however, when stripping itself of corporeal contagion and when considering that it is itself pure, thinks that what feels [*sentit*] nothing is better and more worthy to exist than what lies subject to the accidents of so many different passions. It follows, then, that the soul does not have perfect wisdom. Another reason can be given concerning the same thing, namely, that the soul, when it has put off reason, immediately loves luxury, theft, murder, and other vices, which the wisdom of perfect reason execrates. Whence again it is apparent that the soul's wisdom is imperfect. Thus, it is adequately proven for those who do not believe the Scriptures that there is another maker whose wisdom is perfect in itself, just as it is evident through the reason allotted to us by him that works of the soul without that very reason are defective and, in some sense, disgraceful. It follows, then, that the one from whom we receive reason is not the soul but some other, since it cannot happen

that one who abhors or execrates some thing should wish to
make it. It also follows from this that the soul is the giver of an
imperfect wisdom, whereas the giver of reason is [the giver] of
a perfect wisdom. And since reason operates in the soul, the
giver of reason necessarily is the maker of the soul. Since this is
the case, and the soul, as was proved above, has formed all composites in matter, then without doubt one can conclude that
the one who gave reason both made all things and exists as the
cause of all. And this is certainly the philosophical opinion regarding the soul. For the philosophers say that the rational soul
proceeds from the universal [soul].[85] As you know, however, the
Jews assert that all souls are created at the same time at the beginning of the world, and repose in one place, and until all are
embodied, the day of judgment will not come, and when they
are embodied, then immediately the end of the world will arrive.[86] Now Christians assert that new souls are procreated daily,
and, having been formed new, they are infused into bodies in
the womb [*in ventre*].[87] Whatever you choose to believe, how-

85. For Plato every soul is formed from the enduring substance of the world
or universal soul (see *Timaeus* 41D). Cf. Pseudo-Bede, who, following a discussion of Plato's view on the soul, adds, "Certain people say that there is only
one soul—that is, the world soul—which animates all things, granting to each
thing powers according to its aptitude; for example, reason to the stars; to men,
whom <alone> among corruptible things it found to possess a spherical head
and an erect face, it also poured in reason and sensuality . . ."; *De mundi celestis
terrestrisque constitutione* 2, p. 65.

86. *Tanhuma Pekude*, quoted in the *Jewish Encyclopedia* 11: 473–74. Pseudo-
Bede also attributes to the *Hebraica veritas* and to the philosophers the view that
"all souls were made together at the beginning of the world," later to descend
into bodies. See *De mundi celestis terrestrisque constitutione* 2, p. 67.

87. Alfonsi appears to allude here to a debate concerning the origin of the
individual human soul. This debate grew far livelier at the end of the eleventh
and in the early twelfth century. Some—called traducianists—insisted that the
individual soul descended from Adam just like the individual human body, or
as a part separated from a whole. This view was challenged and overcome by the
thirteenth century by those who insisted that God creates new souls for each
new body, and infuses the soul into the body at some moment after conception.
Pseudo-Bede gives expression to this debate, writing, "Others say that souls are
born from the passing of the sperm, and, just as the body of the son is separated from the substance of the father, so the soul of the son <is separated from>
the soul of the father. They infer this argument from the similarities of character. . . . Steadfast faith convinces us that souls . . . are born together with the
body itself. And there is a certain time after the conception of the seed which is
fashioned into the human body, when the soul is born in the body"; *De mundi ce-*

ever, concerning the soul, without a doubt, as was said, the one
who gave reason made all things and exists as the cause of all.
It is necessary then for this creator, who has perfect wisdom, to
exist as eternal and to be neither created nor new, since if this
one should be believed to be created or new, then certainly it
would be necessary to have another creator, or initiator [*nova-
tor*]. To be sure, nothing can ever create or initiate itself, and
thus the number of creators or initiators will be without end.
Moreover, creation [*factura*] will never reach a fixed limit when
there are fashioners without end. Therefore, one must believe
that the first creator is neither created nor initiated, but is necessarily eternal. Moreover, it is appropriate to believe that he
is not composite, but simple. In fact, every composition is the
motion and act of a simple thing. Likewise, what is first cannot
have a beginning. Every composition, however, has a beginning.
Therefore, the first creator is neither a composite nor corporeal. Indeed every thing that is corporeal, as we discussed in
depth above, is composite. In the same way, neither is he subject to motion [*mobilis*]. For everything that is moved consists of
parts. But whatever consists of parts is composite. That which is
the first of all things, however, is not composite. Therefore, neither is it subject to motion. And again, every motion occurs in a
body, whether it is rectilinear [*recta*] motion, as when someone
abandons one place and occupies another, or it is motion in
a circle, namely, when something existing in the same place is
turned in a circle [*orbis*], like the firmament. Or there is a motion of the parts of something toward one another, from the
extremes to the middle or from the middle to the extremes,
as occurs in the parts of the air, or there may be a motion of a
thing existing in the same place, but expanding to this side and
to that by certain increments, as it were, as occurs in some sense
in the branches of trees that gradually grow out to all sides. All
of these motions can only occur in a body. But that which is the
first of all has been proven to be incorporeal. Therefore, it is

---

lestis terrestrisque constitutione 2, p. 67. The most extensive treatment of this problem, however, will be found in Odo of Tournai's *De peccato originali*, which was
written in the decade before Alfonsi's *Dialogus*. For a discussion and translation
of Odo's text, see *Two Theological Treatises of Odo of Tournai: On Original Sin, and
a Debate with the Jew, Leo.*

not subject to motion. And again, neither is it changed or corrupted. To be sure, each of these is a motion. But the first of all
is immobile. Therefore, it is not changed or corrupted. Again,
neither does it grow through itself nor is it increased by an external agent. For every thing that receives growth or increase
is without a doubt a composite. But we showed above that that
which is the first of all is not composite. Therefore, neither does
it grow nor is it increased. Likewise, it does not decrease. For
what decreases is corrupted. But it has been proved that the first
of all is not corrupted, and therefore neither does it decrease.
And again, it has no likeness in any respect to any creature. For
likeness [*similitudo*] is a quality. But that which is the first of all
is not subject to any quality, and therefore neither is it subject
to likeness. Again, let us propose that it have a likeness to some
creature. But it is evident that a likeness of two things renders
one like the other, just as, if the two are said to be the same in
whiteness, then the whiteness of one ought to be like the whiteness of the other. And it is the same for blackness and for every
thing that causes a likeness among others. If this were the case,
this is why what is first of all would be first and last at the same
time, and what is last would be last and first at the same time.
How unsuitable each of these [claims] would be is not hidden
from anyone. Again, since matter that is created has no form or
image in itself, how much less should God, the creator of nature itself, who is of a simpler and subtler nature, be thought to
have any likeness. I believe we have clearly proved, by reason,
that God has no likeness, fulfilling then what was promised.

MOSES: I thank God and you, because I have recognized without any hindrance of doubt that the creator of all is unlike any
creature, and has neither beginning nor end. For it was clear
from your words that God is the creator of all things, that [God]
is principally the root and foundation, whereas the soul and
matter exist in a secondary sense, and that God made the soul,
and that the soul that is made by God works in matter. But I earnestly entreat that one scruple, however, which is still gnawing
at my mind, be untangled by your sagacity. For I have read in
many books of the philosophers that five things existed before
the establishment of the world, namely, God, who holds the ori-

[*consistit*] through another whole, if any part is corrupted of that
which is the cause of the one existing [*consistendi*], certainly a
part is corrupted also of that for which it is a cause. Whereas if a
part of that which exists through another is corrupted, it nevertheless is not necessary that any part of that which is the cause of
the one existing be corrupted. Therefore, although place is the
cause of existing for a thing which exists in it, it is not necessary
to conclude, for this reason, that some part of place is corrupted
because some part of the thing existing in it is corrupted. Once
this has been granted, it follows that place does not exist for the
sake of another. As evidence for this argument, let us introduce
this analogy. If we say that some mountain has been removed
from any part of the world, the place in which it existed is not diminished for this reason. Certainly it has lost the original name,
because it can no longer be called the place of that mountain,
but the name and nature of a universal place have remained
there. Again, if you say that the slave of some man is dead: Now,
because the slave has died, has his master ceased to exist for that
reason? No, but he has only lost the name of "master," which he
had in relation to him. It is clear, then, that once a thing which
is in some place has been removed [from it], certainly the name
of the particular place [*partialis loci*] is changed, but in no way is
the substance of place abolished. Moreover, he says that time is a
substance existing *per se* and not as an accident which subsists for
the sake of another. For example, if we set up a vessel with water[90] in order to know the time of the individual hours, it should
not be thought that that vessel is the cause of its [time's] existing, but only that it is an indicator [*signum*] for discerning time.
For even if the vessel did not exist, time would not pass any differently. In this way, too, we ought to understand that the firmament is never the cause, but only the measure and the indicator
of time. Because even if the firmament did not exist, still time
would not cease to exist: but then time would only be simple,
without an indicator and without measure and without any distinction, just as even the time of the hours of the day would remain undifferentiated [*indiscretum*] if a vessel were not marked

90. I.e., a water clock.

out with water. Now, in order to conclude all these things briefly, it has been proved that God is the creator of all things, whom his works show to us because they come forth from a perfect wisdom, whereas the soul is both created and a creator because it creates something in matter, yet nevertheless [it is] not corporeal; moreover, time and place existing in their own right [*per se*] are not corporeal, but nonetheless they are substantial, whereas indeed matter is created but is not a creator.

MOSES: Clearly, the clarity of your argument has expelled all darkness of doubt from my breast. Indeed, I knew that the world with all that is in it was created, and not eternal. But for the completion of your task this remains for you: namely, to provide some argument which will destroy those who say that the world has existed from eternity. For they say, how was such a sudden and novel creation of things conceived by the highest creator, when he had not already created them a long time ago? To be sure, they say that it is wicked to believe that God either remembered something or suddenly saw something that previously he had forgotten or had not seen. Up to now, I have found no solution to this question of theirs.

PETRUS: You ought to know that there are three reasons for all actions. For there is one action that ought to be; a second, that ought not to be; and a third that is good absolutely [*simpliciter*]. That which ought to be is of a sort that, if you do it, you will receive thanks, whereas if you do not do it, you will be blamed. Whereas for that which ought not to be, you will be blamed if you do it, but if you do not do it, you will be praised. If, however, you perform that action which is good absolutely, you will be thanked, whereas if you do not do it, you will still not be blamed. This last one lacks measure and time and limit, just as if someone should give alms today, one does not ask why he did not do so yesterday. Similarly, if he gave one coin, one ought not investigate why he did not give two. And since the creation of the entire world is a good, as even Scripture attests, which says: "God saw all that he had made, and they were very good,"[91] one ought not ask why he did not do this earlier.

91. Gn 1.31.

MOSES: With justice, I would like God to give you a great reward because you have solved in so subtle a manner the question of those not believing in the creation of the world, who
oppose believers. Now I would like you to make clear what you
said above, how all things are made gradually by the union of
the soul and matter.

PETRUS: The philosophers say that when the soul was united
and conjoined to matter, the first of all to be formed and composed was the greater firmament, in which there are no stars,
and which makes all the circles be moved.[92] After that, however,
the sign-bearing circle was formed, in which the twelve [zodia-
cal] signs gleam. In third place was the circle of stars formed,
which remain always fixed in their places, guarding their position. In fourth place, the circle of Saturn was set. Moreover, in
fifth was set [the circle] of the sphere [*orbis*] of Jupiter. Sixth
place, in turn, the sword of Mars claims for itself. Moreover, in
seventh place the circle of the sun shines. The sphere [*globus*] of
Venus possesses the eighth. Mercury is assigned the ninth. Tenth
place belongs to the parts below the moon. Once all these circles
and all that is in them were completed, then that spherical motion began, which is said to be simple and perfect. That motion
gave birth in matter to heat, which heat is dispersed by matter,
and [the matter] itself received heat, and in this way were the
four elements made: fire, air, water, and earth. It happens, moreover, that every motion that proceeds from some moving thing,
and every power of some empowered thing [*virtuosi*], the nearer
they are to those from which they proceed, the greater the power and the strength they achieve. The more distant they have
been from them, the weaker and more yielding [*molliora*] they
are rendered. Since this is so, it is clear[93] that the heat which proceeds from the movement of the firmament glowed much more
and was burning up in the places nearer to it, and fire, namely,
was made of a dry and hot nature. Whereas because that heat
gradually receded further from the firmament, already moder-

92. Marie-Thérèse d'Alverny suggests that this section echoes the "Chapter"
ascribed to Isaac Israeli on the pseudo-Aristotelian *De elementis*. See her "Pseudo-
Aristotle, *De elementis*," 66–68.

93. Reading *patet* (A) for *pater* (B).

ately losing its power, little by little it grew tepid and was made weaker, but still it moved itself hither and thither, for which reason the nature of air was made hot and moist. For every heat, so long as it is very strong, dries out and burns. Whereas when it becomes merely warm, it causes a thing to soften and to liquefy. Moreover, when it withdrew still further from the firmament, as if from a root existing nearby, it lost its vigor, and this is why a frigid nature flowed forth, and it was made liquid and heavy, and this is water. And when it withdrew still further than it was from the firmament, this very nature of frigidity, owing to its extreme withdrawal, was rendered stronger, thicker, more congealed, and harder, and it was made dry and cold, and this is earth. Once the creation of the elements was completed in this way, the nature and power of the firmament moved them to accomplish the will and command of God. And when the power of the firmament moved all these toward one another, they were equally mixed and united among themselves, and by their mixture were born the other, lesser bodies, the inanimate, the animate, and the animals. Indeed, the inanimate, like rocks and metals and others like this that are contained within the earth (like quicksilver, sulfur, and the rest) do not grow, whereas the animate, like trees and plants, do. Moreover, both the irrational animals, like the brute beasts, and the rational, that is, the human, who was made after all these, do. Therefore, every creature takes its beginning from the universal soul, and it [the universal soul] reaches its limit at the human, gradually passing from one into another. Therefore, the soul and matter are simple and are the makers of all subjects, at the disposition of the ineffable providence of the highest creator. Whatever is inferior to these, however, conforming to the will of the supernal director, holds equally the office of maker and made. For each individual one of these both comes to be from its superior and makes its inferior. Whence even the prophet David prophesied in this way concerning them, saying: "Bless the Lord, all his powers, his ministers, who do his will. Bless the Lord, all his works, in every place of his dominion."[94] Moreover, divine power so restrains all these,

94. Ps 102.21.

although they are diverse, that deep down they seem in no way
repugnant or discordant to each other. The same David attests
to this in another place, saying: "Let them praise the name of
the Lord, because he spoke, and they were made, he commanded, and they were created. He established them for ever and
ever, he established a command, which cannot be passed by."[95]
But each and every one of the inferior ones is said to be simple
with respect to the superior, whereas it is said to be composite
with respect to the inferior. The human body, however, which
is inferior to all, because there is nothing under it to which it
is said to be simple, is not improperly said to be entirely composite, and a human is made from a creature that is altogether
simple (that is, the soul) and from a body that is altogether composite. And God filled him and illuminated him with the wisdom
of his lofty height, through which he may discern and know all
things. Therefore, from among all the species of animals the human species was made better and more elegant and in all things
more excellent, whence he is called—hardly unjustly—a micro-
cosm [*minor mundus*].

MOSES: You have adequately demonstrated a matter that is
difficult, obscure, and unknown to many, with a brilliant and
welcome exposition. Now, according to philosophy, from these
words of yours I understand clearly what Moses was able to show
at the beginning of the book of Genesis. For he said, "In the
beginning God created the heaven and the earth,"[96] that is, the
universal soul and matter. And he enumerated step by step all
the creatures, until he arrived at the human, who, through the
succession of days, finally was created on the sixth day. But in
this respect, another question arises among those who do not
at all believe that God is the creator of the world, which is this:
If all worldly things, they ask, were not created through themselves [*per se*], but if there is another creator who created them
all, since he, as you say, is omnipotent, why did he not complete
all these things in one day, instead of by working little by little
over a period of many days? I do not know how to answer, how
one ought to respond to this.

95. Ps 148.5–6.
96. Gn 1.1.

PETRUS: Reason does not maintain that since one creature is created later than another, the highest creator should be believed to be less powerful for this reason. For no weakness of his was responsible for this, but rather that one of these creatures was more pliable and another was harder with respect to receiving its creation and form, just as if you were to receive one mass in which were placed iron, brass, lead, tin, pitch, and wax at the same time, and you were to cast this entire mass which was a mixture of all of these into a fire at the same moment, would all liquefy at one and the same time?

MOSES: Certainly not. Instead, first the wax would liquefy, and then the pitch, and then the tin, and next the iron, and after that the bronze, whereas the iron would liquefy last.

PETRUS: Do you impute this—that some liquefy more quickly than others—to the power of the fire, or do you attribute it in different ways to their weakness?

MOSES: No one doubts that the fire's power is the same toward all, but that those that are softer liquefy more quickly, whereas those that are harder liquefy more slowly.

PETRUS: In the same way, for the creatures of the world a delay of just so many days passed for no other reason than that some of them were slower to receive form.

MOSES: Now that the error of doubt has been removed, I see the light of truth.

PETRUS: This discourse, which the proof both of the arguments and of reason everywhere supports, is sufficiently clear and firm for everyone. But your sages, when pertinaciously they attempt to oppose us in certain things, are discovered to be opposed to this same view.

MOSES: I wish you to show me, if you please, what the error is.

PETRUS: Indeed, they say that when God established the firmament he was unwilling to complete entirely the space of a certain large aperture in the northern region, and abandoned [it] as incomplete. They assert that he did this for this reason: namely, so that if someone were to say someday that he is a god, rising up and making himself equal to him, God himself could confront him with the incompleteness of this space, saying: "If you are God, as I am, close that space, if you can, which I left open." But a sharp eye reveals how clearly this is a lie. Moreover, we see that the axis of the north pole is always very high above us and is never hidden, and we see that it is entirely whole and complete. Therefore, do you understand how evident that error is?

MOSES: Certainly I understand, and I recognize that this opinion [*sermo*] lacks the power of every argument.

PETRUS: Is it not even more mendacious, more dishonest and absurd, what they invent about the keys of Korah?

MOSES: In what way do they seem to you to be deceived?

PETRUS: They said, as you know yourself, that when Korah passed through the desert with Moses and the children of Israel, he had 300 laden camels, carrying nothing but the keys of his treasure, all of which keys were made from cowhide so that they could be lighter to carry.[97] Let us consider this for a moment, O Moses, if you please, to see whether this can stand. Let us grant that there are at least six keys to a pound, and that each camel carried at least 600 pounds, and then that one camel carried 3,600 keys. And let the number of keys of 300 camels be 1,080,000. But since each key would be for at least one chest, without doubt there would be just as many chests as there are keys. Let one grant therefore that there are at least two chests for each camel, and there would have to be 540,000 camels carrying the chests. But given the custom among rich men, who take greater care for the guarding of riches, it would have been necessary to have at least one guardian for two camels, who would watch the treasures with the greatest care, barely even sleeping, and the number of guardians for the camels will be found to be 270,000. But we learn—and the book attests to this—that the host of Korah, with the households and relations and their families, was only 8,600. Like this, it is not less ridiculous when they say that the sons of Esau carrying their father to the sepulcher came with a great host upon the sons of Jacob, likewise carrying their father to his sepulcher. And since each was a great host, and the individual parties wished to claim the

97. For the biblical Korah, see especially Nm 16.1–40. For this extra-biblical legend, see B.T. *Pesachim* 119a; *Sanhedrin* 110a.

sepulcher for themselves, they say that Dan ascended a mountain and cut off a rock of such a massive size, that it could be as
large as the size of the entire host of Esau; that he removed the
mass of rock and carried it on his head, casting it down upon
the battle line of the enemy host to lay all of them low with one
blow. And when, arriving there, he found both battle lines in
harmony, he cast into the sea the mass of rock which he had
carried, from whose great size the water of the sea, exceeding its
two bounds, destroyed two cities by its outflow, and these are
the ones which Pharaoh, king of Egypt, commanded the children of Israel to build much later.[98] Does not this invention, I
ask, seem to you justly to deserve the greatest laughter? For
there were still only 12 sons of Jacob, while there were 40 men
of Esau, from his tribe. Now, then, given that the number of the
sons of Jacob had increased, how much larger can one think
the number of Esau's children was? For it was necessary that
their size be large enough to be able to oppose both the sons of
Jacob and the entire Egyptian people, which had come with Joseph. Now, judge, then, which of these things is more worthy of
admiration: namely, either where he found a mountain so large,
or on what mountain he found a rock mass of such wondrous
size, or how he could have carried a rock of such great weight
upon his head, so that he could overthrow so great a company.
Not less stupendous is this marvel: that Og, king of Bashan,[99] seeing the vast army of Israel, namely, 603,500 men, 20 years and
older, not including the women and children who could not be
counted, bore a rock mass of a magnitude unheard-of on his
head, and with it he wished to overthrow the entire expedition,
but a hoopoe, the smallest bird, alighted upon that rock mass
and pecked at it for so long with its beak that, when it had made
a large opening appropriate for the size of his head, the rock
mass slipped over his head and settled on his shoulders.[100] More-

98. See B.T. *Sotah* 13a and *Pirke de Rabbi Eliezer*, ed. G. Friedlander (London,
1916), pp. 308–11.

99. Bashan is described as "the land of the giants" (Dt 3.13) which Moses
overthrew (Jos 13.12).

100. The details of this tale are largely found in B.T. *Ber.* 54b, although there
it is an army of ants, and not the hoopoe, that gnaws a hole in this rock mass.
For the hoopoe, see Ginzberg, *The Legends of the Jews*, 6: 120. This legend of Og

over, with his head and his entire body uninjured, he might still
have lifted it up off his neck except that the size of his teeth
(which had suddenly increased) prevented it. For as soon as the
rock dropped onto his neck, his teeth grew so quickly, that then,
when he wanted to do so, he could not raise it at all. When Moses saw this—whose body you assert was ten cubits, and you attribute just as many [cubits] to his rod—he raised himself ten cubits off the earth like one leaping up, to strike him some place
on his body with a rod.[101] If, then, you calculate the ten cubits by
which he was raised up above the earth, and the ten cubits of
his body, and add the ten other cubits of the rod extended
above, you will find that from the ground to the tip of the rod
was 30 cubits. But although Moses was raised up this much, nevertheless the tip of the rod, with which he intended to strike
him, could never reach further than to that joint [*nodum*] which
joins the calf to the foot, which the vulgar call the ankle.[102]
When he struck him there, he expired, falling immediately.
Anyone can recognize in this that from the sole of the foot,
which he held fixed on the earth, up to the joint on which he
was struck, there were 30 cubits. Therefore, from that spot as
far as the top, there were not less than 80 cubits, and his head
alone could easily consist of 10 cubits, whence it follows that
that bird bored out that rock mass for ten cubits. I do not know
how many marvels are in this deed, or, when I consider it, how I
could be more amazed. For where could he find such a large
rock, or how could he carry so much weight? Or how was only
such a small bird able to penetrate so hard and so thick a rocky
body so quickly, or why did his teeth grow so suddenly? Or for
what reason must one believe that it was of such immense and
unheard-of magnitude, when the law says precisely that his iron
bed was only nine cubits?[103] Or why must one believe that a man
so large was felled so easily by so slight a wound? It is appropri-

---

became a staple in subsequent Christian polemics or disputations. See, for example, Nicholas Donin's remark from the Parisian disputation of 1240, in Maccoby's *Judaism on Trial: Jewish-Christian Disputations in the Middle Ages*, 161.

101. Cf. B.T. *Ber.* 54b.

102. "Ankle": *cavilla*. Cf. modern French, *cheville du pied*, or modern Italian,
caviglia.

103. Cf. Dt 3.11.

ate to reveal their foolishness by taking note of something else still more ridiculous. For they say that Moses ascended to heaven to receive the law, and there he quarreled with the angels in this way. Indeed, they say that the angels said: "Under no condition do we permit you to bear this law, which we know to be more necessary for us than for the children of Israel." Moses, terrified by so unaccustomed a sight, did not presume to respond to them. But, with the Lord strengthening him so that he could respond safely, and commanding it, he said to the angels: "Since this law contains the precepts for governing bodies, I do not consider that it would be so necessary for you, who are a spiritual creation." The angels were overcome and, having nothing to say to this, became silent. Thus you say that God laughed and greatly rejoiced over Moses' victory, and so Moses descended with the law after his quick triumph. I ask you, how many different types of foolishness are contained in this insolence? For how could Moses ascend to the height of heaven when restrained by the weight of a body, or how could the angels hold back from giving the law, when God willed it? Again, what is even more stupid than to say that God exulted when one conquered and the other was overcome, and laughed in a childish manner? Likewise if, as you say, the angels were so determined to keep his law, why did they not seek it from God earlier, or how did it benefit them to rage violently in arguments? For they could still observe that same law with the Jews, nor was there a reason why they had to hold it back from Moses. Something else that they recall as having occurred stands out for anyone as not less ridiculous than these. For they say that the angel of death appeared to a certain man named Joshua, the son of the sage Levi,[104] and said to him: "You know that I have come for this: that you die and I receive your soul." "Never," he said, "will I do what you require, unless first you show me paradise." Then the angel, having taken him up on his wings, led him to a place from which

104. For the legend of R. Joshua ben Levi, see B.T. *Ketubot* 77b. It was a popular tale in the medieval world, and was included as well in the influential *Alphabet of Ben-Sira*. For a translation, see *Rabbinic Fantasies: Imaginative Narratives from Classical Hebrew Literature*, ed. David Stern and Mark Jay Mirsky (Philadelphia and New York: Jewish Publication Society, 1990), 194–95.

he saw paradise. But that cunning man, having slipped off the angel's wings, allowed himself to fall into paradise. The angel, pained that he had deceived him, said with an exceedingly angry countenance: "Go forth so that you may die." He said: "I will never go forth." And when for a second and third time the angel repeated himself with a great cry, and he ignored his words, the exceedingly distraught angel, approaching God, entered a complaint over this affair. God, however, asked him to return, to order that man to go forth from paradise in the name of God. And when the angel came to paradise, he said: "God commands that you go forth." And he swore and said: "I will not go forth for God [*per deum*]." The angel returned to God and said: "Swearing an oath, he confirmed that he will never go forth from there." And so God, rendering a judgment, responded: "Carefully reread and turn over again all the pages of his life and his deeds. If you find that he swore but perjured himself at some time, then he, too, will now be unable to swear on his own behalf. If you prove, however, that he has never foresworn himself, he will not be afraid in this instance."

And once the angel studiously examined all the pages, he found that he had never perjured himself. Therefore, conquered, [the angel] released him who, as you say, remains safe and alive to this present day. Consider, I beg you, how things very deserving of laughter can be known in this little story. For what is more amazing? The foolishness of the angel who did not know beforehand the man's cunning stratagem; or that the man, once he heard God's command from the angel, dared to swear against that very command? Or should we say that it was the impotency of a God that was only able to expel him from paradise by a deception? Or should we attribute it to God's ignorance that he could not know in any other way whether he had foresworn himself except by ordering that the pages of his life be reexamined? Are not these the most foolish things? If we lay out all the things which your sages have written down similar to things like these, we would fill up many books with tales of nonsense, just as they have. Here, however, we have mentioned just a few things so that either their wisdom or their foolishness would be evident to all. Certainly this is what I said to you before, that the words of your sages seem to be

SECOND *TITULUS*

OSES: SINCE YOU have demonstrated by the light of incontestable arguments that whatever our sages apply, unworthily, to the divine majesty cannot stand either on the authority of Scripture or on the power of any sort of reason [*ratio*], let us turn now to the second part of our proposed project, in which you have spoken of our captivity, if it is agreeable to you. Indeed, if I remember correctly, you have said we can never escape from captivity in such a way as we hope. Now then I ask you whether on account of this you accept that we cannot escape [this captivity] in the way in which we believe, but rather can do so in another way, or whether you believe—let it not be so—that we cannot escape it at all.

PETRUS: I do not believe that it can be escaped in the way in which you think, but I do not deny that you will escape it in another way.

MOSES: I would like to hear why we are never able to be freed from it in the way we say, and what the means of liberation will be.

PETRUS: As long as you deny that Christ is the Son of God or that he came into the world for the redemption of the human race, and as long as you are unwilling to keep his precepts, you will be unable to be freed from captivity. But if you will believe both that he is the Son of God and that he has already come, and if you will safeguard his commandments, you will immediately go forth from captivity.

MOSES: Can you bring some authority to bear on this claim?

PETRUS: First we ought to see what the cause of your captivity was, so that we may better understand the means for escaping it, following the practice of the wise physician who first examines the illness, so that he can know what medicine is necessary.

MOSES: I praise this as well said.

PETRUS: First I want you to tell me the cause of the Babylonian captivity, which lasted only 70 years, because that cause, when we have heard it, will assist us in recognizing the cause of this great captivity.

MOSES: Many sins, which are too many to enumerate, were the cause of the first captivity.

PETRUS: I agree that this is so, but I want to hear from you something about them.

MOSES: I will introduce a few of them, which are proved by prophetic authority: to wit, usury, or accepting a reward for iniquity; swearing a false oath; giving a false coin when buying or selling; giving false testimony; disparaging each other; dishonoring parents, places of sanctification, and the Sabbath day; uncovering the nakedness of a mother, sister, daughter, mother-in-law, or of any illicit woman;[1] committing murder; adoring idols; sacrificing to the stars; denying God and slaying the prophets of God, like Uriah, Zechariah, and Isaiah; and many others. These [sins], as I said above, are too many to enumerate. They grew so great that God said to the prophet Jeremiah: "Run to and fro through the streets of Jerusalem and look and take note, search in her squares to see whether you can find a man, one who does justice and seeks faith, I will pardon her."[2] Likewise, Ezekiel says: "I sought for a man among them who should build up the wall[3] and stand in the breach before me for the land, that I should not destroy it, and I have not found one."[4]

PETRUS: I rejoice and give thanks, because I recognize that you already see some scintilla of truth. Tell me then, if you know, what has been the cause of a captivity so protracted and so harsh that it has already lasted 1040 years?

MOSES: These same sins, and others like them.

PETRUS: You will not be able to establish this argument with any authority, because there was no prophet in Israel for 300 years before the destruction of Jerusalem[5] who prophesied this

1. "Illicit woman": presumably, illicit because of bonds of consanguinity, as outlined in Lv 18.6–17.
2. Jer 5.1.
3. Reading *saeptum* for the nonsensical *sepum* (A).
4. Ezek 23.30.
5. According to B.T. *Sanhedrin* 11a, the spirit of prophecy departed from

or wrote about it, especially since your sages say that this alone
was the cause of Jerusalem's destruction—that one person envied another and became the enemy of another.[6] Moreover, they
add even this besides for the overthrow of your argument: that
once the Temple was built, God handed over into their hands
the prince of sin, from whom, with hands and feet bound, he
plucked out one eye; and from that day on he did not have the
power to be able to beguile into murder and idolatry and to
uncover the nakedness of consanguineous relations. Therefore,
none of those sins that were the cause of the first captivity were
also the cause of the second. Moreover, they say that while the
Temple was in existence there were many people of a good life,
who would have had to be prophets if it had been the time of
prophecy. In addition, many people performed new miracles
beyond the order of nature [*praeter usum*], just as they say that
John, the son of Zachai,[7] was of such great holiness that when
he sat in the chair to read his books, God caused all the birds
flying over his head to burn up and to fall to the earth, to demonstrate the power of his merits.[8] They also add another miracle such as this concerning another person, namely, Huni.[9] For
they say that in his time the land suffered a drought. Once he
had made a circle of stones, he entered into it and said to God:
"I swear in your name, God, that I will not go forth from here
until the rains fall upon the earth."[10] Then it began to rain, bit
by bit, but when he demanded a heavier rain, such a violent
rain fell that it almost devastated the entire land. But when he
pleaded modestly, temperate rains fell, and the earth abounded
with all good things. They also say that every day a voice from
Mount Horeb gave testimony concerning Ananias, the son of

Israel after the death of the last of the prophets, Haggai, Zechariah, and Malachi.
6. B.T. *Yoma* 9b.
7. I.e., Yohanan ben Zakkai, mistaken for Yonathan ben Uzziel.
8. Indeed, it is said of Yonathan ben Uzziel, one of Hillel's disciples, that
when he sat and studied Torah, the birds that flew over him were consumed by
fire. See B.T. *Sukkah* 28a.
9. Honi ha-Me'aggel, the circle-drawer, a renowned miracle worker of the
first century B.C.E. See B.T. *Ta'anith* 23a. For a brief discussion, see "Honi Ha-
Me'aggel," *Encyclopedia Judaica* 8: 964–65.
10. Cf. Mishna *Ta'anith* 19a.

Doza, and of his holiness, saying, "On account of the goodness of Ananias, the son of Doza, I govern the entire world; nevertheless, a very little from that world suffices for him." They adduce still another such miracle concerning him. For although both he and his wife both led a very poor life for the sake of God, he ordered that the oven be warmed every Friday so that his neighbors and relatives would think that they had more than enough food and lived well. When on a certain day, as was his custom, he commanded that the oven be fired, and one of his neighbors observed why he did this, she came suddenly upon the oven to reveal their deeds and to cast shame upon the man as well as upon the woman. When she came to the oven and examined it, she saw that it was full of bread, which she announced to the aforementioned woman, running quickly to her.[11] But she was unwilling to believe her, thinking that she spoke not for the sake of truth but for the sake of a reproach, until she proved it herself by going there. She went there, she saw it, and found it to be just as her neighbor had said; and once she had returned to her husband filled with joy, she told him in sequence how God had changed the desire of a wicked woman to honor. He judged it unworthy, however, that God had performed a miracle, and replied that he would accept none of it for his own use, that he would enjoy none of it, but would give all of it to the poor. In addition, they say that in these times[12] there lived Nicodemus, the son of Guirio, a man whose life was very praiseworthy. Such a drought oppressed the land in his days that those who went forth to the Temple in order to pray were unable to have anything to drink on the way. On the journey for those going there, however, there was a cistern belonging to a certain prince of the gentiles. Approaching this prince, Nicodemus said: "Please give your cistern to me for the need of the entire people, if it please you, and on that day when I am able to, I will restore your cistern with water or return the price of a horse." What more? He obtained what he demanded, and he checked the people's thirst. But when on the designated day the creditor had come to him seeking the price, and the cistern

11. For the tale of Hanina ben Dosa, see B.T. *Ta'anith* 25a.
12. Reading *eisdem* for *isdem* (A).

had no water on account of the terrible drought, Nicodemus, after having poured forth prayer to God, obtained rain from heaven for the entire land, and he restored the cistern full to his lord, just as he had received it. But because at that hour in which the rain descended the day was already tending toward evening, the prince said to Nicodemus, "I received the water because of your prayer; but nevertheless, since a whole hour of the designated day has passed, you ought to pay to me the price for your debt."[13] So then he held back the course of the sun by his prayer, and with the whole world illuminated by its light, he avoided the question of the debt. You also have a text about Akiba, that he obtained whatever he had demanded from God. One reads, too, concerning the magnitude of his sanctity, that when Moses drew near to the mountain to receive the law, and he learned in advance, with the Holy Spirit dictating, all the future times coming after him and all the generations, and he saw that among men Akiba's human life surpasses all measure and is abundant with great merits, he said to God: "Since there will be a man of such a worthy life in the future, why, O Lord, does it please you to administer your law to the people through me rather than through him?" God said to this: "Because the law is necessary in the present world," he said, "whereas Akiba will exist after a long time to come." In these words one is given to understand that Moses foresaw that the one of whom he spoke such things, would be far better than he.[14] These and others like them were judges and elders for you, who commanded the masses [*minoribus*] to do good, and the rest freely submitted to their admonishments. If there had been even one like them in the time of the earlier captivity, as above we showed that God said through Jeremiah,[15] the captivity would never have occurred. And what is even more amazing, in those same days in which their nobles [*meliores*] were strong, once the Temple was destroyed, the Jews were taken captive. Tell me, O Moses, what

13. Recalling that the day, of course, begins at evening. For this tale of Nicodemus ben Gorion, see B.T. *Ta'anith* 19b–20a.

14. Cf. B.T. *Menahoth* 29b. Note that in the talmudic account, Moses is shown Akiba's martyrdom (during the second-century Bar Kokhba revolt), and not that he will live a long time in the future.

15. Cf. Jer 5.1.

the cause of this captivity was, since no firm argument supports what you said above.

MOSES: I have nothing else to say, except that after the Temple had existed for a long time, many sins gradually increased, but they were multiplied with that crime which our sages mentioned.

PETRUS: You say that the Temple had stood for a long time, yet actually it existed only for ten years longer than the other one that had existed earlier, namely, the Temple of Solomon. Moreover, reason does not accept what you say—that sins accumulated on sins. For in the first captivity, sins were added to sins for this reason: that wicked kings presented a bad example to others; to wit, they did not give due reverence to God, they worshiped idols, and they compelled the people to do the same, [kings] such as Ahaziah, Ahaz, Manasseh, Amon, Zedekiah.[16] But the princes during the second period were altogether different from these, because they were living a good life and encouraged the people to live in the same way by their example. With what argument can one show that sins grew to be so many that the captivity occurred for that reason? When you say that the captivity was caused on account of the malevolence they held toward one another, this is not supported by the anchor of right reason.

For this sin was one part of those which they had committed in the first captivity; nevertheless, they would not have to be made captives on that account, unless other sins greater than it had grown along with it. For we do not know how to distinguish between the greater and the lesser character [*quantitas*] of crimes except in terms of the punishment pronounced by God. But the punishment for this one is only forty stripes.[17] There are other crimes for which the punishment is greater, namely, when someone is sentenced to be killed—either to be beaten about the head, or to be hanged, or to be stoned, or even burned by fire. How, then, can it be true that the crime of malevolence ought to be equivalent to one that is greater? Again, reason refuses to believe that this crime reigned to such an extent in those times,

16. Cf. 1 Kgs 22.53; 2 Kgs 1.2; 16.1–4; 21.2–4 and 19–22; 24.18–20.
17. Cf. Dt 25.1–3.

when, once the Temple had been constructed, the words of the prophet Haggai attest that God said: "The glory of this last house will be great, more than that of the first, says the Lord of hosts, and in this place I will grant peace."[18]

MOSES: Since every approach for my arguments has been blocked, I beg you, open the door for me with a key of your own solution to this question.

PETRUS: Since you do not know the cause and the origin of the captivity, you cannot answer why the captivity has been so harsh, so cruel and intolerable. For during the first captivity, when they were led off into Babylon in the manner of other captives, they sustained no punishment other than servitude. They tilled the fields, they planted vines, they built houses, and they lived in safety with the wives and children. In the second, however, they bore so many, so great, and such unheard-of scandals that ones like them or equal to them have never been seen or heard among them. Indeed, they were slain and burned and sold as captives, and the sale increased so much, until thirty captives were given for one piece of silver;[19] nevertheless, no one was found who would buy, just as Moses promised when he said: "You will offer yourselves for sale to your enemies as servants and maidservants, and there will be none who will buy you."[20] There were ships filled with them that were released upon the open sea to drift without oar or helmsman, to their disgrace and shame. Moreover, after you were cast into this captivity you were given intolerable commands—not to read the law or to teach it to your children. If anyone was found either reading [the law] or teaching it to his children, either he was burned by fire or he was flayed by very sharp iron combs. Besides this, you were not permitted to observe either the Passover or the Sabbath. Truly if anyone was found doing so, he was punished very harshly. In addition to this, you were prohibited from circumcising your sons

18. Hg 2.10.

19. This tradition is recorded later in *The Golden Legend*, that "as the Jews had bought Jesus Christ for thirty pieces of silver, Titus had sold the Jews at the rate of thirty for one silver coin." Jacobus de Voragine, *The Golden Legend: Readings on the Saints*, 67, trans. William Granger Ryan, vol. 1 (Princeton, NJ: Princeton University Press, 1995), 276.

20. Dt 28.68.

according to ancient custom, and a long time passed during
which no one dared circumcise his son except in secret. Moreover, anyone found circumcising was punished by the harshest
punishments.[21] And the harshest edict was promulgated against
you: that if any one of you wished to take a virgin girl to wife,
first he would lead her to the prince of the province, so that he
might sleep with her, and then, after returning her to the Jew
at last, she would marry. No one wanted to betroth a virgin because you were so ground down by this thing.[22] Thus, throughout the passage of all ages diverse commandments of evil were
proclaimed against you, as is proved by the testimonies of your
own books.

MOSES: Without a doubt I concede all kinds of evils, but at
this time I long to hear the cause of so much tribulation.

PETRUS: Since you do not know the cause of the evils, certainly this is why you do not know why it is so long. See, you
have already completed 1040 years [in exile] and still you have
no certain knowledge, from any text, concerning how long it
has to last. Legal justice requires that once those who had committed some crime have been punished and have died, those
following after them ought to be freed from captivity; just as
it is written in the law that the spies who were sent to spy out
the promised land, since they chose to rebel against the will of
God, were held for forty years in solitude lest their sin go un-
punished, and in this period of time all those conspirators per-
ished. Once they were punished with such a death, the sons,
who were innocent of the crime of their fathers, entered into
the land that had been promised to their fathers.[23] They tarried for seventy years in captivity [*transmigratione*] in Babylon
until once all had died whose sins had resulted in captivity, the
sons, who had committed no sins, were freed from the yoke.[24]
Innumerable generations, however, have passed in this captiv-

21. Such prohibitions were imposed during the Hadrianic persecution, after
quelling the Bar Kokhba revolt (132–135 C.E.).

22. J. H. L. Reuter (*Petrus Alfonsi*, 57–58, and 58, n. 1) locates the source for
this tale in a medieval Jewish chronicle, possibly *Jossipon*, but adds that the detail
of the boatload set adrift is found in marginal commentaries of prayer books.

23. Cf. Nm 13–14.

24. 2 Chr 36.17–23.

ity, which was caused by Titus, yet still it has no end. But this has occurred contrary to that passage that the Lord spoke to Moses: "The fathers shall not be killed for the sons, nor the sons for the fathers, but each will die for his own sin."[25] Ezekiel said as well: "As I live, says the Lord God, this proverb shall no more be used by you in the land of Judah.[26] Behold, all souls are mine; the soul of the father as well as the soul of the son is mine. The soul that sins shall die."[27]

MOSES: Even if the duration of our captivity is contrary to these examples, yet nevertheless it accords with other written laws. For in Exodus the Lord says: "I am the Lord your God, strong, jealous, visiting the iniquity of the fathers on the sons, unto the third and fourth generations, of those that hate me."[28] In addition there are the words of Jeremiah: "Our fathers sinned, and are no more. And we have borne their iniquities."[29]

PETRUS: The reality is different than you say. For if it were so, then the prophet's words would contradict themselves. Each, however, is resolved in this way. When it is said that the children will not bear the iniquities of the fathers, this means if the children have not committed the iniquity of the fathers. When it is said, however, that the sons bear the iniquity of the fathers, they are said to bear the iniquity in this way: if they have committed the crimes of the fathers.

MOSES: What you say is sound and produces a reasonable and just understanding for the wise. One is given to understand from your words, however, that all the generations to come will certainly remain in the captivity of the fathers, because they follow the deeds of their fathers, so far as they can. But if they abandon the deeds of the fathers, then they will go forth from captivity.

PETRUS: This is the way I understand it.

MOSES: Now, if it please you, reveal the magnitude of such guilt.

---

25. Dt 24.16.
26. Lit., "so will this be beyond comparison in the proverb in the land of Judah."
27. Ezek 18.3–4. 28. Ex 20.5.
29. Lam 5.7.

PETRUS: Because you have slain Christ, the Son of God, saying that he is a magician, born from fornication, and that he led the entire people into error.[30] Your elders proclaimed these things and others like them, until they caused the entire people to share in their depraved will, and they led a just man to a very unjust punishment—they crucified and they slew him. The magnitude of a crime so great is the cause of such a long captivity. And as long as you abide in your paternal faith just as in their will, you will without any doubt remain in the same judgment of damnation.

MOSES: It will be necessary to argue further whether that man was the Son of God, since the author of so important a question needs the very strongest argument as a vehicle. In the interim, I want to be shown in what way or by what authority you attempt to assert that that man, of whom you speak, was the cause of our tribulation.

PETRUS: Why, I ask you, do you demand an authority from me on this, when above you already conceded to me that an altogether unheard-of sin was the cause of an affliction so unheard-of? And since you were unable to show it to me in any way whatsoever, a balanced judgment commands that you should hear [it] from me, not that you ought to investigate on what basis I will prove it, but rather to destroy it with whatever means you can, or to concede what you are unable to deny. Although it is true that the judgment of a legal proceeding does not constrain me, still I will provide not just one but many authorities on this matter.

MOSES: That is what I desire with all my heart.

PETRUS: You ought to know that, forty years after the death of Christ, Titus destroyed the city of Jerusalem. And again, forty

---

30. Magic is often said to be learned from the Egyptians. See B.T. *Shabbat* 104b; Mishna *Yebamoth* 4.13 (49a). Nestor the Priest (*The Polemic of Nestor the Priest*, 1: 70) claims that Herod sought to kill Jesus because he practiced magic, and the claim that Jesus had learned magic during his sojourn in Egypt became a staple in Jewish attacks on Christianity. See *The Jewish-Christian Debate in the High Middle Ages: A Critical Edition of the* Nizzhon Vetus, cap. 32, trans. David Berger (Philadelphia: Jewish Publication Society, 1979), 63–64. Alfonsi takes up this theme again in the tenth *titulus*. For additional bibliography, see *infra*, pp. 232–33, n. 29.

years before it was destroyed, portents and signs were seen in the same city, clearly indicating that the destruction of the city and the Temple was about to occur, as the books of your doctrine attest in some way. For they say that forty years before it was cast down, the red wool, which was tied to the horns of the scapegoat [*hedi*],[31] did not whiten in the customary fashion, and the candle of the candelabrum, which looked back on the west, was put out before its customary time. Moreover, the doors of the Temple were spontaneously thrown open with a great noise, though no one was touching them. When one of your sages, named John, son of Zachai,[32] saw that they were often opened in this way, he was very disturbed and finally called out: "Be still!" And he added, "Temple, O Temple, actually I have known that fire will possess your end," just as the prophet said, "Open your gates, Lebanon, and let fire consume your cedars."[33] Therefore, since these wonders were sighted forty years before the destruction, and in the fortieth year from the death of Christ the city was destroyed by Titus, clearly one concludes that these signs occurred because of Christ's death. But John, along with your other sages, understood this as well: that Christ's death is the cause of your captivity.[34] They said, however, that not this but rather the malevolence and envy of men (in fact the cause of the cause) were the cause of the captivity, but they remained silent concerning the [true] cause. Indeed the envy and malice of the Jews were the true cause of Christ's death, whereas Christ's death was the cause of the captivity.

MOSES: If he was a man such as you say, and his death was the cause of our tribulation, none of us would deserve to live. For a sin such as this is greater even than denying God. For one who denies God only estranges himself from the faith that he once

31. For the tying of red wool to the horns of the scapegoat see Lv 16.22 and Mishna *Yoma* 6.5–6. On the meaning of the scapegoat ritual in rabbinic literature, see especially Hyam Maccoby, *Ritual and Morality: The Ritual Purity System and its Place in Judaism* (Cambridge: Cambridge University Press, 1999), 85–91.

32. I.e., R. Yohanan ben Zakkai.

33. Zec 11.1.

34. Here is a good example of Alfonsi's claim that the rabbis of the Talmud *knew* that it was the crucifixion that caused the destruction of the Temple, even if they hid the fact from other Jews. Cf. B.T. *Yoma* 39b.

received. Whereas he who denies the Son of God, beyond denying the deity that is invisible, even adds that sin that he removes
from the mind's faith the visible object as well that it sees with
bodily eyes, since what is seen should lead the mind to greater
faith than what is not seen. Besides this, however, our fathers
fastened him to the Cross, covered with spittle, beaten by blows,
and afflicted with various and multiple wounds, and innocently
bound over to death. Not undeservedly, this crime was greater
than the one that they committed in the desert, when they worshiped a golden calf as a god. We read that at that time God
truly wanted to destroy the people of Israel altogether. But Moses averted God's wrath by intervening on their behalf, with a
great deal of weeping, fasting, and prayer. For forty days and
forty nights he afflicted himself with the torment of an assidu-
ous fast for the sake of this same sin, just as the law proclaims
when it says: "I fell down before the Lord just as before, for
forty days and forty nights, eating no bread and drinking no
water, on account of all your sins, which you have committed
against the Lord . . . for I feared his wrath and indignation, because of which, being moved against you, he wished to destroy
you."[35] Thus, had the prayer of Moses not intervened, no one
from among the entire people would have remained. Since,
then, they planned in advance this other crime that exceeds the
measure [*quantitas*] of [all] crimes (that is, to slay the Son of
God), and there was no one to intervene on their behalf, certainly none ought to have lived. You see, however, that this is
not the case, that God permits us to live and daily shows us how
much he loves us, since he shows us favor in the sight of our
enemies and fills us with riches and exalts us with honors, just
as he promised us through the mouth of the prophet Moses,
saying: "When they are in the land of their enemies, I have not
spurned them nor despised them, in order to consume them
and to render void my covenant with them, for I am the Lord,
their God."[36]

PETRUS: You do not conceive a proper understanding of this
matter. For God does not suffer the remnant of your people to

35. Dt 9.18–19.
36. Lv 26.45.

live because he plans something to their advantage, but only so that you serve all the nations and so that you would be in the eyes of all a reproach and a byword and a curse, just as the giver of the law promised, saying: "You will become a horror in a proverb and a byword among all peoples, to whom the Lord will lead you"[37] and so that you will be for the whole people in a parable and a proverb for all those seeking and asking one another: What do you think is the reason that God has subjected to perpetual servitude this people, which is dispersed everywhere across the earth, and why has he condemned it with the penalty of so many evils? And another person will answer: on account of a sin such as this, that they slew the Son of God solely because of envy; for this reason they arrived at these evils. If at the time that you committed this sin he had annihilated the entire Jewish lineage at the very root, then once many years had passed and the guilt had been eliminated by forgetfulness, then it would be known by no mortal. In this way you would escape the opprobrium of infamy and the peril of [other] evils, just as occurred to many kings and peoples whose acts were eliminated by the passing of time. And there is another reason why God was unwilling to allow the Jewish people to perish. To be sure, he saw that, at some time, some of your seed would believe in him and that they would be saved. For this reason, he did not want to destroy your stem altogether, just as Isaiah said: "As if a grain be found in a cluster and it be said: 'destroy it not, because it is a blessing,' so I will do for my servants' sake and not destroy them all."[38] But the testimony of divine compassion that was extended to you, which you proclaimed was promised to Moses in the book of the law, does not concern the present captivity but has to do with the Babylonian captivity that has already passed, since already he led you forth from it at some time.

MOSES: According to what authority do you prove that that promise pertains only to the Babylonian captivity?

PETRUS: If you look a little bit before that place where God made this promise to Moses, you will find that the same Moses spoke [these] prefatory words: "Then shall the land enjoy

37. Dt 28.37.
38. Is 65.8.

its sabbaths all the days of her desolation; when you will be in
the enemy's land she shall keep a sabbath and rest in the sabbaths."[39] Ezra, in the book of Chronicles, proves, however, that
this was fulfilled among those who were led off in captivity to
Babylon, saying, among other things: "He was led into Babylon
and there served the king and his sons, until the land might celebrate its sabbaths. For all the days of the desolation she kept a
sabbath."[40] It appears quite clear in these passages that he was
speaking of the first captivity.

MOSES: That authority does not suffice for my doubt, because
it does not demonstrate that we have fallen into this captivity on
account of that man.

PETRUS: What clearer testimony do you require that you
have been subjected to this captivity on account of the death of
Christ, than what you read before you: that in the beginning of
that captivity there was a certain prince of your land who sent
ten from among the best of the entire Israelite people, namely, Hananiah, the son of Teradyon,[41] Symeon, the son of Gamaliel,[42] Ishmael, the son of Elisha, and Akiba, and other captives
into prison, learning that they had sold a just [person]. He said,
"The law decrees that any man who shall sell a Jew will be punished with a sentence of death, and therefore you ought to die
according to this judgment."[43] Once this decree was given, he
gave [their] bodies over to various deaths. For not all are bound
to one punishment, but specific types of death are established
for different individuals. One he burned with fire, another expired torn by the teeth of an iron comb, whereas some different
type of death consumed another, just as the book of your teach-

39. Lv 26.34–35.
40. 2 Chr 36.20–21. Note this conflates two passages, omitting the beginning of verse 21.
41. I.e., Hananiah ben Teradyon, one of the ten martyrs put to death during
the Hadrianic persecutions of the second century. The names in this list of ten
martyrs are not consistent across all sources, nor are all the ten always identified
as contemporaries. For a discussion of the traditions, see "Ten Martyrs," *Encyclopedia Judaica* 15: 1006–1008. For a translation of one version found in Adolph
Jellinek's *Beit ha-Midrash* (1853; repr. Jerusalem: Wahrmann, 1967), 2: 64–72,
see *Rabbinic Fantasies*, 143–65.
42. Presumably Simeon ben Gamaliel I (1st century C.E.), traditionally included among the ten martyrs who met that death at Roman hands.
43. Dt 24.7. N.B.: the final clause is not in the Vulg. text.

ing has explained these deaths. Your sages, however, changing the name of the just man in that deed for which they were punished, actually were silent concerning Christ. For they said that the prince understood the just one to be named Joseph the son of Jacob, whom his brothers sold in Egypt, and, demanding his blood from them, he afflicted them with such punishments because of this. It seems ridiculous, however, to reason that he would demand it from them for something that had happened at least 1500 years earlier, especially when at the time that Joseph was put up for sale there was as yet no law under which that prince could convict them of crimes subject to death.[44]

MOSES: Your arguments do not satisfy me, since you do not confirm them with any authority, but rather you fabricate [them] according to your own will, nor is there any necessity about them with which you ought to compel me to believe you. If you are able, however, I want you to introduce some authority from the prophets by which you may demonstrate that that captivity is because of that man, and that he is, of necessity, Christ, and that for us there can be no fixed termination to this tribulation.

PETRUS: The prophet Isaiah said: "From the ends of the earth we have heard praises, the glory of the just one."[45] These words show that the praises of this just one have been from all the earth. Never have we heard, however, that there were such praises of a just man that they reached the ends of the earth. Because he foresaw the tribulations which he was about to suffer without cause, he had compassion on the just one, saying in these words: "Woe is me, the prevaricators have prevaricated, and with the prevarication of transgressors they have prevaricated."[46] For foreseeing the tribulations that would be borne by the prophets proclaiming the advent of God, the prophet said: "the prevaricators have prevaricated." Moreover, having considered that they were filled with envy and that, not content with the limbs, they were going to oppress him in whatever ways they

44. Our author's sense of chronology here seems especially weak.
45. Is 24.16. See *supra,* p. 72, n. 66, where Alfonsi cites this passage according to the *Hebraica veritas.*
46. Is 24.16.

could, in terms of the body's capacity for suffering, and cut off the head,[47] he repeated the name of prevarication, thus adding: "with the prevarication of transgressors they have prevaricated." But foreknowing what punishment they had to suffer for this sin because the Spirit was speaking [to him], he added to this and said: "Fear and the pit and the snare are upon you, O you inhabitor of the earth."[48] Among other things, he also said of this same people: "And its iniquity will be heavy upon it, and it shall fall and not rise again,"[49] where he took away from you completely a fixed term for escaping from captivity. The Lord proposed things similar to these in another place, saying through the same prophet: "Now then go in and write for them upon a box, and note it diligently in a book, and it will be in the latter days a testimony forever. For it is a people that provokes to wrath, and lying children, and children who refuse to hear the law of God. Who say to the seers: See not; and to those that behold, Behold not for us those things that are right. . . . Take away from me the way, turn away the path from me, let the Holy One of Israel cease from before us."[50] A box is hard wood and not prone to rot. Moreover, this is why he commands that it be written on a box and diligently noted in a book, so that it would last forever and endure until the end time as a testimony of—and reproach for—your incredulity. Also what he said—"it will be in the latter days a testimony forever"—implies that the error of the Jews will endure even until the end time. He also indicates both how and why it ought to be written in one verse, when he said: "For it is a people that provokes to wrath, and lying children, and children who refuse to hear the law of God." But why is it that he says: "who refuse to hear the law of God"? Of what law of God did he speak? For if [he spoke] of the law of God which he had given through Moses, would the prophet want to say, "who refuse to hear the law of God"? Since they had already heard it very often, the prophet certainly would not say this, but rather that they were unwilling to fulfill it. He was thinking, then, of

47. As Christ is understood to be the head of the body of the Church, and his disciples its members or limbs.

48. Is 24.17.   49. Is 24.20.

50. Is 30.8–11.

that law which was to be given in the future by Christ, which the
prophet foreknew they would refuse to hear. Moreover, what he
concluded—"Who say to the seers: See not; and to those that
behold, Behold not for us those things that are right. . . . Take
away from me the way, turn away the path from me"—he added
on behalf of John the son of Zechariah, the precursor to Christ,
and others who not only prophesied that Christ was about to
come,[51] but even pointed him out with a finger, whom he knew
in advance the Jews would not believe, but only would speak
words like this. Moreover, one should not pass over what they
said in the passages that followed. For they said: "let the Holy
One of Israel cease from before us." Who is this Holy One of Israel? Is God visible, so that they would say of him: "let him cease
from before us," or can one say of something invisible, that it
should cease from before human sight, since it cannot be seen
by us? If, then, you look for a God that can be seen, you will discover only Christ. For he is God himself, and one with the Father,[52] and nevertheless appeared in visible form to the world
through [his] humanity. When, however, he set forth their many
prevarications, he suggested the punishment for their sin, saying: "Because you have rejected this word, and have trusted in
oppression and tumult, and have leaned upon it, therefore shall
this iniquity be for you as a breach that falls and is found wanting in a high wall, for its destruction will come on suddenly,
when it is not expected, and it shall be broken small, as the potter's vessel is broken all to pieces with a mighty breaking, and
not a shard of its pieces will be found, in which a little fire may
be carried from the hearth or a little water drawn out from the
well."[53] Christ is the Word of God. Therefore, he who rejects
Christ certainly rejects the Word, and vice versa. Certainly they
have been punished because they rejected the Word of God,
and the ones punished are confined because they have rejected
Christ and trusted in the word of their sages. Consider, too, how
hard is the destruction that will befall them for that sin. For that
breach will befall them suddenly, he says, and for that reason it

---

51. Cf. Jn 1.6–7.   52. Cf. Jn 10.30.
53. Is 30.12–14.

will be the more damaged, and from a high wall, since the greater the height from which something falls, the more it is broken
at the bottom. This destruction is likened to a broken potter's
vessel, and the breakage will be so great, as was said, that not a
shard of its pieces will remain. Indeed, every break in a vessel
can be repaired, and it can be restored to some useful purpose.
If, however, the vessel with a small potsherd is broken by a
mighty break, its parts can be put to nothing useful, and the
longer a potsherd remains broken, the larger the break becomes. Since, then, their destruction is compared to such a potsherd, which is not even able to carry a little fire from the hearth
nor to draw a little water out from the well, clearly one is given
to understand that your captivity results in being so cast down
that it will never return to [your] original freedom. God, however, has chosen to preserve your seed for the sake of those who,
at some time, will believe in Christ and will be saved for that reason, and this is why the prophet added this, under the description of a blessed grain, saying: "As if a grain be found in a cluster, and it be said: destroy it not, because it is a blessing";[54] in
the same way he promised that he will not utterly destroy you
when he says: "So will I do for the sake of my servants, that I may
not destroy the whole."[55] He also revealed why he promised this,
saying: "And I will bring forth a seed out of Jacob, and out of Judah a possessor of my mountains and my inheritance. My elect
and my servants shall dwell there," that is, calling the apostles
"mountains," who, like tall mountains, are visible to the entire
world, although in the following passage one understands that
Christ is the holy mountain, indicated in the singular, but calling "elect" and holy "servants" any others for whose future salvation you are to be preserved. Hear that punishment he imposes
on those who are not going to believe: "You that have forsaken
the Lord, who have forgotten my holy mountain, who set a table
for fortune and offer libations upon it, I will number you in the
sword, and you shall all fall in slaughter, because I called and
you did not answer, I spoke and you did not listen, and you did

54. Is 65.8.
55. Ibid.

evil in my eyes and you have chosen the things that displease me."[56] Having chided them for their iniquity, he condemned them in one way and in another, namely, by praising his faithful and by reproaching the unfaithful, with these words: "On account of this the Lord God says: 'Behold, my servants shall eat, and you will be hungry; behold, my servants shall drink, and you will be thirsty; behold, my servants shall rejoice, and you will be confounded; behold, my servants will praise for joyfulness of heart, and you shall cry for sorrow of heart and you will howl for grief of spirit, and you shall leave your name for an execration to my elect.'"[57] And because even after all these evils have come to pass, some hope of avoiding captivity could still remain for you, he added something else that would remove all solace of assurance from them. For he said: "The Lord your God will slay you."[58] One who is slain is never restored beyond what he had been. Therefore, those who remain in infidelity will not be able to be repaired. Having said this about the faithless ones, he added this about those who will believe: "And he will call his servants by another name."[59] For when they are servants of Christ, they will be called Christians, from Christ. This follows, however: "And you shall leave your name for an execration to my elect," just as if to say, my elect will swear in your name, just as still today Christians say, swearing, when they are asked to do something they do not want to do: "May I be a Jew, if I do that!" Similarly, the prophet Amos clearly proved that, saying: "Hear this word which I raise up over you as a lamentation: the house of Israel has fallen, and it shall rise no more as the virgin Israel. She is cast down upon her land, and there is none who will raise her up."[60] Again, elsewhere he says: "The end is come upon my people Israel, I will not pass by them any more."[61] Thus he removed from you utterly any hope whatsoever of escaping captivity. He himself confirmed that this evil befell you because of Christ, saying: "Thus says the Lord God: For three crimes of Israel and for four I will not convert him, because he has sold the just man and the poor man for a pair of

---

56. Is 65.11–12.
58. Is 65.15.
60. Am 5.1–2.

57. Is 65.13–15.
59. Ibid.
61. Am 8.2.

shoes."[62] In this place, he used "four" for "a fourth," and when he said, "for four," it was the same as if he had said, "for the fourth." Solomon proclaimed something like this. For he said, as the books of the Hebrews attest: "Three things are hard for me, and four of which I am utterly ignorant."[63] If you want to understand these three *per se* and four *per se*, they will make seven. He only counts "four," however, as the one of which he suggests he is ignorant. It is necessary, then, to understand "four" as the fourth. So, too, the prophet has to be understood in this way. This fourth one, however, is a wicked deed, as he adds there: "Because they sold the just man for silver." He wanted it understood that Christ is the just man.

MOSES: Thus far, you would have said everything properly and in a praiseworthy manner, had you introduced this authority in a manner which is supported by argument [*ratio*], especially since many things can be raised as objections against this. For many ancients before you often produced this same little verse in testimony against the Jews, but they were unable to defend it with any argument. But I am surprised that such a prudent man as yourself has introduced an argument so worthless, which does not rest on any firm foundation, especially since you yourself know very well all those things which customarily are said against this.

PETRUS: Considering that all those who came before me had introduced this authority properly against the Jews, but are said not to have overcome Jewish objections either clearly or sufficiently, in the present place I have introduced the same [authority] on purpose, so that you can make all the objections which can be made as best you can, in their place.

MOSES: First this can properly be objected to these words, since when the prophet said: "For three crimes," he immediately added, "Israel," showing that Israel had committed those three sins, but it was not Israel but Judah that slew the Christ whom you wish to know.

62. Am 2.6. Note that Petrus Alfonsi's text departs slightly from the Vulg., omitting the phrase "for silver"
63. Prv 30.18.

PETRUS: Your objection poses no obstacle for me, since all the scrolls [*volumina*] attest that Israel is very often substituted for Judah.

MOSES: I do not doubt that it is as you say. But since he referred above to the sin of Judah and consequently added the sin of Israel, it is enough to note that Israel's sin is different from Judah's.

PETRUS: This does not withstand my argument. For the sin that only Judah committed is called the sin of Judah, whereas the sin that Judah and Israel committed together is called the sin of Israel.

MOSES: Since the entire people of Israel, which is divided across all the earth, never dwelled in the land of Jerusalem in those times, how can it be held guilty for the death of Christ?

PETRUS: Do you deny that at that time a large portion of the sons of Benjamin and Levi were in Jerusalem with Judah?

MOSES: Who would dare deny what is clear to everyone?

PETRUS: Then the part rightly ought to receive the name of the whole. There is also another, not inferior cause: that although the people Israel was not physically present then for the death [of Christ], once they had heard what their co-religionists [*socii*] had done, they became accomplices[64] in the crime, applauded it and gave consent and became willing participants. Certainly the will has to be reckoned the same as the deed among them.

MOSES: And if I concede that it is as you say, nevertheless I do not see that what the book says can pertain to Israel—that this shall have happened to them for having sold the just man. For one does not read that they sold the one whom you call Christ, but only that they bought him from Judas Iscariot.

PETRUS: Your objection is supported on no anchor of reason, for those who provided consent, aid, and counsel to sell Christ committed the crime no less than if they had sold him themselves.[65] Now, Solomon did not fashion idols, but because

---

64. Reading Migne's *consortes* for *ex(s)ortes* (A). *Ex(s)ortes* would suggest just the opposite of what is implied here, resulting in a clear non sequitur.

65. Cf. Rm 1.32.

he gave his assent to his wives and concubines to fashion idols, the text says that he fashioned them.[66]

MOSES: Although I may confess that you have spoken the truth in the things said above, no necessity compels me to concede that it is necessary for Christ to be understood to be this just man, since by a sound understanding he ought to be understood to be Joseph, whom his brothers sold for twenty pieces of silver.[67]

PETRUS: If the prophet had wanted Joseph to be understood to be the just man, he would not have said the fourth, but rather the first, sin. For they committed that transgression earlier, for which later they suffered the very harsh yoke of Pharaoh. But since, once they had performed penance, they were already freed from the sin, why should they be incriminated again by a sin that had already been pardoned?

MOSES: And if I am unable to defend that this was said of Joseph, nevertheless I can still assert that it refers to some other just man.

PETRUS: It seems unworthy and unreasonable that when there is a crime so great that no pardon will follow, for which divine judgment rages against the whole people of Israel, its person, on whom it was blamed, should be hidden and unknown, especially since that guilty condition is described in the Hebrew language by a word of a sort that is imposed on one who has denied God. Moreover, the sale of a Jew is not equal to the denial of God. But these have sold such and so great a man, namely, the Christ, the Son of God, that they are equal in their guilt to one denying God.

MOSES: I would like you to show the four sins that are all manifestly equal to the denial of God.

PETRUS: I do not know how to reveal that about which the book is silent, but perhaps the first sin was when in the desert they worshiped the molten calf instead of God, by which act it is true enough that they denied God, and because this sin was perpetrated by all, for that reason it was common to all.[68] The sec-

66. Cf. 1 Kgs 11.4.   67. Cf. Gn 37.28.
68. Cf. Ex 32.4.

ond, in which likewise they denied God and in which all sinned together, was, namely, when Jeroboam similarly fashioned calves and established that they should be worshiped by all.[69] But the third was when all, with the same will, slew the prophets of God and condemned their words. Truly, the fourth was worse and more serious than all these, and is said not to be subject to forgiveness: when they wickedly sold Christ, the Son of God and a man who was a stranger to every contagion of sin, and unjustly condemned him to death. Behold, in this authority which I have set forth against you, I have demonstrated that everything to which you may be able to object stands without force, and reasonably I have concluded that it applies to Christ. I think, then, that it has been proved beyond doubt by all the things mentioned above—authorities established with unshakable firmness—that this long captivity has occurred on account of the death of and malevolence toward Christ. In addition, having concluded that the captivity occurred on account of Christ, it follows that you will not escape it until you correct the sin of your fathers, that is, until you believe what they did not believe. Once the mind has been purified of this sin, divine piety immediately follows it. One of your sages, however, wanted that to be expressed by subtle and dissembling words, had that penetrated the hardness of your mind. For, asked when the son of David would come, he said: "Today, if you will believe his words."[70] By these words he let it be understood that anyone, at any time, who will believe and obey the commands of Christ—to him the Son of God will come. I believe that I have revealed to you clearly and manifestly whatever I have proved by the authority of your books. Implore the mercy of this same Christ with me then, brother, so that, once having drawn away the error of all falsehood, he will pour forth in equal parts the love and splendor of every goodness and of true faith upon your mind's eye, and, in the future, compensate the right faith with a worthy reward, so that by it you would escape from captivity. Amen.

69. Cf. 1 Kgs 12.28.
70. See B.T. *Sanhedrin* 98a, where this is revealed to R. Joshua ben Levi. Cf. Ps 94.8 (Vulg.).

OSES: YOU HAVE demonstrated with the most clear and indisputable arguments what pertained to the present heading, namely, what the cause of our very long captivity was, or in what way are we able to escape it, and all the things necessary to be said about it. Nor do I see that there is anything further that should be investigated or doubted concerning it. As a result, I eagerly desire that we pass over to the other matters, just as they were listed above. Therefore, I entreat you to explain why you said in the beginning of the book that we err, because we believe that after escaping from captivity an extraordinary miracle will occur among us: namely, that the dead who are resurrected by God will dwell on the earth again. Why does it seem to you that we err in this belief?

PETRUS: You yourselves claim that this miracle is extraordinary [*preter usum*]. Whatever occurs, however, beyond the customary [order of nature] should not be believed without an authority or argument, before it happens. Therefore, I determine that [you] believe an error that you cannot prove with any authority.

MOSES: But surely we are able to prove this with many authorities. This is demonstrated by Moses' testimony when speaking to the people of Israel: "See that I alone am he and that there is no other God besides me. I shall kill and make alive, I shall wound and I shall heal."[1] Since, then, God himself promises that one who dies will be made to live again, why does it seem to you that our belief concerning this ought to be rejected?

PETRUS: That authority departs from the path of reason. For he spoke this passage [*verbum*] to show his omnipotence, not because he is about to revive your dead.

MOSES: Do you concede that at any time God has performed

1. Dt 32.39.

this miracle, from the day when God promised that he would do it, until the present day?

PETRUS: Certainly he has done all things. For he himself afflicted Miriam, the sister of the prophet Moses,[2] [and] Job,[3] Hezekiah,[4] Naaman,[5] and several others, when he wished, and when he wished to do so, he healed them. Likewise, in a single night he killed all the firstborn of Egypt,[6] and in the space of one night he slew 185,000 in the camps of Sennacherib.[7] But, on the other hand, he revived the son of the Shunnamite by the hand of Elisha,[8] and by the hand of Elijah he revived the son of the widow.[9]

MOSES: Since you believe that he has indeed already done these miracles, what prevents you from believing that he will yet perform the same miracles at some time in the future?

PETRUS: I do not deny that the almighty can raise the dead, since I confess and I believe that on the day of judgment all men will be revived by him. Yet I do not believe what you add [to this], namely, that they will dwell on the earth again.

MOSES: This ought not appear to you to be contrary to faith, since the one revived by Elijah or Elisha still enjoyed a long life, had a wife, begot sons, and fulfilled all the original functions of human life.

PETRUS: It is true, and it could well be the case that, either by a miracle or by the prayer of a holy man, the body had not yet been destroyed, although we should never believe this unless we have some prophetic testimony concerning it. The faith of men is not easily accustomed to accept as true those things which are wont to occur beyond the usual order, unless they are confirmed by the authority of such prophets, whom the approbation of all who hear them acclaims, and unless the prophets speak of these things very clearly. No prophet, however, openly proclaimed this. But although your sages said this, none of those who lived before Christ predicted it. Their disciples invented this error, however, so that the race of the Jews would persist in its infidelity.

2. Nm 12.9–10.
3. Jb 1.13–19.
4. 2 Kgs 20.1–11.
5. 2 Kgs 5.1–14.
6. Ex 12.29.
7. 2 Kgs 19.35.
8. 2 Kgs 4.32–35.
9. 1 Kgs 17.17–24.

MOSES: And if you assert that our sages have fabricated these things for the sake of misleading us, what will you say about the prophets who do the same thing? For Isaiah says: "Your dead shall live, my killed will rise again. O you who dwell in the dust, awake and give praise."[10]

PETRUS: These words never demonstrate that your dead are revived in order to inhabit the earth again, since if we pay careful attention to what is said, we do not find that the resurrection of the dead is clearly presaged there. Otherwise, the prophet would seem to contradict himself when he says in passages above this one: "They are dying and will not live, they are shades and will not arise."[11] Therefore, unless a necessary reason requires that it be understood in this way, what departs from the rule of nature and stands opposed to the meaning of the prophet ought never to be explained in a sense contrary to nature or according to anyone's free interpretation, since it can be understood in a different way by a sound intellect.

MOSES: I should be delighted to hear how the interpretation of this passage can be understood correctly in some other way.

PETRUS: This passage can be understood in two ways: namely, one may believe either that it was said concerning the resurrection at the last judgment, or that under the heading [*nomen*] of the resurrection, it indicated escape from captivity. Moreover, this latter interpretation seems more pertinent to the text, since just a little above this the prophet wept over the captivity and affliction of his people. Immediately after that he reported the consolation of the divine promise and love, saying: "Your dead shall live, my slain will rise again."[12] Nor does he imply that this end to captivity will occur at some indeterminate time, but that it will come to an end after a modest period, saying: "Come, my people, enter your chambers, close your doors behind you, hide for a little while, until the wrath has passed."[13] These things appropriately refer to the captivity.

MOSES: Can you deny that some such thing is found among Daniel's words? For he said: "Many of those who sleep in the

10. Is 26.19.
11. Is 26.14.
12. Is 26.19.
13. Is 26.20.

dust of the earth will awake, some to life everlasting, and others to a shame that appears everlasting."[14]

PETRUS: The further this authority departs from your premise, the more clearly it is understood to have been said about the last judgment. To be sure, at that resurrection they will go either to life eternal or to eternal opprobrium.

MOSES: Will you find something that you can say against the prophet Ezekiel? When he had revived many of the dead by divine power, he also prophesied about things to come with these words: "Thus says the Lord God: I will open your graves and I will lead you forth from your tombs, my people, and I will bring you into the land of Israel."[15] And a little later, [he says]: "And I shall make you rest upon your own soil."[16] See, here the prophet clearly and indubitably shows that the dead will be raised and will dwell in their own lands.

PETRUS: First we ought to discuss this, namely, so that we will be able to understand in what manner he will raise them: that is, whether they will fulfill all the functions of the human body after being raised up, or not. For this appears in doubt among many people.

MOSES: As my sages attest, he has made them to rise up not in sleep but awake. And in order to indicate this even more clearly, they proclaimed that all the dead whom he raised were from the tribe of Ephraim, who, they said, had died in the region of the Philistines during the people's exodus from Egypt.[17] Moreover, this resurrection was a sign of the one to come, so that just as all these were raised up by him, so, too, all the rest are believed to have to be raised up, at some time.

PETRUS: How did he bestow upon them a true and perfect resurrection, when he never restored a rational soul to them?

MOSES: How do you contend that they did not receive a rational soul, when by God's command the same prophet prophesied with regard to the spirit, with words such as these: "Thus

14. Dn 12.2.   15. Ezek 37.12.
16: Ezek 37.14.

17. For the claim that Ezekiel has already raised from the dead the Ephraimites who attempted to escape from Egypt before the Exodus, see Ginzberg, *Legends of the Jews*, 4: 332.

says the Lord: Come forth from the four winds, O spirit, and breathe upon these slain, that they may live again. And I prophesied, just as the Lord commanded, and the spirit entered into them, and they lived and they stood upon their feet, an exceedingly great host"?[18]

PETRUS: This spirit, which was commanded to come forth from the four winds, is never a rational soul, but is only what results from the conjunction of the four elements.

MOSES: From your words, one understands that the corporeal spirit is one thing, and the rational soul something else. But if this is so, then their effects [*opera*] are different as well.[19]

PETRUS: No sensible person doubts that this is so.

MOSES: I would like to hear about the difference between them.

PETRUS: The corporeal spirit is a very light and subtle body, which is made in a human's heart from the conjunction of the four elements. It is distributed from that location to all the veins, and it bestows upon the very body life and nourishment, a continuous pulse to the arteries, and natural movement to a human. This [spirit] is corrupted at the same time with the body that it vivifies.[20] By contrast, the rational soul is a substance subsisting in itself, incorporeal, and causing the body to be moved by a voluntary motion, although it itself remains unmoving. It exists as incorruptible even in the corrupted body to which it

18. Ezek 37.9–10.

19. This discussion illustrates Alfonsi's utilization of medical doctrines to criticize Moses' interpretation. He identifies the "spirit" mentioned above with the doctrine of three spirits—the spiritual, animal, and natural—that effect the various operations of the body. These spirits are located in different principal organs of the body, but they are themselves corporeal. Reason, memory, and imagination—faculties of the incorporeal soul—are depicted as being independent of these corporeal spirits, and are distinctive to the human being. For a discussion of the medical doctrine of the spirits, see James J. Bono, "Medical Spirits and the Medieval Language of Life," *Traditio* 40 (1984): 91–130. See, too, a discussion by the roughly contemporary author William of St. Thierry in his *Nature of the Body and Soul*, 1.5–6, trans. Benjamin Clark, in *Three Treatises on Man: A Cistercian Anthropology*, ed. Bernard McGinn (Kalamazoo, MI: Cistercian Publications, 1977), 112–15.

20. This discussion of corporeal spirit seems to recall that of Costa ben Luca. See his *De differentia animae et spiritus liber translatus a Johanne Hispalensi* 1, ed. Carl Sigmund Barach (Innsbruck: Wagner'sche Universitäts-Buchhandlung, 1876), 121–24.

cleaves; moreover, when it is united to the genus it perfects the human species.

MOSES: I recall that many before us have said that the rational soul is created from the conjunction of the four elements. When this conjunction occurs subtly and has in itself no density, they said that it is a subtle soul; if, however, it has some thickness and darkness about it, they said that that soul is obtuse and sluggish, proving it with an argument such as this. They say that from the union of certain things, we often see there are born things such as colors, powers, and effects, which are not produced from any of these if they are received separately. In a similar way, too, the rational soul is produced when water, fire, air, and earth are equally united; nevertheless, the soul is not detected if it is sought out in the individual [elements].

PETRUS: If a rational soul arises from a body with the four elements in perfect conjunction, then when the strength of the body fails, the power of the soul ought to fail as well. Moreover, if the soul's power fails with the body's strength, then it follows that the soul's power equally is destroyed with the beginning of the destruction of the body's vigor. But if this is admitted, then once the body has been corrupted, it follows that the soul also is corrupted. To be sure, the correct order of the conclusion demonstrates that it happens this way. But the argument's conclusion impugns the reliability [*fides*] of the eyes. For it often happens that the more the body is weakened and approaches death, the more the soul gains strength. This is wont to happen often to many sick people, so that the nearer one is to death, the more he recalls and foresees all things with more than the customary acumen of a perspicacious mind, and at that very moment when the soul thrives best, the person dies. When, however, as I said, the soul thrives with such full awareness, then all the functions of the languishing body deteriorate more. Moreover, we have found that for many old people who, when they approach such an advanced age that no more bodily strength remains in them, it is just then that the soul becomes powerful in every counsel and wisdom. Certainly, from this a clear argument is assembled: that a rational soul will never arise from a union of the elements, but rather, just as we said above, it is a self-subsistent substance. Indeed, whatever is one in number and is capable of receiving contraries while remaining immutable in its nature, is certainly a self-subsistent substance. Since, then, the soul is one in number (just as is the soul of Plato, Socrates, or any other individual human) and since the soul is not changed in any way in its nature but is capable of receiving good or evil, it remains necessary that it be a self-subsistent substance. In this way it is proved that it is not corporeal. For every quality of a body is subject to the human senses. It is not the case, however, that the qualities of every thing whatsoever are subject to a bodily sense, nor can it be said to be corporeal itself.[21] Indeed, the qualities of the soul are good and evil, which are not perceived by any bodily sense. Therefore, the soul is not corporeal. Again, the same thing is proved by another argument. Every body is perceived by some bodily sense. The soul, however, is not subject to any sensory power of a body. Therefore, it is not corporeal. Moreover, this soul is not corrupted once the body is corrupted. For the body's corruption occurs in three ways: either when something begins to grow feeble and dry out, as we see in trees and plants; or when it suffers some loss to itself, like salt or hay when it is moved from place to place; or when it is demolished, like a house or a wall when it is destroyed or like some vessel when it is broken. But these only occur in a body or in a thing that belongs to a body. But a soul is not a body, nor does it depend on a body. Therefore, it is not corrupted in any of these ways. Besides, this rational soul perfects the human species, since it makes a man rational.

MOSES: Certainly I was aware that a corporeal spirit is different from a rational soul. But since the philosophers say that there are three souls in a man, I ask that you clarify for me what these are.

PETRUS: The three that they mention are the vegetable soul, the irrational soul [*anima bestialis*], and the rational soul.

MOSES: I urge you to tell me about the effects and functions [*officia*] of these individual souls.

PETRUS: It is proper to ascend gradually from the lowest to

21. The antecedent for the pronoun "it" remains vague in the original. It could refer to "every thing" or to the soul.

the higher. There are two functions of the vegetable soul. It causes things to grow, and it provides nutriment to the bodies themselves. It only does these things, however, by means of the four powers of nature, namely, the appetitive [power], the retentive, the digestive, and the expulsive. And this soul is found in every plant [*virgultis*] arising from the ground and in all the species of animals. Moreover, the functions of the irrational soul are the five senses of the body, and motion from place to place. This one is only found, however, in animals, and this soul is united with a bodily spirit as if by a certain nexus. Moreover, these are the functions of the rational soul: to contemplate, to remember things contemplated, to discern, to establish something as fixed or certain, to have memory and will, to discuss the causes of things, and to approach the truth of the matter from those that were discussed. This abides in no animal species other than the human alone.

MOSES: I do not know how, and I marvel at how, these three souls come together in one human, whereas there are two in irrational animals, but only the third is in all the things arising from the earth.

PETRUS: I have read in the books of certain philosophers that when it pleased the creator of things to generate bodies for all animated and growing things, he mixed the four elements together and tempered their qualities—each one with its contrary—and from this mixture their aforementioned bodies were generated. From the tempering of the qualities arise the four natures, which we previously called powers, to wit, the appetitive, the retentive, digestive, and expulsive. The vegetable soul cleaves to all the generated bodies of this type and exercises its functions in them: that is, growing, nourishing, and generating. The irrational soul, however, is joined to the more subtle ones, so that it may perform its functions in them: to wit, being responsible for sensation and motion from place to place. The rational soul joined itself to the one that is most subtle and lightest of all of these and that was most tempered and best suited to receive reason, and freely performed its functions, which we previously mentioned. In this way, according to the will and disposition of God, these three souls all come together in the human, whereas in irrational animals there are only two, and only the third is in trees and plants, which are born from the earth.

MOSES: My thanks to you that you have shown me what I did not know. But one thing still remains which I want you to clarify for me. For since all bodies are composed from the four elements, I greatly wonder why it is that some are lighter than others.

PETRUS: Clearly this results from the diversity of the elemental quantities that were unequally conjoined at the creation of bodies, and from the diverse ways in which their qualities were tempered. If you would like to know more, you will discover it in the books of the philosophers, because at present we have neither the time nor the place for explaining a matter of this sort. Instead, it is better for us to return to our proposition.

MOSES: Up to this point you have treated quite philosophically the difference between a corporeal spirit and a rational soul. But since simple minds do not at all penetrate the depths of the subtle arguments of the sages, I beg you to prove the same distinction by the testimony of the law and the prophets, if you are able to, so that at least authority would create faith among those for whom the gravity of [these] profound arguments has not illuminated the mind.

PETRUS: In the beginning of the book of Genesis the prophet Moses says: "God formed man from the dust of the earth and breathed upon his face the breath of life, and man was made into a living soul."[22] Understand that the corporeal spirit is the breath of life, and understand that the rational soul is the living soul.

MOSES: We can understand the breath of life to be the rational soul.

PETRUS: What you say cannot stand. It is written in the following passages in the same book: "And all flesh was consumed that moved upon the earth, of the winged things and the living beasts and crawling things which creep upon the earth, and every man and all things on earth in which there is the breath of life, were dead."[23] See that after having enumerated flying

22. Gn 2.7.
23. Gn 7.21–22.

things, living beasts, and crawling things or men, suddenly he reported: "all things in which there is the breath of life, were dead." If he wanted the rational soul to be understood as the breath of life, then all would have a rational soul. But since no creature except man has a rational soul, it follows that he never denoted the rational soul as the breath of life. Also, sensing the same thing, the very wise Solomon said: "Who knows if the spirit of the children of Adam goes upward, and if the spirit of the beasts goes down below?"[24] See that the spirit of man goes upward, because it remains incorruptible after the body, whereas he claimed that the spirit of beasts, which is corrupted and perishes at the same time with the body, descends down below.

MOSES: I have learned clearly that the rational soul is one thing, the corporeal spirit is another, and that this corporeal spirit comes into being from the conjunction of the four elements from all the parts [of the world]. Whereas the spirit, which, by God's command, the prophet Ezekiel commanded to come from the four parts of the world,[25] I now know ought to be understood as the corporeal spirit, and I confess that I find no authority concerning the dead whom he raised—that is, that they received a rational soul, although many believe this to be so. Nevertheless, I say and I also believe that the resurrection that was in some way accomplished was a sign of the future resurrection: namely, that at some time God will revive our dead who will dwell on earth a second time. The prophet showed the same thing up above, when he said: "And you will know that I am the Lord when I will open your graves and lead you from your tombs, my people, and I will give my spirit unto you and you will live, and I will make you to rest upon your land."[26]

PETRUS: Certainly this could be said about the raising of the dead on the day of judgment.

MOSES: If he wanted it to be understood to be about that judgment, he ought not to have said at the end of the sentence: "I will make you to rest upon your land." For at that time no one will be allowed to rest upon his land.

PETRUS: This rest can be understood in this sense: to signi-

24. Eccl 3.21.
25. Cf. Ezek 37.9–14.
26. Ezek 37.13–14.

fy that the soul rests in the body, which is not improperly expressed by the word "earth," from which it has arisen; which the Scripture witnesses as well, which frequently calls it by the name "earth." For Moses says: "God formed man from the dust of the earth."[27] See how man, since he is perfected from the conjunction of the four elements, is said not inappropriately to be made only from earth, which is one of the elements, since he indicates a body by the name "earth." Therefore, we can understand what he says—that he will make them rest upon their land—to mean that he will restore the soul to the body and each will be judged. Moreover, this meaning can be grasped by a sound intellect for the explanation of this prophet, so much so that neither any Scripture nor reason would seem contrary to it. In addition, something can be understood in many ways from the obscure words of the prophets, so much so that when explaining them one departs neither from the testimony of Scripture nor from the path of reason, and it is not at all inappropriate if one explains them in a different but correct sense. If the explanation is of such a sort that it is or seems to be foreign to Scripture or reason, then a proper judgment should consider these to lack force. Since your explanation, then, is found to be contrary to Scripture as well as to reason, it should be rejected by a fair judgment.

MOSES: It would be pleasant to hear in what way my opinion may be contrary to Scripture.

PETRUS: The prophet David speaks in this way of the dead: "Their graves are their homes forever, their dwelling places in all generations."[28] Again, on the same subject: "He will go to the generation of his fathers and never more will he see the light."[29] And again, elsewhere: "The spirit in him will pass away, and he will not be, and he will know his place no more."[30] Again, elsewhere: "Just like the wounded sleeping in the grave, like those whom you remember no more, for these are cut off from your

27. Gn 2.7.
28. Ps 48.11.
29. Ps 48.20. Note that the biblical text here and immediately above departs from the Vulg.
30. Ps 102.16.

hand."[31] Moreover Job, thinking the same way, says: "Remember that my life is a breath, and my eye will never again see good, nor will the sight of man behold me. Your eyes are upon me and I do not exist. As the cloud fades and vanishes, so he who goes down to hell will not rise up again nor return once more to his dwelling, nor will his place know him any more."[32] And again elsewhere: "I will go and return no more to a land that is dark."[33] And again the same author [says]: "A man, once he falls asleep, will not rise up again."[34] Solomon also held views akin to these, saying: "For the living know that they will die, but the dead know nothing further nor do they have any more reward, for their memory is forgotten. Love and hate and envy will perish at the same time, and they have no share in this world and in the deed which is done under the sun."[35] See that Solomon the most wise is in agreement with the other authorities, namely, that the dead will not be raised in order to dwell again on earth, yet nevertheless he does profess that at some time they will rise up again, saying that they have no share in the things that are done under the sun (in earthly things, that is), but implying by this that they will have a share in the things which occur beyond the sun, that is, in the heavens.

MOSES: Half of the arguments or authorities introduced would suffice fully for any wise man; nevertheless, since you said that our explication is contrary to both Scripture and reason, it remains for you to show how it departs from reason.

PETRUS: Do you not believe that, when your dead have been resurrected, once the anointed one [*unctus*] comes, Adam as well as Seth, Methusaleh, Abraham, Isaac, and Jacob, Moses and Aaron, and the other patriarchs and the prophets and all the righteous, who died before his advent, will be resurrected equally along with them? And do you not believe that those performing and undergoing all the functions of the human race and practicing the original rituals of things according to ancient custom, will again inhabit the earth, and that Aaron and his sons

31. Ps 87.6. Note departure from Vulg.
32. Jb 7.7–10.   33. Jb 10.21.
34. Jb 14.12.   35. Eccl 9.5–6.

will offer sacrifice as before and will be clothed by Moses again with priestly vestments?

MOSES: I cannot deny that our sages have said all these things.

PETRUS: Who then, I ask you, will be the high priest?

MOSES: Who could be higher than Aaron?

PETRUS: What then will happen to Eleazar, Phineas, and the many others who all were high priests in the past? Will all at one and the same time and in the same moment be high priests, or will they be deprived of the dignity of this order? If you say that when Aaron is alive they cannot be charged with the high priesthood, then what good does resurrection do them? For them, to rise again will entail dishonor and misfortune more than honor and benefit, and it would be better for them to remain dead than to lead a life filled with hardship; and the law of Moses, in which there is a precept that one who had been elevated to a higher order should not be reduced again to a lower order, will be destroyed in this deed. If you concede, however, that they will all be equal in the order of the high priesthood, then you deprive Aaron of his honor, since among many equals no one can have a preeminent honor. Besides, many temples are necessary for so many pontiffs. And because of this there follows something else that is unbecoming: that is, there follows the destruction of the law that commands that there should not exist more than one priest or more than one temple.

MOSES: I have no argument to oppose your reasoning. For I see that either we concede that we will have a new law, or that the law of Moses could not have been complete.

PETRUS: I rejoice that the light of truth casts itself now on your mind's behalf. Tell me, then, will you have many kings, or just one?

MOSES: Certainly we ought to have but one king, just as the prophet Ezekiel proclaimed, saying: "All will have one shepherd."[36] If there are many, there can be no concord, and they will deprive the kingdom of peace.

36. Ezek 37.24.

PETRUS: You have begun to respond wisely, but can you tell me who that king will be?

MOSES: The anointed one, at whose arrival we will be brought forth from our captivity and our dead will be revived, should rightly have the government of our kingdom.

PETRUS: What you say could be well said if the anointed is both man and God. For if, as you believe, he will be only a man, what then will become of Abraham, Isaac, Jacob, and Moses and the other prophets? Shall they be subject to his command?

MOSES: It should not seem surprising if they are subject to his power. For in this way was even Samuel subject to Saul and Elijah to King Ahab and Elisha to Joram and many other prophets to their kings.

PETRUS: The analogy to things in the present does not work. For even if the prophets (who were hardly kings) were subject to kings, it does not then follow, nor is it necessary, that a king-prophet—like Abraham, David, and Joshua, each one of whom was both king and prophet, or Moses, who was king and prophet and lawgiver for the entire people—should be subject to any earthly king. The book of the law offers this testimony concerning him, saying: "There arose no more a prophet in Israel like Moses, whom the Lord knew face-to-face, in all the signs and portents which he sent by him."[37] When such great men as this are revived to be subject to the law of the anointed one, would it not, I ask you, would it not have been better for such men not to be raised up again? Besides, two unbecoming things arise from this. For if Moses is less than he is, then Scripture deceives, but if he is greater, then so much more is he [the anointed one] demeaned.

MOSES: Then let us propose that Moses himself be king.

PETRUS: Then what will become of the anointed one? What then will become of Abraham, Isaac, and Jacob, whom Moses himself, while he lived, held in such regard that when he implored God for something, he prayed that he would obtain it because of their love? If you pay careful attention, you will be

---

37. Dt 34.10–11.

in great difficulty. But I would have you tell me, if you know, whether those who are dead and who then are to be revived will have the nature and power to beget children?

MOSES: In order to hear what you would answer, let me deny that they will be able to beget [children].

PETRUS: I would have you answer first, whether it is nature that will deny to them the function of procreation or whether a commandment of the law will prohibit it.

MOSES: I answer that they will be constrained by a precept of the law.

PETRUS: Since, then, the law commands that sons and daughters procreate, you prove that they will have a new law that is contrary to your faith.[38]

MOSES: I will prove, then, having reversed my position, that they are restrained from procreating by a nature that has changed, not by the law.

PETRUS: What you say cannot stand. For the ear abhors and the mind refuses to believe that any animal exists in such a way that, according to nature,[39] it has no power to generate, unless some accident should intervene. Whereas in truth any man who loses the power for procreating when some accident has intervened, will be unable to be a priest[40] or to offer testimony or to pass judgment. If you say that this is a *new* nature,[41] you should not say that they will be revived, but that there a new creature will exist, similar only in form to the first but not similar in its whole nature, for they will eat and drink but will not procreate.

MOSES: Whatever we have said up to this point in this debate we have said not so much in defense of the truth as from the tangles of syllogistic arguments. Now, it is our faith that just as they will have the other functions of humanity, so, too, they will have a nature for procreating, so much so that we believe that daily a woman will conceive and daily will give birth.[42]

PETRUS: Human ears can barely listen to what you are saying. For me to confess that the things you say are true—namely,

38. Jer 29.6.
39. Reading *naturale sit* (A) for *natura lesit* (B).
40. Lv 21.20.   41. My italics.
42. Cf. B.T. *Shabbat* 30b.

that they all will believe in the anointed one and will be resurrected—since they beget children daily, in fact the earth will not contain them, even if it should become twice the size or if the earth became the sea. And this is why the limited expanse of the space will confine them, because they will not have arable lands that they can cultivate; instead, because of this there will always be strife among them and conflict over the limited spaces of the earth. Again, when all are raised, will a man return to the wife he had, or will he have a new one?

MOSES: Each one will certainly have his own again, and this will be the consummation of happiness.

PETRUS: But that woman who has died after having had three or even more husbands, which of them will she have in the resurrection?[43] Now if you answer that she will have the first, then the law of Moses, who says that after a second husband she ought not to return to the first, is destroyed.[44] But if you say that she will have a husband other than the first, the law is destroyed by this as well, for the law commands that while the first husband still lives and while he does not repudiate her, she will be unable to marry anyone else. But look, since so many are raised and so many are born after them, will any of them die at any time?

MOSES: From that point on they will remain immortal.

PETRUS: Reason demonstrates that what you say cannot stand. For when a man shall eat, drink, and have the power [*usus*] of generating, it is necessary that he be composed from the four elements. But whatever is composed in this way, necessarily will be corrupted. Therefore, necessarily it follows that they will be subject to the corruption of death, since they are composed in this fashion. Again, if they are immortal, then in that case they will never be subject to the specific definition that belongs to the human now, because it [immortality] does not pertain to his definition. For the definition of a human is: a rational, mortal animal.[45] But that definition cannot be predicat-

---

43. Cf. Mt 22.23–30.   44. Dt 24.1–4.

45. This definition of the human *qua* species was commonplace in both ancient Greek and medieval Latin philosophy. For medieval examples, see Augustine, *De ordine* 2.10.31, ed. Pius Knöll, CSEL 63 (Vienna, Leipzig: Hölder-

ed of immortal humans, which is why it is not a human species. Whence, by this middle [term] one correctly deduces that those whom you call humans will not be human, which is inappropriate. Again, just as we said above, the expanse of the entire earth could not be adequate for this multitude, if we assert that the largest multitude is immortal. Since we said above that they will beget without impediment, even if they are placed on top of each other like rocks, in no way will they be accommodated even if the expanse of the earth has been doubled.

MOSES: Since I am unable to defend the claim that they are immortal, I concede that they are merely mortal.

PETRUS: Since you concede that they will die, I want you to tell [me] whether their resurrection will be a punishment or a crown [of glory].

MOSES: Their resurrection will be to glory and honor, so that they will look upon the glory and the kingdom of the anointed one, and enjoy a perfect joy of heart and body.

PETRUS: I would like to hear what you think about the status of good men in the interim, until they rise up; namely, whether they will remain subject to punishments or are at rest until the time of the resurrection.

MOSES: It is absolutely certain that they enjoy the blessedness of rest with God.

PETRUS: If it is as you say, then the future resurrection is a punishment rather than a crown [of glory]. For since now they are glorified by the gift of life eternal, why are they thrust back again into the prisons of bodies, if not to be disturbed again by hunger, thirst, sleeplessness, and finally various and innumerable punishments? In addition, according to your opinion, they

---

Pichler-Tempsky, 1922), 169; idem, *De quantitate animae* 1.25.47, ed. Wolfgang Hörmann, CSEL 89,1.4 (Vienna: Hölder-Pichler-Tempsky, 1986), 190. Elsewhere, Augustine explains that the human falls midway between angels and beasts, sharing rationality with angels and mortality with beasts. *De civitate Dei* 9.13, CC SL 47, p. 261. See also Boethius, *In Porphyrium dialogi* 1, PL 64: 35C; *Commentaria in Porphyrium a se translata* 3, PL 64: 104D; *In Categorias Aristotelis* 1, PL 64: 163D, 165B; *In librum De interpretatione, Editio prima*, PL 64: 315C; *Liber de divisione*, PL 64: 880C; Isidore of Seville, *Etymologiarum* 2.25.2–3, PL 82: 143A–B, and 2.29.2, PL 82: 149A; and Ratramnus of Corbie, *Liber de anima ad Odonem Bellovacensem* 2, ed. D. C. Lambot, *Analecta mediaevalia Namurcensia* 2 (Namur: Centre d'Études Médiévales, 1951), 27.

will endure the fright and punishment of a second death. It is clear to everyone from all these considerations that this resurrection brings shame to them more than honor or glory.

MOSES: Even if they remain now in rest and in delight, from which they will be returned to the straitened circumstances of bodies, nevertheless their exaltation will be so great as to see the presence of the anointed one and to exult in his reign, to dwell in Jerusalem as they did once in the past, and to sacrifice in the Temple according to ancient rite. As a result, the punishments of bodies will be nothing for them, and the rest that they have now will later be viewed as a very small thing.

PETRUS: What you say deviates from the path of truth. For no honor and glory of the present world bears any comparison to the delights and rest of eternal life, because no one has been able [to enjoy] the delights of this world for even a single moment without pain and labor. Moreover, the glory of that blessed life remains permanent and continuous without any trouble interrupting it, especially since your sages attest that all the honor and glory of this world are to the delights of that life as one is to sixty.[46] Moreover, it is clear to anyone, unless he is altogether lacking reason, that it is an incomparably greater joy to see God than to see the one whom you call "the anointed," who will only be a man.

MOSES: Whatever we have said up to this point, we have said for the sake of reasoning and arguing. Actually, this is the certitude of our faith: that in fact those being raised will have the use and nature of eating, drinking, and procreating. After a course of one thousand years has been completed, they will be transferred to a realm of perpetual beatitude and immortality, without any death.

PETRUS: If you agree that they will be immortal, you return unsuitably to the earlier [problem]. In less than one thousand years so great a multitude of them will be propagated that they will be unable to be accommodated in any way within the compass of the earth. Much less will there be any room for cultivat-

---

46. See B.T. *Ber.* 57b, where it is avowed that the Sabbath is only one-sixtieth part of the world to come.

ing fields. Besides, even that which we said above is in doubt, since the patriarchs and the prophets and all the just, who already shone in glory, will, once they are restored to the body, undergo at the end new punishments. And also the other [problem], that every being that eats, drinks, and begets, and experiences delight or sadness, is undoubtedly composed of the four elements, without any doubt. Then how will one composed of them or afflicted with the aforementioned passions be transferred to this kingdom, without a change in these same passions? But, let us agree to all these things. What will you say about those who will be born after the coming of the anointed one? Do you claim that they will die, or not?

MOSES: Certainly they die at the end of the reign of the messiah [*Christus*].

PETRUS: What, then, will their parents do at their death? For it would be better for them not to rise up again than to undergo all the pain of their deaths.

MOSES: Then let us say they will not die.

PETRUS: Then Scripture misleads [us], when David says in the Psalms: "Who is the man who will live and will not see death?"[47] If you consider it, the pathways of reason and the passages for flight are closed to you on all sides, because the resurrection of the dead can in no way occur in the way that you say. This is why we had overturned the same claim earlier with the testimony of the law. How then, brother, can your mind forebear to listen to fables of this sort? Invoke with me the compassion of the Lord, then, so that he will free me as well as you from the error of this unfaithfulness. Amen.

47. Ps 88.49.

FOURTH *TITULUS*

OSES: NOT UNDESERVEDLY, I give thanks[1] to the one who illuminates hearts and drives away the darkness of such great blindness from our mind, even if only very late. Not unjustly I also repay you with the greatest thanks, you who have lifted the error of infidelity from me with the light of the clearest and most unconquerable arguments. Now, if it please you, following the order already established, explicate the next part of our proposed tasks. For you said that we observe hardly any of the law's precepts, and that that is not itself pleasing to God. Eagerly I would like to hear why, or for what purpose, you said this.

PETRUS: Since what I said—that you keep hardly any of the commandments of the law—is so clearly evident, it does not require proof from either authority or reason, considering that it can be proved with those very sacrifices that you never celebrate. For you do not present an offering of a lamb as a sacrificial victim in the morning and evening,[2] as was done in the past; nor do you celebrate the burnt offerings at the time of the new moon,[3] or the burnt offerings of the Sabbath rituals,[4] or those of bread, wine, and oil, which similarly you have neglected. Neither do you offer the libations, nor that which was prepared daily on the table, nor that bread of presentation which your forefathers were accustomed to offer on the seventh day.[5] They also kindled from evening time to morning the lamps that were prepared,[6] and at the same times they had the incense placed in censers burned in the Temple.[7] They also guarded the ordinations and anointings of the priests, and the various changes of their vest-

---

1. Reading *gratias* (A) for the nonsensical *ratias* (B).
2. Cf. Ex 29.38–39.   3. Cf. Nm 28.11–15.
4. Cf. Nm 28.9–10.   5. Cf. Ex 25.30.
6. Cf. Ex 27.21.   7. Cf. Ex 30.7–8.

ments and the different varieties of the foods they consumed;[8] and they guarded the performances [*vicissitudines*] of the ministers taking their turns according to the precepts of the law during specific weeks. They consecrated the Levites as well,[9] chosen according to the law, and performed the psalms with musical instruments, just as Moses had instituted. They presented one portion of the firstlings of a cow, a sheep, and a goat as an offering, and another portion they reserved for the priests to consume.[10] Moreover, they redeemed the firstborn of man and of unclean animals for a price,[11] and they gave the first fruits of the trees[12] to the priests as food. They did not assign the use of any of the fruits remaining on the trees for the first three years. In the fourth year, all of their fruits were sanctified as praise to the Lord. Moreover, they offered the first fruits to the priests, and to the Levites they gave one of the two tenths,[13] and they carried another to Jerusalem to be eaten in the holy place. In addition, the Levites rendered a tenth of the tenth that they received to the same priests. The seventh year was a Sabbath for the land, and the fiftieth year was a jubilee year.[14] In addition, there was subject to the judgment of the priests the law of every kind of leprosy that would strike them: of the leprosy of garments and dwellings, of a scar and blisters breaking out, of a shining spot and various types of changed colors, so that it might be known when a thing is clean or unclean.[15] Also, the law concerning him who suffered an issue of seed,[16] as well as the law regarding a woman who is separated during her monthly times,[17] and the sacrifices of their purification, was established according to the decision of the priests. If any man entered the tent of a dead man[18] or had touched the cadaver of a man that was slain,[19] or his bone or his grave, both he himself and all the vessels in his tent were unclean, until they were cleansed—sprinkled with the

---

8. Cf. Ex 29.1–7.
10. Cf. Nm 18.17–18.
12. Cf. Nm 18.8.
9. Cf. Nm 8.6–13.
11. Cf. Nm 18.15.

13. Cf. Nm 18.26–30. "Tenths": i.e., the tithes presented for the maintenance of the Levites and priests.

14. Cf. Lv 25.4, 10.
16. Cf. Lv 15.2.
18. Cf. Nm 19.14.
15. Cf. Lv 14.54–57.
17. Cf. Lv 15.33.
19. Cf. Nm 19.16.

ashes of a calf that had been consumed by fire. Besides these, several other precepts are commanded in the law, which for a long time now you have entirely neglected.

MOSES: We ought never to be reproached for observing very few of the precepts of the law, since we are exiles from our country, and we have no temple and lack legitimate priests.

PETRUS: You have offered a feeble excuse. For if your sacrifices were accepted by God, he certainly would not have thrown you out of the land so that you would be altogether unable to fulfill these precepts which he commanded.

MOSES: Let it not be thought that he expelled us from our only fatherland so that we should be unable to comply with his precepts, seeing that it would not be an act of one who is wise or just to command something, the very thing which, later, he would prevent from being done; and again, would he have a reason to demand from us why we did not do these things, except that because we had failed in his sight he became angry with us and threw us out of the land to a place where we cannot fulfill his precepts? Thus our impossibility [for doing these things] will not be culpable until the time arrives when we are returned to the land of our dwelling, and then we will complete in act the things which the Lord commanded us, and our sacrifice will be acceptable to him, just as the prophet Malachi attested, saying: "And the sacrifice of Judah and Jerusalem shall please the Lord, as in the days of old and in the ancient years."[20]

PETRUS: The testimony of this prophecy contributes nothing to our theme. For if you examine the history that precedes and follows it, you will find that it was said concerning the sacrifices of the Temple built in Ezra's time. Again, I confirm what I said about your exile: namely, that he threw you out of the land so that you would make no sacrifices; so that you not observe the new moons or any other festivals according to the original custom; so that you not wear down the thresholds of the Temple. For although God commanded through Moses that sacrifices be performed, he did so for this reason: so that those believing in him and loving him rightly with all their mind would guard the

20. Mal 3.4.

precepts of his law with as much solicitude and purity as was fitting, and so that they not treat the law as something unworthy
by committing thefts, murders, rapes and other vices and, likewise, sacrificing to idols, nor so that those who are unworthy
and polluted by many impurities enter his holy Temple to sacrifice to the true God, just as the prophet Jeremiah attests, saying:
"Behold, you put your trust in lying words which shall not profit
you, to steal, to murder, to commit adultery, to swear falsely, to
offer up to Baalim, and to go after strange gods that you did not
know, and you have come and stood before me in this house, in
which my name is called upon, and you have said: We are delivered, because we have done all these abominations."[21] God has
detested your works and your offerings presented with songs,
then, and has expelled you from his Temple and from the land,
just as the prophet Isaiah clearly indicated with words such as
these: "Why [do you offer] me the multitude of your victims?
says the Lord. I am full. I do not want burnt offerings of rams,
and the fat of fatlings, and the blood of calves and lambs and
goats. When you come to appear before me, who required these
things at your hands, that you should walk in my courts? Offer
sacrifice no more in vain. Incense is an abomination to me. The
new moons and the Sabbaths and other festivals I will not abide.
Your assemblies are wicked. My soul hates your new moons and
your solemnities. They are become troublesome to me. I am
weary of bearing them."[22] Jeremiah confirms this, saying: "To
what purpose do you bring me frankincense from Saba and the
sweet-smelling cane from the far country? Your holocausts are
not acceptable and your offerings are not pleasing to me."[23] And
elsewhere, "When they fast I will not hear their prayers, and if
they offer holocausts and offerings, I will not receive them."[24]
The prophet Amos, moreover, said concerning this: "I hate and
I have rejected your festivities, and I will not receive the odor of
your assemblies. And if you offer me holocausts, and your gifts,
I will not receive them, neither will I regard the vows of your
fat beasts. I will sweep away the tumult of your songs and I will

21. Jer 7.8–10.   22. Is 1.11–14.
23. Jer 6.20.   24. Jer 14.12.

not hear the canticles of your harp."[25] Again Malachi says about this: "I have no pleasure in you, says the Lord of hosts, and I will not receive a gift from your hand."[26] And the psalmist [says]: "Sacrifice and oblation you did not want, whereas you have perfected ears for me."[27] [God] also says, through the prophet Hosea: "And I will cause all her joy to cease, her solemnity, her new moon, her Sabbath, and all her festival times,"[28] and many other passages [like these], which take too long to enumerate. These are the greater and chief precepts of your law, which God never wants to receive from your hand, as prophetic authority and the epoch of the present era indicate.

MOSES: We say and we believe that all the words that you have introduced from the prophets were prophesied about the Babylonian captivity and were fulfilled at that same time. For after it, divinity both looked upon us and accepted our sacrifices.

PETRUS: My understanding agrees perfectly with your explanation. For when God returned you to your country and to the Temple, after having led you out of captivity, it is clear that he fulfilled the threats of the prophets and regarded your offerings as acceptable for sins that were pardoned. But when later you returned to your original crimes, you were punished once again with the original penalties, and it is clear that this second captivity was greater and more severe than the first to the same extent that God's wrath toward you was greater in this one than in that.

MOSES: You contradict yourself with this claim, since previously you said that the people at that time were religious and just and faithfully guarded the law's precepts, whereas now you affirm that their acts were displeasing to God.

PETRUS: I do not deny that they guarded worthily that law which the lawgiver Moses had received from God and proclaimed to them. But after Christ arrived—who revealed the hidden teachings of the prophets and, once the veil of the law

25. Am 5.21–23. "I will take away . . .": note that the text reads *auferam* for the Vulg. *aufer a me.*
26. Mal 1.10.
27. Cf. Ps 39.7; the Vulg. reads "you have pierced [*fodisti*] ears for me."
28. Hos 2.11.

had been removed, revealed the spiritual sense that it concealed—from that point on, they had to guard the legal insti-
tutes not according to the letter that kills but according to the
lifegiving spirit,[29] since he who gave the law understood it better
than the prophets who were the ones who heard it. Since they
neglected to do this, God refused to receive their ancient observances for that reason, just as they were forbidden to perform
the ancient rituals which they had observed before the law had
been received from the hand of Moses, after that same law had
been received: for example, the practice of marrying two sisters
at the same time[30] or taking a wife who had been put aside,[31] or
eating every animal.[32] Doing these things and others like them
before the law was not considered a crime, but afterwards no
one could do them without sin.

MOSES: I believe and I think that we ought to observe our law
in every respect just as Moses gave it and just as every generation of our fathers practiced it from ancient times.

PETRUS: If the old observances of the law had been acceptable to the Lord, he never would have thrown you out of your
homeland and from the Temple when you fulfilled them in act.
But, let me accept your words in order to show you that you
ought to be reproached for your judgment since, just as I said,
you observe only a few precepts of the law and you do not even
guard those in their entirety, as the law commands, since indeed you do not have the offerings and other things commanded which are necessary for the Sabbath, for solemnities, or for
your fasts. Even the prayers which you pour out to the Lord in
place of the sacrifices do not rise up to his ears, that they may
be granted. You are unable, nor do you dare, to attribute this to
my malevolence, since your own sages attest that God has not
accepted your prayers since the time when the Temple was destroyed. They even confirm this with the authority of the prophet Jeremiah, saying: "When I cry and entreat, he has shut out my
prayer."[33] And again, "You have set a cloud before yourself, lest
prayer pass through."[34] And Isaiah [says]: "And when you stretch

29. Cf. 2 Cor 3.6.
31. Cf. Dt 24.4.
33. Lam 3.8.
30. Cf. Gn 29.21–30.
32. Cf. Lv 11.1–23.
34. Lam 3.44.

forth your hands, I will avert my eyes from you, and when you multiply prayer, I will not hear."[35] Moreover, you are all unclean according to the law of Moses. For there is no one among you who is not polluted by contact with the dead. This stain is only removed by spreading the ashes of a red heifer,[36] which you cannot have at the present time; therefore, you cannot be delivered from uncleanness. All your women are believed to be polluted by an issue as well, since there no longer exist the priests of old to whom the judgment was left to discern between a menstrual woman and one polluted by a flux of blood;[37] and the children are born from pollution. Also, all of your foods are proven to be unclean according to the law's judgment. O Moses, since your entire nation [*gens*] is shown to be polluted,[38] the women are polluted, and for this reason all the children are born from pollution; and since all foods are unclean, and their prayers never reach God's ears, and their works do not please him, how, I ask you, can you have any assurance that there will be an end to these evils, or that they will be considered to have any value before God? I give due thanks to him because he delivered me from their error, and devotedly I pray to him to deliver you as well. Amen.

35. Is 1.15.
36. Cf. Nm 19.1–10.
37. Although rabbinic authority undertook to make this same discrimination. For a discussion of talmudic taxonomies of issues of blood, see for example Charlotte Elisheva Fonrobert, "Yalta's Ruse: Resistance Against Rabbinic Menstrual Authority in Talmudic Literature," in *Women and Water: Menstruation in Jewish Life and Law*, ed. Rahel R. Wasserfall (Hanover and London: Brandeis University Press, 1999), especially 62–69.
38. Cf. Is 64.6.

FIFTH *TITULUS*

OSES: UP TO THIS point, you have shown how worthless and inconsistent the faith of the Jewish nation is in every respect, and how irrational and unwelcome is its service to God; or you have demonstrated and disclosed, with the clearest arguments, why you have withdrawn from the faith of this same nation, and you have shown me the extent to which I have remained in error up to now. But I wonder why, when you abandoned your paternal faith, you chose the faith of the Christians rather than the faith of the Saracens, with whom you were always associated and raised. For I should like to bring to bear whatever obstacles I shall be able to, not only in regard to the Hebraic [sect] but even against that sect, so that, just as you hold out an argument about our [faith], so, too, you will hold out an argument concerning that one, with which it can be demolished. For you were always, as I said, associated with them and you were raised among them; you read [their] books, and you understand the language. You ought to have chosen this [part] before the rest, which is known to be more pleasing and more suitable than the others, so that I would take their role for myself. Indeed [their] law is generous. It contains many commands concerning the pleasures of this present life, by which fact divine love is shown to have been greatest toward them. Equally, it promises ineffable joys to its practicing members in return. If you should investigate the basis of this law, you will find that it is grounded on an unshakable foundation of reason.[1] A sign of

1. It is interesting that a somewhat "enlightened" Moses here acknowledges that Islam is grounded in reason, whereas, just above, Judaism has been dismissed as irrational. This does indeed reflect a view held by some of his Christian contemporaries or near-contemporaries, for whom Muslims shared certain core beliefs with Christians (e.g., the Virgin Birth) that Jews had ridiculed as irrational. From the first half of the twelfth century, see Amédée de Lausanne, *Huit homélies mariales* 4 and 5, ed. Jean Deshusses and trans. Antoine Dumas,

this, namely, that God loved them and was unwilling to burden
them with many precepts but spared them instead, is that he
only commanded them to pray five times each day, but that to
have perfect purity always before they pray, they should properly wash the buttocks [*culum*], sexual parts, hands, arms, mouth,
nose, ears, eyes, hair and, last, the feet. Once having done this,
they declaim in public, confessing the one God, who has none
like or equal to him, and that Mohammad is his prophet.[2] Also,
they fast for an entire month during the year.[3] On the other
hand, when fasting, they eat at night time, but abstain during
the day, so that, from that time of day when they will be able to
distinguish a white thread from a black one by sight, until the

---

Sources chrétiennes 72, Série des Textes Monastiques d'Occident 5 (Paris: Les Éditions du Cerf, 1960), 122, 163–65, and 146, 128–31 (where "Gentiles" seems
to refer to Muslims). Moreover, it has sometimes been argued that the "Philosopher," the symbol of Reason in Abelard's dialogue between a philosopher,
a Jew, and a Christian, is modeled after the Muslim philosopher Avempace. Indeed, the "Jew" seems to acknowledge that the "Philosopher" has been circumcised, like the descendants of Ishmael. See Petrus Abaelardus, *Dialogus inter Philosophum, Iudaeum, et Christianum*, ed. Rudolf Thomas (Stuttgart-Bad Cannstatt:
Friedrich Frommann Verlag, 1970), 68, 731. For the identification with Avempace, see Jean Jolivet, "Abélard et le philosophe (occident et Islam aux XIIᵉ
siècle)," *Revue de l'histoire des religions* 164 (1963): 181–89. As Payer points out in
his introduction to his translation of Abelard's text—see Peter Abelard, *Dialogue
of a Philosopher with a Jew and a Christian*, trans. Pierre J. Payer (Toronto: Pontifical Institute of Medieval Studies, 1979)—this identification remains conjec-
tural so long as the date for its composition remains uncertain. By contrast, in
twelfth-century polemics, Jews would be more frequently demonized as irrational beasts. This claim is found most notably in Peter the Venerable's *Adversus Judeorum inveteratam duritiem*, pp. 57–58. For a consideration of this text, see Anna
Sapir Abulafia's "Twelfth-Century Renaissance Theology and the Jews," in *From
Witness to Witchcraft: Jews and Judaism in Medieval Christian Thought*, ed. Jeremy
Cohen, Wolfenbütteler Mittelalter-Studien 11 (Wiesbaden: Harrassowitz Verlag,
1996), 135–37. Also see Anna Sapir Abulafia, *Christians and Jews in the Twelfth
Century* (London and New York: Routledge, 1995), 124–25; eadem, *Christians
and Jews in Dispute. Disputational Literature and the Rise of Anti-Judaism in the West
(c. 1000–1150)*, XVI: "Bodies in the Jewish-Christian Debate," (Aldershot: Ashgate, 1998), 123–37, previously published in *Framing Medieval Bodies*, ed. Sarah
Kay and Miri Rubin (Manchester: Manchester University Press, 1994); Gavin I.
Langmuir, "The Faith of Christians and Hostility to Jews," *Christianity and Judaism. Papers Read at the 1991 Summer Meeting and the 1992 Winter Meeting of the Ecclesiastical History Society*, ed. Diana Wood (Oxford: Blackwell Publishers, 1992):
77–92.
    2. Cf. Qur'an 4.43.
    3. I.e., during Ramadan.

sun sets, no one eats or drinks, nor presumes to befoul himself by intercourse with his wife.[4] After the setting of the sun until twilight of the next day, however, it is always permitted to them to enjoy food and drink and their own wives, as much as pleases them. If someone is burdened with an illness or is on a journey, however, for as long as the period of his languor or his journey shall last, he is permitted to eat and to enjoy whatever he will; yet nevertheless later he should correct, when he is at liberty to do so, what he had fulfilled less from the necessity either of the illness or of the journey.

Moreover, all are commanded to go to the house of God once each year,[5] which must be seen in Mecca, and there to worship, for the sake of a solitary self-examination; and, having clothed themselves with seamless garments, to circle it and, just as the law commands, to throw rocks backwards from between their legs to stone the devil. Moreover, they say that Adam constructed this house for the Lord when he had been banished from paradise, and it was a place of prayer for all his children, until Abraham came.[6] Abraham, the servant of God, strengthened and restored it, however, and offered vows to the Lord in it, and offered sacrifices, and after [his] death left it to his son named Ishmael, and across all the centuries it remained for him and for all his children a place for praying, until Mohammad was born. After he was born, God promised it as an inheritance to him and to all his generations, as they claim. Besides this, their prophets are commanded to despoil, to capture, to slay, to pursue, and to blot out in every way the adversaries of God, unless they have chosen to repent and to be converted to their faith, or unless they have paid the tax of servitude imposed on them. All flesh is permitted to them to eat, moreover, except the flesh and blood of the pig [and] likewise carrion.[7] And they reject whatever has been consecrated in the name of anything except God. In addition to this, it is permitted to them to have four lawful wives at the same time, and, having divorced one, to accept another at any time, though only so long as they never exceed the number four. This is observed in divorce, too: that it is

4. Cf. Qur'an 2.183–87.   5. Cf. Qur'an 2.189.
6. Cf. Qur'an 2.125.   7. Cf. Qur'an 2.172–73.

permitted to divorce and to remarry the same one, up to three times.[8] It will be permitted to have female slaves [*empticiae*] and captives, as many as [a man] will, and he will have unrestricted power for selling them and buying them back again, [yet] in such a way that once he has made one pregnant, he can in no way bind her by the yoke of another servitude. It is also granted to them to take wives from their own kin, so that the bloodline [*sanguinis proles*] may increase and so that the bond of amity grow stronger among them.[9] You yourself know very well that among them legal judgments regarding claims to property are the same as they are among the Hebrews, so that the plaintiff proves [his case] with witnesses and the defendant defends himself with an oath. Moreover, they accept only the most worthy and proven persons as witnesses, and those whom they can believe without an oath. In certain other respects, as well, they keep to the practice of the law of Moses, so that he who has shed the blood of a man is punished with the same punishment,[10] and a man who has been caught in adultery is stoned along with the adulterous woman.[11] Moreover, a man who has engaged in fornication with another woman will be subject to eighty lashes. Such a punishment as this is laid down for a thief: for the first and second offense he will endure eighty lashes, for the third he will lose a hand, for the fourth a foot, and one who has removed a limb from any man may redeem [it] with an appropriate price. All these precepts were set forth by God, lest, if any license for acting were too broad, ruin should quickly befall the entire people. They are commanded to abstain always from wine, since it is the kindling for, and the seedbed of, all sin.[12] These are [only] the principal commandments of the law, since it would take too long to tarry over individual ones.

And God promised to those believing in him and in Mohammad, his faithful prophet, and to those fulfilling the commandments of his law, a paradise, that is, a garden of delights, irrigated with flowing waters, in which they will have thrones everlasting. The shade of trees will protect them, and they will not

8. Cf. Qur'an 2.230. 9. Cf. Qur'an 33.56.
10. Cf. Gn 9.6. 11. Cf. Lv 20.10.
12. Cf. Qur'an 2.219.

suffer from either cold or heat.[13] They will eat from the kinds of every fruit and of every food.[14] Whatever appetite suggests to any one, he will find immediately set before him. They will be clothed with silk garments of all colors.[15] They will recline in delights, and the angels will pass among them as table servants with gold and silver vessels,[16] offering milk in the gold ones and wine in the silver,[17] saying: "Eat and drink in complete joy, and, behold, what God promised you has been fulfilled." They will be joined to virgins, whom neither human nor demonic contact has violated,[18] more beautiful in form than the splendor of hyacinth and coral.[19] These goods will be given to believers, whereas for those who do not believe in God and his prophet Mohammad there will be infernal punishment without end. Regardless of the number of sins by which every man is bound, yet on the day of his death if he shall believe in God and Mohammad, he will be saved on the day of judgment with Mohammad intervening for him. Since from childhood, no less, you have known that these things and many others, which would take too long to enumerate, were written and were held in the greatest veneration by the entire race of the Saracens, then why have you followed the Christian rather than the Muslim [*Muzalemitica*] religion? Will you better enjoy the felicity of the present life and equally enjoy that of the future life as well?

PETRUS: Although the web of your discourse, which has so much elegance and sweetness, is not less convincing than if Mohammad himself were present, for those who consider the delights of the body the highest good, nevertheless it is strange that you hope to instruct me in this, in order to convince me of that in which you believe I can in no wise be deceived.[20] For you are certain that it is not unknown to me who Mohammad was, how he falsely fashioned himself a prophet with a clever deception, and who his advisor was in contriving this. One thing remains uncertain to you, I reckon: how useless I will judge that

13. Cf. Qur'an 76.13.
14. Cf. Qur'an 55.52.
15. Cf. Qur'an 18.31.
16. Cf. Qur'an 43.71.
17. Cf. Qur'an 47.15.
18. Cf. Qur'an 55.54–56; 50.56, 70–74.
19. Cf. Qur'an 55.58.
20. To say that this passage is troubled is a gross understatement.

doctrine that they call Mohammad's. When, though, you have heard his life and character summarized in my narration, then you will easily be able to discern whether I do or do not know what is true about him.

MOSES: I eagerly wait to hear this from you.

PETRUS: Mohammad then, after he was orphaned, passed the years of childhood under the protection of his uncle, Manephus,[21] serving the worship of the idols of the time, with the entire race of the Arabs, as he himself testifies in his Qur'an, saying that God said to him: "You were an orphan wandering aimlessly, and I received you and I guided you; you were poor, and I enriched you."[22] After the passage of a few years as a hired servant with a certain most noble widow, named Khadijah, he so possessed, in a brief time, the mind of his mistress, that he would take possession by law of marriage both all the goods and the mistress of the goods herself. Once he was transformed from the humblest pauper into a very rich man by this wealth, he burst forth into such arrogance that he expected that the kingdom of the Arabs would be offered to him, except that he was afraid that his kinsmen would not accept him as king, since they were his equals and his betters. Nevertheless, devising a path by which he could be made king, he chose to fashion himself a prophet, relying upon that wit for eloquence which, when he exerted himself in business dealings among various nations, he had received by the facility of his intelligence. He relied, too, on the fact that the greater portion of the Arabs at that time were common soldiers [*milites*] and farmers, and almost all were idolaters, except for some who embraced the law of Moses in a heretical way, following after the Samaritans, and others who were Nestorian[23] and Jacobite[24] Christians.

21. According to tradition, Mohammad was raised by his grandfather, 'Abd al-Muttalib; after his grandfather's death, he was taken in by his uncle, Abū Tālib. The error here, according to J. H. L. Reuter, stems from Petrus Alfonsi's use of Ps.-al-Kindi's *Apology*, which gives the tribal name for Mohammad's uncle, Abdu Manaf, which appears as Manephus in a Latinized version. See her *Petrus Alfonsi*, 85–86.

22. Qur'an 93.6.

23. That is, followers of the heretical patriarch Nestorius (d. ca. 451).

24. That is, Syrian Christians utilizing the Jacobite liturgy.

The Jacobites, however, are heretics named after a certain Jacob. They preach the circumcision,[25] and believe that Christ is not God but only a just man, conceived of the Holy Spirit and born of a virgin; nevertheless they do not believe that he was crucified or that he died. Moreover, there was at this time in the region of Antioch a certain archdeacon named Sergius,[26] a Jacobite and a friend of Mohammad's; he was called from there to a council and condemned. Saddened by the shame of his condemnation, he fled from the region and came to Mohammad. Mohammad, supported by his advice, brought to a conclusion what he contemplated but still was unable to fulfill on his own. There were also two Jews among those heretics of Arabia whom we mentioned, named Abdias[27] and Chabalahabar, and these, indeed, attached themselves to Mohammad and offered their assistance to complete his foolishness. And these three mixed together [*contemperaverunt*] the law of Mohammad, each one according to his own heresy, and showed him how to say such things on God's behalf which both the heretical Jews and the heretical Christians who were in Arabia believed to be true; whereas those who were unwilling to believe of their own free will nevertheless were forced to believe for fear of the sword. But we do not know of any other prophecy of his nor any miracles, as we heard about Moses, Joshua, Samuel, Elijah, and Elisha, who, we read, performed many miracles.

MOSES: We, too, believe in many of the prophets without having read about any miracles performed by them, like Jeremiah, Obadiah, Amos, Hosea, and others.

25. A claim reiterated in the early thirteenth century by Jacques de Vitry, who claims that when he landed at Acre he encountered Jacobites there, who circumcised their children according to the Jewish custom. See his *Lettres de Jacques de Vitry* 2, ed. R. B. C. Huygens (Leiden: E. J. Brill, 1960), 83.

26. Petrus Alfonsi erroneously identifies Sergius (i.e., Bahira) as a Jacobite; tradition maintains that he was a Nestorian Christian.

27. Abdias and Chabalahabar appear to be corruptions of Abdallah ibn-Salām and Ka'b al-Ahbar, two Jews mentioned in Ps.-al-Kindi's *Apology* as having influenced Mohammad. See Barbara Hurwitz Grant, "Ambivalence in Medieval Religious Polemics," 167. The *Apology* was translated into Latin ca. 1142 by Peter of Toledo. For the claim that Peter of Toledo and Petrus Alfonsi may be one and the same, see *supra*, p. 22. For the Latin text of the *Apology*, see Jose Munoz Sendino, "Al-Kindi, Apologia del Cristianismo," in *Miscellanea Comillas* 11–12 (1949): 337–460.

PETRUS: This is why we do not have to demand miracles from them—because they neither introduced any novelty of the law nor in any way contradicted the Mosaic teaching, and what they predicted we know was fulfilled by them.

MOSES: There is no doubt but that the divinely inspired patriarchs Noah and Abraham received[28] new commandments, like commandments concerning sacrifices, the eating of meats, circumcision, and other rituals. Why, then, did their descendants put faith in them without the light of miracles?

PETRUS: Truly, they believed in them because that prophet bore witness to them whose testimony no one doubts, namely, Moses. How should Mohammad, who is not comparable to any of the prophets in any plausible way, be accepted among the prophets, then?

MOSES: Why did you say that he is not shown to be a prophet with any plausibility, when frequently you hear that he was marked out by genuine miracles? Did not a brute animal, namely, the ox Doregele,[29] announce him as a prophet? Did not the moon identify him as a wonderworking prophet, when it entered in through each sleeve [*manica*], and then, made whole again, went forth from his lap? Must one not also take note of the fact that a sheep's teat, once it was rubbed by his hand, offered a drink of milk, pouring it out for the entire population? It was also a wonder that when he called a fig tree to come to him, the tree came to him and he ate of its fruit; and a poisoned shoulder portion of a sheep, which was placed on a platter for him, spoke to him and said: "Do not eat me, because I am poisoned."[30]

28. "Received": reading *data esse*, following MS B1, rather than *dedisse*.

29. P. Sj. van Koningsveld attempts to explain Doregele as a corruption of the name *Darîkh* found in Ps.-al-Kindi's work. See P. Sj. van Koningsveld, "La apologia de Al-Kindi en la Espana del siglo XII. Huellas toledanas de un 'Animal disputax,'" 116.

30. An allusion to the tradition in Hadith (see Sahih Bukhari, 3.47.786; Sahih Muslim, 26.5530) that the widowed wife of Sallām ibn Mishkam, a Jew, attempted to poison Mohammad with a roast lamb. "The Prophet took a bite of the shoulder of the lamb but spat it out . . ." See "Muhammad, The Messenger of God," in *The Concise Encyclopedia of Islam*, ed. Cyril Glassé (New York: Harper Collins, 1989), 283. This tale was repeated in medieval Latin sources, e.g., Vincent of Beauvais's *Speculum Historiale* 23.46.915.

PETRUS: All these which you go on about are frivolous things, nor are they proven to be worthy of belief in the judgment of all of your [sages], especially since Mohammad himself reported no such thing in his Qur'an; but rather whatever had been written about him that is not in the Qur'an, he prohibited altogether from being believed as true. "Many have said many false things," he said, "about all the prophets; so that this may not happen to me, that alone should be accepted as true about me which is proved to be supported by the authority of the Qur'an." Wanting to show why he would not perform a miracle, he introduced the Lord speaking to him, by saying: "The Lord said to me: I do not allow you to perform miracles for this reason, because I fear lest there be something in the miracles to contradict you, just like the other prophets." Therefore, by his own testimony, he is shown to have performed no sign. By what other indications, then, is one proven to be a true prophet? The indications of a true prophet are these: probity of life, a display of miracles, and the firm truth of all [their] teachings. Violence was the good quality of life in Mohammad, by which he had himself proclaimed a prophet of God by force, rejoicing in theft and rapaciousness, and burning so much with the fire of lust that he did not blush to befoul another man's bed in adultery just as if the Lord were commanding it, just as is read about Zanab the daughter of Ias, the wife of Zed:[31] "The Lord has commanded," he said, "that you, Zed, send away your wife."[32] Once she was sent away, he copulated with her himself regularly. The dishonor of his wife, Aissa, brought to light very clearly how empty his prophecy was when, after she had been caught in adultery by the testimony of many people, he confirmed with a message of the false Gabriel that she had not been caught in adultery, because he did not want to send her away.[33] One reads

31. That is, Zaynab bint Jahsh, who had been the wife of the Prophet's adopted son Zayd ibn al-Hārith. According to Thomas Burman, this incident was exploited by other twelfth-century Andalusian anti-Muslim polemics—e.g., the *Liber denudationis*. See his *Religious Polemic and Intellectual History of the Mozarabs, c. 1050–1200*, 105–6.

32. Cf. Qur'an 33.37.

33. That is, 'Ā'ishah, the daughter of Abū Bakr and the Prophet's favorite wife, who was accused of marital infidelity. The accusation of adultery, however,

that he had praised God for the power of his own vice, that is, lust, because the power abounded in him forty times beyond human measure, and he gave thanks that the sweet odor and beauty of women attracted him a great deal, with God granting it. We have already spoken about miracles. Moreover, the great slaughter and flight of his own people, his teeth broken[34] and his face battered in battle, attest to the truth concerning the battles which he acknowledged that he entered, with the Lord commanding and promising victory. This would hardly have happened to him if, as you say, an angel of the Lord guarded him, just as we read concerning Elijah and Elisha, whom an angel of the Lord always snatched from their enemies. And victory would always follow after him if he were such a one as you say, like Moses, Joshua, and David, whom victory always attended, since they entered into battles by divine command. Moreover, if he were a true prophet, as you say, then when about to enter battle he would know whether misfortunes would befall him. How, then, do you say that I, once having put aside my law, ought to follow his[35] law rather than the Christian [law]?

MOSES: Assuredly this argument seems true for one who has investigated the matter lucidly.

PETRUS: From what you said above—that I have read the books, know the language, and was raised almost entirely among the Saracens—it is not therefore appropriate that I would follow their law.

MOSES: I said that you ought to receive it because I believed that it was a good [law].

PETRUS: You said that the basis of their law is constructed on a foundation of unshakable reason; therefore, in the give-and-take of debate let us consider words against words, commandments against commandments, so we will be able to discover if it is well established.

MOSES: I agree.

---

remained unproved, when four witnesses could not be provided. Cf. Qur'an 24.11–14.

34. Reminiscent of the text of Ps 3.8: "Dentes peccatorum contrivisti" ("You have broken the teeth of sinners").

35. Reading *illius* (A) for *ilius* (B).

PETRUS: You say that Mohammad commanded prayer five
times a day, and that certainly he did this for this reason, that—
on his mentors' advice—he wanted his law to be established as a
mediator between the law of the Christians and that of the Jews,
and not for its probity nor from divine inspiration [*adiutorium*].
For the Jews, according to their law, pray three times each day,[36]
and the Christians seven times,[37] but he established as a limit
between each of them neither three nor seven, but instead five
times for praying. What you praise—that, before they pray, they
wash the hands and arms and other members of the body—
is not important to prayer. For prayer it is important to be
cleansed inwardly, not outwardly. A purity resulting from the ablution of the members, however, was important to the worshipers of the planet Venus,[38] who, wanting to pray to her, prepared
themselves as if they were women, coloring [their] mouths and
eyes. He commanded this for the reason that he became king at
the minute of the planet Venus.[39] You admit that at the time of

36. Morning *(Shaharit)*, afternoon *(Mincha)*, and evening *(Ma'ariv)* prayer, a
daily routine which rabbinic tradition claims was established by the three patriarchs.

37. See *Benedicti regula*, c. 16, ed. Rudolph Hanslik, CSEL 75 (Vienna:
Hölder-Pichler-Tempsky, 1975), 64–65.

38. "Worshipers of the planet Venus": perhaps a notion that arose because
the Muslim "Sabbath" occurs on Friday, lit., the "Day of Venus" *(dies Veneris)*.
Thus, in the early thirteenth century Bishop Jacques de Vitry remarked that
Mohammad commanded Muslims to observe the sixth day, namely, the day of
Venus, as their Sabbath. See his *Historia Orientalis* 1.6, ed. Franciscus Moschus
(Douai, 1597), 29. Michael Camille notes, too, in early Byzantine Christian po-
lemics the equation of Muslims' veneration of the black stone of the Ka'aba with
worship of a sculpted head of Venus. See his *The Gothic Idol* (Cambridge and
New York: Cambridge University Press, 1989), 140, for this, and for a broader
discussion of Christian attempts to stigmatize Muslims as idolaters. Finally, Paul
Alvarus insists that Mohammad's excessive libidinal desire was not given to him
by the creator God but by Venus, Vulcan's wife. See his *Indiculus luminosus* 23
(PL 121: 538B–C). Medieval Christian authors therefore sometimes linked Islam to Venus because the Saracens were said to be under the influence of the
planet Venus; because Muslims observed a "sabbath" on the "day of Venus"; and
because the uncontrollable libidinal desire for which Mohammad was chastised,
and with which other Muslims were associated, was linked with Venus. For this
last characterization, see Jeffrey Jerome Cohen, "On Saracen Enjoyment: Some
Fantasies of Race in Late Medieval France and England," *The Journal of Medieval
and Early Modern Studies* 31/1 (2001): 113–46.

39. My thanks to Charles Burnett for drawing my attention to the passage in
Abū Ma`šar's ninth-century *Book of Religions and Dynasties* 2.8, where it is noted

prayer they declaim [prayers] in a public voice, which is not appropriate to prayer except that he was unable to impose another new sign. He commanded that they fast throughout an entire month, as you say, to restrain the vices of the flesh, which is the beginning of penance.[40] But tell me, I beg you, what good does it do to fast during the day and then at night to eat three or four times, and to enjoy both good meats and the best foods, and to indulge in women? These do not weaken but rather strengthen the flesh. You say that they go once a year to the house of God, which is in Mecca, for the sake of self-examination and to worship there; they say this was the house of Adam and Abraham, not from some authority they have, but as if some legend [which] they concoct. For before he had preached the law, this house was full of idols. But if you knew, O Moses, what kind of house this was, and what secret was contained in it, and why Mohammad commanded [them] to go there and to do the things found in the law, you would be sorely amazed.

MOSES: I beg you to tell me what you are alluding to. For although I may preach this law to you, I do not know why he commanded them to make a journey there, and to do the other things which the law commands.

PETRUS: I wanted to mention it to you briefly, but now, since I am asked, I will demonstrate it clearly. The two sons of Lot, Amon and Moab,[41] honored this house, and two idols were worshiped there by these same two: one, executed from a white rock, and the other from a black one. The name of the one that was from a black rock was called Merculicius,[42] and the name of

---

that at the time of Mohammad's accession (i.e., the date of the Hejirah), "Venus was in the sign of its exaltation in the ninth place, signifying religion and, being the indicator of the Arabs by nature, it gave the rulership to them . . ." See Abu Ma'ashar *On Historical Astrology* 2.8, ed. Charles Burnett and Keiji Yamamoto, vol. 1 (Leiden: E. J. Brill, 2000), 127. For the Latin translation and glosses, emerging from the school of John of Seville in Toledo in the early twelfth century, see *op. cit.* 2.8, vol. 2, p. 83.

40. Qur'an 2.185.

41. The Ammonites and Moabites were descendants of Lot. See Gn 19.36–38.

42. I.e., Mercury. For this passage and its description of the cult at Mecca, see especially Bernard Septimus, "Petrus Alfonsi on the Cult at Mecca," *Speculum* 56/3 (1981): 517–33.

the other one was Chamos.[43] The one that was from the black rock was constructed in honor of Saturn, and the other, which was from the white, in honor of Mars. Twice a year their worshipers went up to them to worship them, to Mars, indeed, when the sun entered into the first degree of Aries, because Aries is the dignity of Mars.[44] At [the time of] its departure, stones were thrown, as was the custom. [They go up to] to Saturn, when the sun enters the first degree of Libra, because Libra is the dignity of Saturn.[45] Naked, with shorn heads, they burned incense, which [rites] are celebrated daily in India even now, as I said. In fact, the Arabs adored idols with Amon and Moab. Mohammad, however, coming much later, was unwilling to remove this early practice, but permitted [them] to circle the house, covered with seamless clothing, as if having changed the practice in some way. But lest he seem to command sacrifices to idols, he built a statue [*simulacrum*] of Saturn into the wall, in the corner of the house. Only the back was placed to the outside so that the face would not appear. Because it was sculpted in the round, he placed the other idol, namely, the one of Mars, under ground and placed a stone over it, and he ordered the people who gathered there in order to worship it, to kiss these stones and, with their shorn heads bowed, to throw rocks backwards from between their legs, who, bowing down, bare their backsides, which is a sign of the ancient law. Tell me, then, Moses, for what purpose he commanded these things, if not the one I say.

MOSES: I have told you that I do not know the purpose, since I have never found it written down. Nevertheless, I know one [purpose] for throwing the stones, because they say that they do these things to banish the demons. I have seen it written in their books that Omar, one of Mohammad's ten companions, when kissing the stones in the customary manner, began to speak in this way: "I say," he said, "to you stones, I know that you are able

43. "Chamos" can be identified with Amon or Moab. Cf. Nm 21.29; Jgs 11.24.
44. That is, Mars is the ruling planet for the astrological sign Aries.
45. According to Monnot, Alfonsi reiterates here an older Islamic tradition that identified the Ka'aba with a temple to Saturn, prior to Mohammad's reforms. See Guy Monnot, "Les citations coraniques dans le 'Dialogus' de Pierre Alphonse," 265 and 275, n. 12.

neither to assist me nor to injure me, yet I practice this custom because Mohammad did."

PETRUS: What you have said—that they banish the demons by throwing stones—does not seem to be a logical argument, because what cannot be perceived by some corporeal sense can never be banished easily. Demons are banished with the [invocation of the] divine name.

MOSES: Since I have heard some say that they have seen demons, and that they have heard them and have spoken with them, I am amazed that you say that they do not perceive them with a corporeal sense.[46]

PETRUS: Although angels cannot be perceived with a corporeal sense, still they become visible to those who walk according to the commandments of God. Likewise, the devil may become visible to his friends.

MOSES: I would like to know, by what teaching or by what art will I be able to see and to speak with them?

PETRUS: Why do you desire to know what does not pertain to God at all?

MOSES: I do not want to perform these acts, but only to have the knowledge.

PETRUS: How is it that you want to learn what may increase your error?

MOSES: You have corrected me well, thanks be to God; I have learned [good] sense in your words.

PETRUS: Enough has been said; let us return to the undertaking. That Mohammad commanded [them] to despoil, capture, and slay the adversaries of God until they decided to believe or to pay tribute,[47] is not among the acts of God, nor did any of the prophets command that anyone be forced to believe, but he commanded this himself out of a desire for money, in order to destroy his enemies. As you know, however, this ought not be done; rather, if anyone wishes to convert someone else, he should not do this with violence, but diligently and sweetly, just as Mohammad himself attested in his Qur'an, saying, in the

46. Other MSS (P1 and P2) read: "because they cannot be perceived with a corporeal sense."

47. This tax or tribute is the *jizyah*. Cf. Qur'an 9.29.

person of the Lord, "If the Lord your God were to will it, the peoples of the entire world would believe. Why, then, do you compel them to believe? Because no one believes except by the will of God."[48] And elsewhere it says, "The will of God has already come upon you nations. He who has believed has done so for his own sake, whereas he who has erred has erred for his own sake, and I am not a custodian over you. Therefore follow, God says, what is revealed to you, and wait until God, who is the judge over all, shall judge."[49] Again, in the same place, "The Lord your God," it says, "would place all under one law, if he wished, without discord."[50] In another place, just as if God were speaking to him, he invents this as well: "There ought to be no violence in the law."[51] He says, "Now justice and truth appear. He who has willed, by his free will will believe."[52] Again, in the Qur'an: "You unbelievers, you do not pray what I pray, neither do I pray to the one to whom you pray, nor do I worship the one whom you worship, and the law is different for me and for you."[53] And in another place he says, "You should argue only with gentle words with peoples of another law."[54] Why, then, did he order [them] to despoil, capture, and coerce the nations to believe by force, and why does he claim that all these are the paths of God? Tell me, Moses, why do you order me to believe a law which contradicts itself?

MOSES: The book of the Qur'an is such that a later order abrogates an earlier order.[55]

PETRUS: The Qur'an was not written by Mohammad's hand, for if it had been, it would be sequentially arranged [*ordinatus*]. Indeed, his companions who had dwelled with him composed the Qur'an after his death, each one declaring his own reading, so to speak; as a result, we do not know which was the ear-

---

48. Qur'an 10.99.   49. Qur'an 10.108–9.
50. Qur'an 11.118.   51. Qur'an 2.256.
52. Qur'an 18.29.   53. Qur'an 109.1–4, 6.
54. Qur'an 29.46.

55. The notion that a later verse in the Qur'an may abrogate an earlier one is an important exegetical device. For a discussion of just this issue, i.e., the role of compulsion in religious belief and the rule of abrogation, see Michael Cook, *The Koran: A Very Short Introduction* (Oxford: Oxford University Press, 2000), 33–36 and 101–2.

lier and which the later arrangement. Moreover, Mohammad ordered [them] to despoil, capture, and slay the nations for this reason: so that the Arabs, who dwelled in the desert but were ignorant of God, would find pleasure in the predations and so that they especially would believe him.

MOSES: I think what you say is true.

PETRUS: You say that they are free to eat all flesh except the flesh of the pig, and blood, and carrion;[56] all flesh is permitted to us as well. We disagree on this alone: namely, with respect to the flesh of the pig. Mohammad, however, did this so that we Christians would differ from his law over this matter. You said that they are free to take four wives and, having divorced one, to take yet another[57]—this is commanded with no logic [*ratio*], for it is commanded to take a wife only for the purpose of begetting children. Moreover, the fact that they can have as many captives and female slaves [*aempticiae*] as they wish is certainly adultery, as far as you are concerned, since very often the father buys a woman corrupted [*stuprata*] by his son, and contrariwise a son or a brother [buys] a [woman] corrupted by his father or brother.

MOSES: Truth is entrusted to your words. When there was such disagreement between these precepts, why did Mohammad, who seemed so wise, order that they be done?

PETRUS: Mohammad loved women a great deal and was too much the voluptuary, and, just as he himself claimed, the power of the lust of forty men dwelled in him.[58] And also, especially because the Arabs were very dissolute, he pandered to their desire, so that they would believe. When you say that they take wives from their own kindred, this was the practice of all at times, so that the bond of an alliance would become stronger among them. And concerning those judgments, which you spoke of above, in some ways they agree wisely with the law of

56. Cf. Qur'an 2.173.

57. Cf. Qur'an 2.236–37.

58. Accounts of Mohammad's dissolute or depraved sexual behavior became a staple of "popular" Christian anti-Muslim polemics. For a good discussion concerning thirteenth-century polemics, see John V. Tolan, "Rhetoric, Polemics and the Art of Hostile Biography: Portraying Muhammad in Thirteenth-Century Christian Spain."

Moses, whereas in others they disagree. And Mohammad did this so that his law would be a little bit different from the law of Moses. This is why they are ordered to abstain always from wine: lest inebriated companions bring about the ruin of the people.[59] And what you mentioned about paradise ought not to be passed over, because these things cannot be proved by reason. Indeed, once a soul has been separated from the body, and the four elements have been separated out from each other, a man does not use those worldly things in the manner in which he did previously; we condemned that [opinion] above in the third book, where we spoke about the resurrection of the dead. A wise man does not believe that paradise is like this at all, and he is not deceived by such words. But the people of Mohammad's time, without a law, without a Scripture, and ignorant of every good, save that of war and the plough, desiring luxury and given to gluttony, could easily be preached to according to their desire. For if he were to do otherwise, he would not impel them toward his law.

MOSES: Without divine help, such and so great a nation would not believe in him.[60]

PETRUS: If he had done all things with divine help, he would not have been defeated so often, nor, as we said above, would his teeth have shattered[61] in battle; like other kings, sometimes he was conquered and sometimes he conquered. Moreover, after his death, they all wanted to abandon his law. For he himself had said that on the third day his body would be raised up to heaven. When they knew that he was a deceiver and saw that the cadaver stank, with the body unburied the greater part [of his followers] departed. Haly ['Alî], however, the son of Abytharius [Abû Tâlib], one of Mohammad's ten companions, obtained the kingdom after his death. He preached flatteringly and cleverly admonished the people to believe, and told them that they

59. Cf. Qur'an 2.219 and 5.91.

60. In the Spanish translation of this text, this passage is erroneously put in the mouth of Petrus, and the previous sentence—"For if he were to do otherwise, he would not impel them toward his law"—is put in the mouth of Moses. See *Diálogo contra los Judíos*, trans. Esperanza Ducay, 304.

61. "Shattered": *crepuissent*. Earlier, it was said that Mohammad's teeth were crushed (or broken) and his face was battered in battle. See *supra*, p. 155, n. 34.

did not properly understand Mohammad's expression. He said, "Mohammad did not say that he would be raised up to heaven before burial, nor while people watched. Indeed, he said that after the burial of his body the angels would bear him off to heaven, with none being aware of it. Therefore, because they did not bury him immediately, certainly he began to stink, in order that they might bury him right away." Therefore, by this argument he held the people a little while in their earlier error. Two brothers, sons of the secretary of Mohammad, Hazan [Hasan] and Hozam [Husayn], tormenting their bodies severely with fasts and vigils, almost killed themselves. Their father often admonished the sons, lest they fatigue their bodies with a torment that lasted too long. When he himself saw, however, that they were stupid and had already arrived at death's door from too much effort, he revealed [to them] the truth about Mohammad. Once they became aware of his wickedness from their father, they began to eat and drink wine, and, just as they had bravely persisted in his law previously, so at last they began to abandon the law, although not totally. But also a certain part of this people followed them in their practice. In all these ways, then, O Moses, we can know that he was not a true prophet and that neither are his words true. Although we pass over many things that we can say about him, let us merely introduce one which both we and you believe, namely, that he denied Christ, whom we believe both to be dead and crucified. For he says, "They neither slew nor crucified Christ, but it only seemed so to them."[62] Moreover, you will find him a deceiver not only in this matter, but reread all the books and sayings of the prophets, and in everything that he said about them you will find him to be a liar. How, then, do you exhort me to believe that liar, when you will find [him] deceitful in everything? I entreat the piety of almighty God to free me from his error and to complete the fulfillment of the law that I chose. Amen.

62. Qur'an 4.157.

SIXTH *TITULUS*

OSES: ENOUGH HAS BEEN ARGUED up to this point against our sect and the sect of the Saracens. You have confounded both, from reason as well as from authority. Now, however, explain what sort of faith yours is and distinguish the nature of your belief [*credulitas*] under [various] chapters.

PETRUS: At the beginning of my book I proclaimed the nature of my belief to you under headings. Now, then, investigate my disputation under any heading and, if it please you, defeat what I said, if you are able.

MOSES: I do desire to do so, if I will be able to. Now, then, I will begin to investigate the first part of your faith: namely, how it is that God is one and yet three persons (which Christians call the Father, the Son, and the Holy Spirit) such that no one of these is by nature [*naturaliter*] prior to another in time, nor separated from another substantially [*substantialiter*]. After that, we will debate other parts of your belief, until we have covered all. Explain, then, how these three persons exist, and do this first in a rational fashion.

PETRUS: I want to call the three persons "substance," "wisdom," and "will." Moreover, I name the first person "substance" for this reason: because wisdom and will are in it and come from it and it itself comes from nothing else. Although there are three persons, all are one substance.[1]

1. Alfonsi's Trinitarian speculation here is unusual, to say the least. The Nicene-Constantinopolitan definition emphasizes that the divine substance is shared equally by the three persons that form the Godhead. Although twelfth-century Christian exegetes sometimes identified the three persons as Power, Wisdom, and Goodness, this model of substance, wisdom, and will Gilbert Dahan suggests may be derived from the Kalam, that is, generally speaking, medieval Islamic natural or philosophical theology, which also influenced Jewish and Christian thinkers. See his "L'usage de la *ratio* dans la polémique contre les juifs, XIIᵉ–XIVᵉ siècles," 302.

MOSES: Can these three be discovered by reason?

PETRUS: They can. Since in the first part of my book we treated resolutely and adequately of substance (namely, that it exists), we do not have to look into it further now, but it remains to explain whether wisdom and will are present in substance itself.

MOSES: This is what I am asking.

PETRUS: Since, then, it truly follows that substance is the very creator of all things and the beginning of all things having a beginning and the maker of all things made, it is necessary that it have wisdom and will. This is so that it would know what it wills to make before it makes it, and even so that it will to make it, because before it may produce a work in reality [*in demonstratione*] it is first formed in the mind by imagining it, and this imagination is wisdom. Moreover, when it knows it in this way, either it makes it or it does not make it. It does not make it, however, if it does not will it. Whereas, if it makes it, it also wills it. And this is will. Therefore, it appears from our discussion that the work is preceded by both wisdom and will. The creator of the world, therefore, is unable to create anything before the knowledge or the will should exist in him.

MOSES: That is true.

PETRUS: Therefore, God is substance, wisdom, and will.

MOSES: That is true. But you still have to prove (as you believe) that both wisdom and will exist eternally in God, and are inseparable from him, and that he does not exist prior to them in time.

PETRUS: I will show that to be true. Certainly, although it follows that God has wisdom and will, we have to know whether this wisdom and will are existent in him and are not separated from him, or whether [they exist] outside him, or whether at some time [they exist] with him and at some time not.

MOSES: It is true that they exist in him and are not separated from him. This is because, were this not the case, then God would be not-wise after he has been wise, or he would be without a will after he has had a will, which cannot happen, since after they are in him they may be separated from him only *per accidens*, and no accident is found in him.

PETRUS: May the Lord bless you, because you have understood the truth well, and you have admitted it, and you have shown that you have good faith. But still you ought to investigate whether this wisdom and will are eternal or whether they have a beginning.

MOSES: Let us suppose that they have a beginning.

PETRUS: Then your words contradict themselves. For you said that God cannot be not-wise after being wise, nor can he exist without will after he has had a will. Finally, because you have proposed that they had a beginning, then at some time they were in him and at some time they were not.

MOSES: This is not in any way contrary to my assertion. For I said above that God is not able to exist without wisdom and will once he has had them. When I posited that these have a beginning, I never contradicted myself by saying that he can have what he has not had.

PETRUS: Clearly, if they had a beginning, either God created them or they created themselves.

MOSES: Without any doubt God created them, because nothing creates itself.

PETRUS: Therefore, since they have a beginning, if God created them, then the creator himself would require another wisdom and will with which to create them, and (as has been said) it is necessary for the creator [operator] to have wisdom and will before something may be created [operetur], and so on to infinity. Therefore, it is necessary for wisdom and will to be in God eternally, and to be inseparable from him; neither may he exist prior to them in time, and this is what we want to explain.

MOSES: That is true. It is correct and useful for us to assent to the truth. But it remains to be said which of these—that is, wisdom or will—is called the Son and which the Holy Spirit.

PETRUS: Wisdom is the Son, and will is the Holy Spirit.

MOSES: Therefore, since neither of these will exist prior to the other in time, nor will substance exist prior to them, can one of these three be prior to another in the order of speech?

PETRUS: Indeed it can, and this is so in the order of the nouns, not in nature. To be sure, wisdom and will are in substance, and for that reason substance is first. Whereas wisdom is prior to will for this reason: that before the creator could will anything, it was necessary for him to know what he would will. Therefore, for this reason, according to the order of the nouns, substance is prior to wisdom and will, and wisdom is prior to will. In the same way [this order exists] among these nouns: namely, Father, Son, and Holy Spirit. We have deliberated with you over a matter of such weight so that in this way you, who do not perceive the more subtle things, may at least be able to perceive something. If we were to speak about this with any Christian, we would be able to discuss it with him with much more subtlety.

MOSES: Since, then, you have shown by reason that God has wisdom and will, can it be found in the context[2] of any authentic book [of the Bible] that, for the creation of the world, the creator had used wisdom and will?

PETRUS: Indeed, yes. For in Proverbs Solomon said of wisdom, "The Lord by wisdom has founded the earth, [and] has established the heavens by prudence."[3] To be sure, in a psalm David [said] about will: "Whatsoever the Lord willed, he has done."[4]

MOSES: And how is it that you call the second person of your trinity by this name, that is, by wisdom, when by others it is called the Word?

PETRUS: Clearly, there is no contradiction in this. For the Word of God is his perfected wisdom, which the psalmist shows as well when he says: "By the Word of the Lord the heavens were established."[5] Therefore, it is clear that the wisdom of God and his Word are one and the same thing.

MOSES: Up until now you have handled the explanation of the trinity well enough in a philosophical manner, but I would like to have it demonstrated that there are several persons in God with at least one authority from the Scriptures.

PETRUS: I will prove it not with one but with several, and not with obscure ones but with clear and intelligible ones.

MOSES: Show me then.

PETRUS: What topic is clearer and more subject to proof than an explanation of the names of God like "Elohim" [אֱלֹהִים]

2. Reading *series* with Migne (col. 608B) for the ungrammatical *seriae* (A).
3. Prv 3.19.   4. Ps 134.6.
5. Ps 32.6.

and "Adonai" [אֲדֹנָי]? Now, "Elohim" indicates a plural, whose singular is "Eloa" [אֱלוֹהַּ]. Moreover, when I say "Elohai" [אֱלֹהַי] it is just as if I were to say "my gods," indicating a plurality of gods but that the one speaking is only one person, whereas when I say "Elohenu" [אֱלֹהֵינוּ] it is as if I were to say "our gods," indicating a plurality of both, both of gods and of those speaking. But if "Eloy" [אֱלֹהִי] is said, it is just as if one were to say "my God." But it is not found in any Hebrew Scripture that any man ever called God "Elohy," although [this] can be said according to the rules of the Hebrew language itself.

MOSES: But in your Gospel one finds already that Christ called out from the Cross, "Eloy."[6]

PETRUS: I have learned that this does not contradict me in any way. For Christ invoked God the Father; that is, only one of the three persons, one only, [invoked] another. It is the same for that noun "adon" [אָדוֹן], that is, "Lord." When we say "adon," it indicates a singular form, and when we say "adonay" [אֲדֹנָי], it is as if I say "my lords," signifying a plurality of lords and the oneness of the one speaking. When, however, I say "adonenu" [אֲדֹנֵינוּ], it is as if I should say "our lords," signifying both many lords and many speakers. Whereas when I say "adony," it is as if I am saying "my lord" [אֲדֹנִי], indicating both that there is one lord and that there is one speaker. Although a man is found to be called this name only by [another] man, God is never found to be called thus. Therefore, when in the sacred Scriptures God is found to be called "heloha" [אֱלוֹהַּ] and "adon" [אָדוֹן], "God" or "lord" is understood in a singular sense, and therefore is one. And again when he is found to be called in other instances "heloym" [אֱלֹהִים] and "adonay" [אֲדֹנָי], this signifies a plurality, and several gods or lords are indicated. Which seems to be a contradiction. For either there will be one God, or many. This contradiction, however, is not found in God. For when he called himself by a singular name, he actually referred to the one substance, whereas when he called himself by a plural, he referred to the several persons. For God is one, in several persons.

MOSES: That these names of God—namely, "elohim" and "adonay"—signify a plural follows from the rules of the art of

6. Cf. Mt 27.46.

grammar.[7] Whereas when God has named himself in this manner, he is constrained by no rules, but has acted just according to his pleasure,[8] and his pleasure ought to be subject to no rules.

PETRUS: It is indeed true that these names ought not to be subjected to any rules, but this is so if these are proper nouns, not appellative. These, however, are appellative, and therefore they ought to be subjected to rules, just as we explained above.[9] Therefore, when they are expressed in a singular manner, they signify singularity, and when they are expressed in a plural manner, they signify plurality, just as in Genesis we find that Lot called the angels "Adonay" [אֲדֹנָי], that is, "my lords,"[10] because there were actually two angels. And in other places in the same book, Laban, speaking harshly against Jacob, said: "Why have you stolen away 'eloay' [אֱלֹהָי]," that is, "my gods"?[11] And one finds written in the Psalms: "I said 'elohim atem' [אֱלֹהִים אַתֶּם]," that is, "you are gods."[12] And when the Lord was speaking to the Israelite people through Moses, he said, "You shall not have 'heloym herim' [אֱלֹהִים אֲחֵרִים]," that is, "strange gods."[13] The books of the prophets abound with similar testimonies.[14]

7. "Art of grammar": *artis litteratoriae*, lit., the art of writing.

8. "According to his pleasure": *iuxta placitum suum*. Also possible is "according to his convention."

9. The issue here is whether Hebrew nouns like "Elohim" are proper nouns or appellatives. Typically, a noun that has a plural is an appellative noun, whereas proper nouns have no plural but refer to a single individual. But proper nouns, or names, then, are not subject to the same grammatical rules as appellatives, because they are not declined throughout all the cases. For a grammarian's discussion, see Cassiodorus (?), *De oratione et de octo partibus orationis* 1, PL 70: 1220. Isidore of Seville identifies some names of the trinitarian Godhead as proper names (e.g., *Deus, Dominus*, etc.), and some as appellative nouns (e.g., *Pater* and *Filius*). See his *Etymologiarum sive originum libri xx*, 7.4.5–6, ed. W. M. Lyndsay (Oxford: Clarendon Press, 1911; repr. 1985). For the application of this principle to a discussion of God's Hebrew name, "Elohim," see St. Bonaventure, *Commentaria in quatuor libros Sententiarum: In primum librum Sententiarum*, I, dist. 4, q. 3, contra, in *Opera omnia*, vol. 1 (Quaracchi: Collegii St. Bonaventurae, 1882), 101. Cf. Alan of Lille, *Theologicae regulae* 28, PL 210: 635A–B.

10. Gn 19.2.   11. Gn 31.30.

12. Ps 81.6.   13. Ex 20.3.

14. Alfonsi's willingness to lead the debate onto the field of grammar seems to contradict the image that Gregory Stone presents. For Stone grammar (which Alfonsi dropped from the seven arts) represents talmudic casuistry and symbolizes Jewish error (see "Ramon Llull vs. Petrus Alfonsi: Postmodern Liberalism and the Six Liberal Arts," esp. 75–76). But here it is Alfonsi who introduces a very traditional argument rooted in grammar, and not the Jewish disputant.

MOSES: Although it is clear that "elohim" and "adonay" signify a plurality, nevertheless, when they are said of God, they signify a singular, and this is known through the action to which they
are joined, since it is expressed by a singular verb.[15] For one says
of God that "he made," "he said," or some other thing like this,
and one does not say that "they made" or "they said."

PETRUS: This is my [scriptural] authority that God's name is
said in the plural and the action in the singular, and it is clear
from this that God is one in several persons. Nevertheless, in
order to cut short all your objections, I can even demonstrate
that both the name of God and the action itself are expressed
in the plural. Although this is the case, we cannot refer that to
many gods, since it was already shown above with many arguments that there is only one God. Therefore, it is necessary to
make reference to one God and several persons.

MOSES: If indeed you will show this, what you have proposed
will now be proved very satisfactorily.

PETRUS: If I show this to you, with God's assistance, will you
believe that there is one God and several persons?

MOSES: I shall make absolutely no agreement with you concerning this matter, but nevertheless I would like to hear it from
you.

PETRUS: Of course I knew the hardness of your heart, but nevertheless I shall show this to you now, for perhaps through this
you will be mindful of some good. It is also written in the book
of Samuel that when the Philistines saw that the ark of the Lord
was coming against them, they said: "Ele hem elohim"[הָאֱלֹהִים
אֵלֶּה הֵם], that is, "these are the gods that struck Egypt with all
the plagues in the desert."[16] Now, here both the name of God
and the action are expressed in the plural.

MOSES: I do not concede that you have clearly demonstrated
with this what you had proposed. For, believing that there are
many gods, this people did not speak of one God, and it considered that there were many gods of Israel, just as theirs were
many.

PETRUS: Seeing that you do not concede this, now let me

15. "Singular verb": lit., singular voice, *singulari voce.*
16. 1 Sm 4.8.

show you a similar passage in the books of the prophets. For it is
written in the book of Genesis: "The Lord spoke to Jacob: arise
and go up to Bethel and dwell there and make there an altar to
God, who appeared to you when you fled from your brother."[17]
Indeed, here both the name of God and the action are expressed
in the singular. Then in the same book it is written that Jacob fulfilled the command of the Lord. For next there follows: "And he
built an altar there and called the name of the place Bethel, that
is, 'the house of God.' For there God appeared to him when he
fled from his brother."[18] Here, however, "God" and "appeared"
are indicated in the plural in the Hebrew. For indeed "elohym"
[הָאֱלֹהִים] and "niglu" [נִגְלוּ] are present there, which signify "they
appeared" [*apparuerunt*] in the plural. Now, if it had wanted to say
"he appeared" [*apparuit*] in the singular, it would have employed
"nigla" [נִגְלָה]. It is the same in the book of Samuel when, praising
God, David says: "And what nation is there upon the earth like
your people, for whom God went forth so that he would redeem
it as a people for himself?"[19] Here again "God" and "went forth"
are plural in the Hebrew. For here again in the same way it contains "helohim" [אֱלֹהִים] and "halchu" [הָלְכוּ] (which means "they
went forth," whose singular is "halach" [הָלַךְ]), whereas "he would
redeem" and "for himself" are likewise singular. Once more one
reads in Jeremiah: "The Lord, however, is the true God, the living God, and the everlasting king."[20] Here again both "God" and
"living" are said in the plural in the Hebrew. Therefore, since in
the Scriptures the name of God and [his] action are sometimes
expressed in the singular, and sometimes in the plural, the two
reveal both that God is one, and that he is several persons.

MOSES: Since, based on the names of God, it is clear that
God is one in several persons, it remains to investigate why there
should be only three persons, as you believe, and not two, or
four, or many more.

PETRUS: We already showed that clearly above—namely, that
there are three persons—when we treated this according to reason. But if you disagree, since now you accept that, based on
the names of God, there are several persons, tell me then how

many persons you wish to believe there are in number, and I will weaken your arguments, if I can.

MOSES: I certainly do not believe that there are two or three or any other number of persons; to be sure, I asked this in order to contradict your arguments.

PETRUS: How subtle and ineffable is the Trinity, and how difficult to explain; the prophets only spoke of it secretly and under a veil, until Christ came as one of the three persons and revealed it to the minds of the faithful according to their capacity. Nevertheless, if you pay attention and you examine that very subtle name of God, which is found explained in the *Secrets of Secrets* [*Secretis secretorum*],[21] a name, I say, of three letters (although it is written with four characters [*figurae*], for one of them is written twice, doubled); if, I say, you examine it, you will see that this same name is both one and three. But that one refers to the unity of the substance, whereas the three refer to the trinity of persons. Moreover, it follows that for the name with four characters—"i" [י] and "e" [ה] and "v" [ו] and "e" [ה][22]—if you join together only the first and second of these (namely, "i" [י] and "e" [ה]), it will clearly be one name. Likewise, if [you join together] the second and the third (namely, "e" [ה] and "v" [ו]), you will now have a different one.[23] Similarly if you connect only the third and the fourth (namely, "v" [ו] and "e" [ה]), you will discover even a third. Again, if you connect all at once in order, there will only be one name, as is apparent in this geometric illustration [*figura*].[24]

Consider then, O Moses, how hidden and subtle and ineffable that name is, and that it can only be known by the insight of a perspicacious mind and by a profound investigation. This is just as Moses attests, who said in Deuteronomy: "Know there-

21. Alfred Büchler suggests that this *Secretis secretorum* refers to a compilation from three sources: the *Sefer ha-Razim, Sefer Yesira,* and an unknown alchemical text. See his "A Twelfth-Century Physician's Desk Book: The *Secreta secretorum* of Petrus Alphonsi quondam Moses Sephardi," *Journal of Jewish Studies* 37/2 (1986): 206–12.

22. That is, *yod, he, vav, he*: the Tetragrammaton.

23. For these two letters as an abbreviation for the divine name, see B.T. *Shabbat* 104a. But, as Klaus Peter-Mieth notes (169, n.), in Jewish tradition one does not find all of the combinations that Alfonsi produces together.

24. This illustration of the Tetragrammaton is reproduced from a twelfth-

century manuscript, Cambridge, St. John's College E.4 (James 107), fol. 153b. It is quite different from the diagram—very much like a Venn diagram—found in the *Patrologia Latina* (PL 157, col. 611C), which displays three interlocking circles inside a fourth circle. There the letters ה and ו are displayed in two areas where the three interlocking circles overlap, whereas the letters י and ה are displayed independently at the two extremes. Klaus-Peter Mieth discusses this diagram in the introduction to his 1982 edition, *Der Dialog des Petrus Alfonsi*, on pp. xlviii–l. There he refers to the earlier work of Beatrice Hirsch-Reich (see "Joachim von Fiore und das Judentum," in *Judentum im Mittelalter, Beiträge zum christlich-jüdischen Gespräch*, ed. Paul Wilpert [Berlin: Walter de Gruyter, 1966], 230–32), who had argued that the diagram in the *Patrologia Latina* reflects the later influence of Joachim of Fiore (d. 1202), who appropriated Alfonsi's discussion of the trinitarian symbolism of the Tetragrammaton and related it to his own trinitarian conception of historical epochs. Alfonsi's own depiction of the Tetragrammaton, it seems, employed a triangular form like the one displayed in St. John's College E.4. John Tolan remarked that he found no manuscript of Alfonsi's *Dialogi* that employed the interlocking circles used in the *Patrologia Latina*, which suggests that the diagram in the *Patrologia Latina* derives from a manuscript of Alfonsi's *Dialogi* that had interpolated Joachim's "Alpha-Psaltery" figure. For the "Alpha-Psaltery" figure, see Bernard McGinn, *The Calabrian Abbot: Joachim of Fiore in the History of Western Thought* (New York: MacMillan, 1985), 163. For Tolan's remarks, see his *Petrus Alfonsi and His Medieval Readers*, 240. My own examination of manuscripts at Cambridge and Oxford universities, and in the British Library, confirm Tolan's result. I am unable to explain, however, the apparently leonine figure within the triangle in St. John's College E.4. Perhaps the lion of Judah (cf. Gn 49.9)?

fore this day and consider in your heart that the Lord [*dominus*], he is God [*deus*], in heaven above and in the earth beneath, and there is no other."[25] Now, where in the Latin "Lord" is written, in the Hebrew you will find the aforementioned name.[26] Yet where it is "God" in the Latin, in the Hebrew it is written "Heloym" [הָאֱלֹהִים], which signifies a plural, and in this way he reveals that he is the same God who is named by both his own proper name in the singular and an appellative noun in the plural. But lest perhaps they think that there are many gods, he added, "and there is no other." Whereas when Moses said: "Know and consider in your heart," truly he implied that the arcane subtlety of this name cannot be apprehended by sight or hearing or the bodily senses, but only by the perspicacious understanding of the mind and by an amazing native genius. Moreover, the Trinity can be denoted in many other instances as, for example, in the fringes which the Lord commanded the children of Israel through Moses to have on their garments, saying: "Speak to the children of Israel and tell them to make for themselves fringes on the corners of their garments, placing among them blue threads that, when they see them, will remind them of all the commandments of the Lord."[27] In fact, these fringes were of four threads, but doubled, having indeed on their upper portion three knots, but two on the lower portion. But the four threads designate the four seasons of the year, whereas the doubling of the threads designates day and night, namely, so that they would be mindful of the commandments of God for the four seasons of the year (that is, for the entire year), and night and day. Now, the Trinity of persons is implied by the three upper knots, whereas the two testaments are implied by the two lower ones, namely, the Law of Moses and the Gospel. The Trinity is also made known by the three benedictions with which Aaron and his sons blessed the children of Israel, according to the commandment of the Lord when speaking to Moses: "Say to Aaron and his sons: thus shall you bless the children of Israel and say to them: The Lord bless you and guard you. May the Lord show his face to you and have mercy upon you. May the Lord turn his countenance to

25. Dt 4.39.
27. Nm 15.38.

26. I.e., the Tetragrammaton.

you and grant you peace."[28] Indeed, during these blessings, the priest who was blessing anyone held both his palms extended before his face. And when he said "Lord," [a word] which we said above, he expressed in Hebrew by that name as threefold and one, he raised up the three primary fingers, namely, the thumb, the index finger, and the middle finger of his two hands, and when he said the word "Lord" he raised the right-hand fingers higher than before.[29] But tell me, O Moses, how can the excellence of the Trinity be expressed allegorically better than by the elevation of three fingers? If you know and are able to indicate something else for them, I wish you would explain it to me.

MOSES: Certainly we have never indicated what you said, nor have we ever indicated anything else about them; but neither have our sages said anything that ought to be noted.

PETRUS: What else except the Trinity of persons can be indicated by what the prophet Isaiah said, namely, by the threefold profession of the angels praising God and saying: "Holy, Holy, Holy, the Lord God Sabaoth"?[30] For why did they say "holy" three times, and not just once, or twice, or ten times, or one hundred times, or some other number? Why, if they wished to praise him briefly, did they not say "holy" just once? Whereas if [they wished to praise him] a great deal, why did they not express praise one hundred, or one thousand, or innumerable times?

MOSES: We know no reason for the threefold profession in the angels' praise except that it was their pleasure.

28. Nm 6.23–27.

29. For this hand gesture accompanying the priestly benediction, still preserved in synagogue culture, see Zvi Ron, "The Priestly Blessing; Hands of the *Kohen*," *Journal of Jewish Music and Liturgy* 21 (1998–1999): 1–5; and "Priestly Blessing," in *Encyclopedia Judaica* 13: 1060–63. One can also find an illustration of the hands raised in priestly blessing from the mystical *Shefa tal* by Shabbatai Sheftal ben Akiva Horowitz (ca. 1561–1619) in *Encyclopedia Judaica* 10: 514. The illustration treats the raised hands as a cosmic symbol. At the base of the hands above the wrist are the letters of the Tetragrammaton. The illustration shows all five fingers of the hands extended, although in two groups. One group consists of the thumb, forefinger, and middle finger; the other, of the last two fingers of the hand. These groupings are separated by a gap in the form of a "V." Alfonsi's attempt, then, to identify the hand gesture as a trinitarian symbol either ignores, perhaps intentionally, that all five fingers of each hand are used in the ritual, or reflects a different practice in his Andalusian community.

30. Is 6.3.

PETRUS: If to the individual cases I have introduced you will answer [only], "we do not know," what else are you saying but that you have been overcome and do not know how to contradict me? Clearly even David attested to the Trinity of persons when he said: "Seek the Lord and his strength; always seek his face."[31] What is the meaning of what he says, "Seek the Lord and his strength and always seek his face" if not to seek the Father and Son and Holy Spirit? For what is meant by the Lord's "strength" if not his Son, or what is meant by "face" if not the Holy Spirit?[32] Explain what you understand, if you understand it differently. Certainly these testimonies of the holy Scriptures concerning the Trinity of persons have been able to suffice for those with an adequate understanding. Now, if I should introduce all the testimonies I am able to besides these, a huge book would not contain them. Therefore, [I have introduced] only so much as this concerning these matters. If, however, you have something else to ask, you should not delay.

31. Ps 104.4.

32. Again, Alfonsi avoids an anthropomorphic interpretation of this verse, and insists that it can only be understood allegorically as a reference to the persons of the Trinity.

SEVENTH *TITULUS*

OSES: NOW I WANT you to explain about Mary: how you believe that she gave birth without a union with a man, and I will oppose you, if I am able.

PETRUS: Clearly we believe that with the Holy Spirit coming upon her and with the power of the Most High overshadowing her,[1] the powers from its members[2] combined in one, as was pleasing to God, so that she conceived without a union with a man.

MOSES: It is an amazing and difficult thing to understand that in some way a son could be engendered from a mother without a carnal father. For we see in the customary manner of generation of human beings that unless two natures come together, namely, a male and a female, a human being cannot be generated.

PETRUS: Why does this generation seem to you to be amazing and indescribable when you have already heard something like it, which both we and you believe, namely, that Eve was generated without a mother from a father, that is, from the flesh of Adam?[3]

MOSES: Certainly that generation could occur miraculously, just like this one, but for that one that has occurred we have an authority, namely, the authority of Moses, whom no legitimate authority contradicts, whereas concerning that other one, I think you will find no authority. Nevertheless, if you learn something else in the books of the prophets, bring it forward.

PETRUS: I will mention not just one authority concerning a matter of this sort, but many, since the prophets foretold Christ's future birth in many places.

---

1. Cf. Lk 1.35.
2. "From its members": *de ipsius membris*, seems able only to refer to the members of the Trinity.
3. Cf. Gn 2.22.

MOSES: If you accomplish what you say, you will undoubtedly defend your faith.

PETRUS: At the outset, recall what is said through Isaiah to Ahaz, King of Judah. For Isaiah spoke to him in this way concerning his enemies, namely, the king of Armenia and the king of Israel, who were descending upon him: "'Do not be afraid, O Ahaz,' he said, 'because Jerusalem will not be destroyed and you should not doubt that. Seek then a sign from the Lord your God, whether from the depth of hell or in the height above.' And Ahaz said: 'I will not seek, and I will not tempt the Lord.'"[4] Since, however, Isaiah knew that Ahaz did not speak in good faith—rather, that he neither feared nor loved God—he responded: "Hear then," he said, "O house of David. Is it a small thing for you to be irksome to men, that you are irksome to my God as well? For this reason the Lord himself will give to you a sign: Behold, a virgin shall conceive and bear a son, and shall call his name Emmanuel."[5] And indeed this prophecy was pronounced in regard to Christ and was repeated to the blessed Mary by an angel.

MOSES: And how will this be able to stand, that these things which Isaiah announced to Ahaz were said in regard to Christ and Mary, as you assert, when, as you yourself know, many centuries would pass between Ahaz and Mary?

PETRUS: If you do not believe that they were spoken in regard to Christ and Mary, concerning whom, then, do you think they were proclaimed?

MOSES: Actually, concerning the wife of Ahaz and his son Hezekiah, who was born from her.[6]

---

4. Is 7.11–12. It was the king of Syria, not the king of Armenia, who had joined forces with the king of Israel. Note that the first part of this passage—"Do not be afraid, O Ahaz, because Jerusalem will not be destroyed and you should not doubt that"—does not appear in the Vulg. For a discussion of Petrus Alfonsi's arguments here and his exegesis of Is 7.10–14, see C. Jódar-Estrella, "La interpretación de Is. 7, 14 en el *Diálogo* de Pedro Alfonso y su fundamentación hermenéutica," *Cristianesimo nella storia: richerche storiche esegetiche teologiche* 22/2 (1999): 275–98, and especially pp. 286–95.

5. Is 7.13–14.

6. Joseph Kimhi provides the same explanation in his *Book of the Covenant*, pp. 56–57. For the identification of Hezekiah with Emmanuel, see *Midrash Rabbah*, Exodus 18.5, trans. S. M. Lehrman (London, 1939).

PETRUS: What you say is false, and you affirm this either through ignorance [*imperitia*] or because you hold neither reverence nor honor for God; rather, you presume to judge wrongly or to lie about him. For at the time when these things were said to Ahaz, he was already king, but his son Hezekiah had already passed nine years of age. Moreover, on the first day of his reign, Ahaz was himself twenty years old, and he reigned sixteen years.[7] His son Hezekiah, however, who succeeded to the kingdom next after him, was twenty-five years old when he began to reign.[8] Accordingly, Hezekiah was nine years old when his father was made king. Therefore, this prophecy which concerns us was pronounced neither in regard to Ahaz's wife nor in regard to his son Hezekiah.

MOSES: I want you, then, to show me and to explain to me how this prophecy was pronounced in regard to Mary and her son.

PETRUS: I will undoubtedly find many things in the words of the prophecy with which I may easily convince you that it was produced not in regard to Ahaz or his son, but rather in regard to Mary and her son, Christ. To be sure, although the prophet was speaking to Ahaz, the prophecy was not pronounced only for him or only for his age. For this reason it was said, "Hear, O house of David," and not, "Hear, Ahaz." In the same way, when the prophet said, "the Lord himself [*ipse*] will give to you a sign," because he added "himself" as if to say "no other," one can understand from this that the Lord is himself the sign to come in the future.[9] Moreover, when he said, in the plural, "to you [*vobis*]," and not "to you [*tibi*],"[10] he hinted that this was not said in regard to Ahaz or to him alone. But also what follows—"Behold, a virgin shall conceive and bear a son, and shall call his name Emmanuel"—clearly indicates that the prophet was speaking not about Ahaz's wife or about his son. For he would not have

7. Cf. 2 Kgs 16.2.
8. Cf. 2 Kgs 18.2.
9. Grammatically, Alfonsi's argument would be more persuasive had Isaiah said, "Dabit Dominus [*se*]*ipsum* vobis signum" (my italics), that is, "The Lord will give himself as a sign to you."
10. That is, he used the plural form of the personal pronoun and not the singular.

called a married woman a virgin, nor would it be any kind of miracle or sign that a woman who had a husband should conceive or should bear a son. In addition, when one reads there, "she will call," two things must be noted: namely, that God wanted the son to be called in this way, and that a virgin would produce a child [*puer*] without a carnal father. For he said, "she will call," as if to say that she alone will call, and not the father. Moreover, we know that no son of Ahaz, nor any other man of that time, was called by this name, that is, Emmanuel.

MOSES: I am certainly amazed that you, a man so skilled in our language, would so confuse the words and pervert the Scriptures. For as you know yourself, the prophet did not use the word in Hebrew that in Latin would be translated as "virgin." If he had wished to do so, he would certainly have used "bethula" [בְּתוּלָה]. Rather, he used "halma" [עַלְמָה], which only indicates an unmarried girl [*puella*].

PETRUS: In fact, Moses, you contradict me unjustly, and you seem to be unaware either of the use or nature of the Hebrew language. For a woman can be called "bethula" [בְּתוּלָה] so long as she is a virgin, whether she is young or old. She can, however, be called "nahra" [נַעֲרָה] so long as she is young, whether she is a virgin or whether she has been corrupted. Whereas she is not called "halma" [עַלְמָה] unless she is both young and intact. Moreover, what the prophet added about the child, saying: "He shall eat butter and honey, that he may know to reprove evil and choose the good,"[11]—tell me, I beg you, O Moses, what did he want to be understood by honey and butter? Did he want to hint at some allegory there, or did he present honey and butter in a simple sense [*simpliciter*]?

MOSES: Indeed, we have never understood that other than in a simple sense, namely, that he will be wise and will have the ability to distinguish both good and evil; for that reason he said he will eat honey and butter, which is sweet and good.[12]

PETRUS: Certainly one cannot be considered wise just because he eats honey and butter. For although these are sweet,

11. Is 7.15.
12. For the claim that he will eat honey and butter, see *Midrash Rabbah*, Numbers 14.2, trans. J. Slotki (London, 1939).

they are not goods, since they are not healthful.[13] And how will a person be wise who eats what is neither good nor healthful? But if you understand this passage in another way (as it is possible to do), namely, that he eats honey and butter for this reason, to know how to reprove evil and to choose the good, that is, so that by eating honey and butter he would have a knowledge of good and evil (that is, he would be wise); if this is how you understand it, I say that you do not seem to me to be wise. For where does one find in the natures of things that the consumption of honey or butter confers wisdom?

MOSES: Clearly, nowhere.

PETRUS: It remains, therefore, that we should understand this allegorically.

MOSES: And how can you understand an allegory there?

PETRUS: Indeed, through these two words both laws can be understood, both the law of Moses and the Gospel. For clearly in many places in the prophets we find that the words of the Lord are compared to honey and milk.

MOSES: Then how is what follows [understood]: "Before the child will know to refuse the evil and to choose the good, the land which you despise shall be forsaken of the face of her two kings"?[14] What, I ask you, did the prophet want to be understood through words of this sort? For these words imply that the child whom the prophecy concerns had been born at that time.

PETRUS: I ask you, O Moses, do you want to understand the prophets' words according to the customary order of human speech? This can never be. For they are like the words of their dreams, and just as the words of people suffering from a severe fever or raving on account of some other illness are not con-

13. Reuter links this remark (*Petrus Alfonsi*, 126, n. 2) to the *Liber dietarum particularum* of Isaac Judaei, who notes that although a mixture of butter or curd and honey may prove useful as an antidote for poison, nevertheless the mixture damages the stomach.

14. Is 7.16. Moses' reading of this passage, following the Vulgate, differs from the Hebrew, for which the NRSV offers the more accurate translation: "For before the child knows to refuse the evil and choose the good, the land before whose two kings you are in dread will be deserted." Moses' reading is all the more peculiar since, at the beginning of the *Dialogue*, he had insisted that Alfonsi acknowledge and employ the Hebrew version, or *Hebraica veritas*. Alfonsi calls his attention again to the *Hebraica veritas* in the next paragraph.

nected in an ordered way, so, too, the words of the prophets were not produced in a coherent sequence, and only later, as the Holy Spirit reveals it to them, do they consider what they might have said earlier. So, why then are these words connected in this way: "He shall eat butter and honey, that he may know to reprove evil and choose the good," seeing that he will know to reprove evil and choose the good before one hears how he eats? Indeed, this is the Hebrew truth [*Hebraica veritas*], and so finally that prophecy that was said to the house of David because of Ahaz's unbelief is concluded. For what follows immediately after, "the land shall be forsaken," etc.,[15] is said for another reason, just as we find in another place. For one reads in Exodus: "And Moses said to the Lord: Who am I that I should go to Pharaoh and bring forth the children of Israel out of Egypt? He said to him: I will be with you, and you will have this sign that I have sent you. When you bring forth my people out of Egypt, you will offer sacrifice to God on this mountain."[16] "When you bring forth my people," etc., seems to be a sign for this, when he says "that I have sent you," but it is not. For once the people had been brought forth from Egypt, and Moses had made sacrifice on that mountain, they all knew already that Moses was a prophet and had been sent by God. Therefore, Moses began to say something different there from what he had said before, in the manner of a prophet. But if you contradict this and ask what that sign was, you should know that the sign was when he said, "I will be with you."[17]

MOSES: If that is the case, then how [do you explain] what one reads in the following [passage]: "For before the child knows to call his father and his mother, the strength of Damascus and the spoils of Samaria shall be taken away before the king of Assyria"?[18] For were not all these things said about the same child, namely, one who was born before the destruction?

PETRUS: Clearly we do not understand that they all were said about Christ. Certainly these could not have been said about him, but about that child or about some other child who was born at that time, of whom the Lord said to the prophet: "Call

15. Is 7.16.   16. Ex 3.11–12.
17. Ex 3.12.   18. Is 8.4.

his name, hasten to take away the spoils, make haste to take away the prey."[19]

MOSES: I will certainly show you that boy who was called Emmanuel, because he was born at that time. For when the prophet spoke about the appearance of King Assur in the land of Judah, he said of him: "And the stretching out of his wings shall fill the breadth of your land, O Emmanuel."[20] Now this shows that at the time of his appearance, Emmanuel already existed.

PETRUS: You do not really convince [me] with this that Emmanuel was already born at that time. For this was not his name, with respect to the body, but with respect to divinity, according to which it follows that Emmanuel existed at that time, and both before and after.

MOSES: Now from your words I understand what you did not say earlier concerning these matters. For you seem to imply that the child of whom you speak will be both God and man.

PETRUS: Certainly I believe, without doubt, that which I have made known in the explanation of my faith, and I will explain it to you anytime you ask.

MOSES: I do not inquire about this at present. Instead, first I want you to answer whether you still have some authority from a prophet that that boy, the son of Mary, was born from a mother without a carnal father.

PETRUS: Certainly I do. For he said: "Drop down dew, you heavens, from above, and let the clouds rain the just; let the earth be opened and bud forth a savior, and let justice spring up together: I the Lord have created him."[21] He said, "Drop down dew, you heavens, from above, and let the clouds rain the just," because he knew that the Holy Spirit would descend from heaven. Moreover, what follows—"let the earth be opened and bud forth a savior"—we understand to have been said with respect to the body of the virgin, who, once the Holy Spirit had come down upon her, was about to conceive and to give birth to the savior. But he also indicates with this—"I the Lord have created him"—that the Lord begot him without the assistance of a carnal father.[22] Wherefore he concluded in the following passage,

19. Is 8.3.
20. Is 8.8.
21. Is 45.8.
22. Cf. Ps 109.3.

against those who do not believe him, "Woe to him who contradicts his maker, a sherd of the earthen pots."[23] And, "Shall the clay say to its potter: What are you making, and is your work without hands?"[24] And, "Woe to him that says to the father: Why do you beget? And to the woman, Why do you give birth?"[25] For in this way he inveighs against those who doubt this and who ask how God shall have produced him, and they give as a reason that the blessed Mary gave birth without a union with a man. Again, speaking against the unbelievers, the prophet said: "Shall not I that make others to bring forth children, myself bring forth? says the Lord. Shall I, that give generation to the others, be barren? says the Lord, your God."[26] Thus is it shown that God begot him without a carnal father. I believe that these things really are sufficient for those with intelligence, [to show] that that child was born from a mother without a carnal father.

23. Is 45.9.   24. Ibid.
25. Is 45.10.   26. Is 66.9.

EIGHTH *TITULUS*

OSES: UP TO THIS point, you have treated the generation of the child from authority, and the explanation [*ratio*] allows well enough that it could have happened in this way. But more amazing than all of these things is how the deity, which is simple, could have been joined and united to a human body, which is composite. Therefore, I beg you to explain fully by reason, as you promised, how that could be done.

PETRUS: Certainly, what was accomplished by the goodness and solely by the will of God did not have to occur for any necessary reason. For had he not himself willed it, he would not have united himself to a human nature. Nevertheless, no reason prevents it from having had to occur. For just as the soul, which is simple, is joined to a composite body, and these two become one human being (and this without any contradiction of reason), so, too, God could unite himself to the human, reason notwithstanding.

MOSES: If it please you, I also want to hear something else from you. For although you say and believe that the Father and Son and Holy Spirit are one, I would like you to explain why you believe that the Son alone is incarnate, and not the Father or Holy Spirit.

PETRUS: I think that what we do not believe to be astonishing, certainly is astonishing and is impossible to you. For although this cannot be shown in the deity because it is something subtle and spiritual, nevertheless we can find an analogy in corporeal things by which you can know this, just as in fire (which is a substance) brightness is always present with heat. Indeed, you will not find the substance of fire without brightness and heat, nor will you find brightness and heat together without the substance of fire. Sometimes, however, heat comes to us without brightness, and sometimes even brightness without heat.

MOSES: Certainly it is true that sometimes brightness comes to us without heat. We can perceive this from a candle, whose brightness we see even when we do not sense the heat. But I do not see how heat may come to us without brightness.

PETRUS: I can show this very easily. Certainly, if you take something metal and heat it in such a way that you could heat another body from it, then if you touch it, surely you will sense the heat, but you will not see the brightness.

MOSES: On the basis of your words, you seem to believe, then, that just as sometimes brightness occurs without heat, and heat without brightness, although nevertheless they are not separated from fire, so in this way the Son received flesh without the Father and the Holy Spirit, yet did not separate from them on account of this.

PETRUS: Certainly I believe it in this way, and if you would believe this, then you have understood well.[1] For Truth itself said: "I am in the Father, and the Father is in me."[2] And again, "I and the Father are one."[3]

MOSES: I fully concede that the deity could unite itself to a man; nevertheless, since it was not necessary for this to happen, why should we believe that it has happened?

PETRUS: Clearly we, who do not believe that the prophets were deceived, should believe that they spoke truthfully when they foretold that in the future Christ would be God and man.

MOSES: I would like you to show to me where the prophets proclaim this about him. For I certainly desire to hear that from you beyond anything else.

PETRUS: We read correctly in Genesis that the Lord said: "Let us create man to our image and likeness."[4] And elsewhere: "God created man to his image and likeness."[5] Tell me now, I beg you, what is this image or likeness of God? In what respect are the image of God and the image of man alike?

MOSES: Certainly it is good to know the truth, and truthfully I say that they are alike in no respect. For this was even shown above by reason as well as by authority, and we conceded that God bears a likeness to nothing.[6]

---

1. Reading *bene* (A) for *vene* (B). 2. Jn 14.10.
3. Jn 10.30; 17.11. 4. Gn 1.26.
5. Gn 1.27. 6. *Supra*, p. 73.

PETRUS: Then Scripture lies when it says that God created man to his image and likeness?

MOSES: Never.

PETRUS: Therefore, which of these two prophets should one believe, the one who says that God has a likeness to nothing, or the one who says: "God created man," etc.? Now, have both of them spoken truthfully?[7]

MOSES: Clearly one must say that neither of them has lied.

PETRUS: And how can two contraries exist in the same thing, namely, that God both has and does not have an image?

MOSES: I want you to explain this to me, how you understand it yourself.

PETRUS: Actually this is true, namely, that God, as we proclaimed, bears a likeness to nothing, and we knew that Moses said truthfully that God created man to his image and likeness. For he was himself truthful in all things. But it is necessary for us to understand by that image of God, of which Moses spoke, that image (that is, human form) which the incarnate Son of God assumed.

MOSES: And how will this be able to stand, since at the time when Adam was made he had not yet assumed that image which you believe God assumed?

PETRUS: Even if that image did not yet exist in actuality [*in opere*], nevertheless it already existed in his providence and will. Moreover, since his will does not change, there is no reason not to believe that his image has always existed. Indeed, we find elsewhere in the prophets that they describe something future as if it were past, just as Isaiah says, in the person of the Lord: "The day of vengeance is in my heart, the year of my retribution has come."[8] Actually, the day or the year had not yet come; nevertheless, he said it had already come because it was already in his heart.

MOSES: Do you have yet another authoritative statement from the prophets, by which you can demonstrate more clearly that that child had to be both God and man?

---

7. The two prophets here seem to refer to Moses and Isaiah. See *supra*, p. 74.

8. Is 63.4. The Vulg. reads, "the year of my redemption is come" *(annus redemptionis meae venit).*

PETRUS: Certainly, I have many. For Isaiah said about him: "For a child is born to us, and a son is given to us, and his name shall be called: Wonderful, Counselor, God, Mighty, the Father of the world to come, the Prince of Peace."[9] Now, all these names only befit the deity.

MOSES: You understand Scripture badly. For it should be read not so that the child is said to be Wonderful, or Counselor, etc., but rather, in this way: He who is wonderful, who is counselor, who is God, who is mighty, and who is the father of the world to come, he, I say, will call him the prince of peace.[10] If not, then of whom is it said, "he will call"?

PETRUS: This certainly presents no difficulty for me, because God called himself in this way, and this is clearly permitted in the Hebrew language. This is just as one finds in the book of Numbers: "This is the law of consecration: when the days which he had determined by vow shall be expired, he shall bring him to the door of the tabernacle of the covenant."[11] Now, "he shall bring" and "him" have been said of one and the same one. But the prophet says this as well in the same place [above]: "His empire shall be multiplied and there shall be no end of peace; he shall sit upon the throne of David and upon his kingdom, to establish it and to strengthen it with judgment and with justice, from henceforth and forever."[12] All of this shows, I say, that that child will have to be God and man. For whatever pertains to a human being will have to have an end; however, God and that which pertains to God remains for eternity. Moreover, beyond all of these things, you contradict me unjustly with reference to the names written above. Your sages have said that the messiah [*Christus*] will have seven names, and they have established these very same ones. Moreover, you did not establish an agreement at the beginning of the disputation, just to contradict me unjustly.

MOSES: I remember, and it is true that our sages have said this.

9. Is 9.6.
10. For precisely this argument concerning this passage, see Joseph Kimhi, *Book of the Covenant*, 29–30.
11. Nm 6.13.
12. Is 9.7.

PETRUS: Yet I will provide you with another authority, if you like, that this child will be God and man. For the same prophet said about him: "And there shall come forth a rod out of the root of Jesse, and a flower shall rise up out of his root, and the Spirit of the Lord will rest upon him, the spirit of wisdom and of understanding, the spirit of counsel and of fortitude, the spirit of knowledge and of piety, and he will be filled with the spirit of the fear of the Lord. He will not judge according to the sight of his eyes, nor reprove according to the hearing of the ears, but he shall judge the poor with justice and reprove with equity for the meek of the earth, and he will strike the earth with the rod of his mouth, and with the breath of his lips he will slay the wicked."[13] Now what he says—"he will not judge according to the sight of his eyes"—and the other things which follow, without a doubt are appropriate only for God alone. For a mere man [*homo . . . purus*] will only be able to judge justly what he will hear or see.

MOSES: Clearly part of that authority which you adduced for your aid stands in the way of demonstrating what you strive to prove. For one reads there: "and the spirit of the Lord will rest upon him, the spirit of wisdom and of understanding, the spirit of counsel and of fortitude, the spirit of knowledge and of piety, and he will be filled with the spirit of the fear of the Lord."[14] Now if he were to be God, he would give these, and not receive them.

PETRUS: Your objection is nothing. For I said to you at the beginning of the explanation of my faith that Christ is three substances, namely, a body, a soul, and God.[15] And according to divinity seven of his attributes are named, whereas according to the soul he was able to receive the seven aforementioned gifts. This soul—beyond the fact that it was united to divinity—was also the most worthy of all souls *per se.*

13. Is 11.1–4.
14. Is 11.2–3.
15. Alfonsi's suggestion that there are three substances in Christ is certainly an incautious one. The Chalcedonian definition of the Incarnation would have us understand that there are two substances—humanity and divinity—in the Incarnate Logos. Even though Alfonsi might respond that the substances of body and soul combine to form the single substance of a human nature, his claim could easily be misunderstood.

MOSES: Since, then, he will have received seven names according to divinity and these seven gifts according to the soul, certainly I would like you to show me what you attribute to him according to the body.

PETRUS: Although you mention this facetiously [*ridiculose*], nevertheless, if you like, I will tell you what I attribute to him according to the flesh. Indeed, the same Isaiah says: "I will plant in the wilderness the cedar and the thorn and the myrtle and the olive tree, and I will place in the desert the fir tree, the elm, and the box tree together."[16] Clearly, the body of Christ is indicated by these seven trees. For why would he say this about some desert, when trees of this type always abide together in the desert? Therefore, the world is understood by the desert, because it was a desert and emptied of every good at the time of the coming of Christ.

MOSES: Since he indicated his body by the trees, why, I ask you, did he not establish the most precious and fruitbearing trees for his designation?

PETRUS: He did this clearly with the greatest insight and reason. For just as these trees always flourish and are never deprived of leaves, so, too, the body of Christ is always living and remains always whole and integral. In addition, I have another argument from authority to prove that man and God could be united. For Isaiah also said: "And they shall say in that day, Behold, this is our God. We have waited for him and he will save us."[17] Certainly we do not care to explain this verse in a way differently than your sages explicated it long ago. For through this verse they taught that a time would come when the world would see God and the people would point him out one to another with a finger.[18] This could only occur if someone were both man and God. This, too, which the prophet said: "The voice of your watchmen: They will have lifted up a voice and they will praise together, for they will see eye to eye when the Lord will convert Zion."[19] I say that your sages have explicated this verse in the same way that we have already said, with respect to "they will see eye to eye." But the prophet established another [verse]

16. Is 41.19.
18. Cf. B.T. *Ta'anith* 31a.

17. Is 25.9.
19. Is 52.8.

through which the aforementioned can be proved no less. For he said: "And the glory of the Lord shall be revealed, and all flesh together shall see that the mouth of the Lord has spoken."[20] Indeed, the voice of a spiritual reality [*res*] can be heard, just as the children of Israel heard the voice of the Lord on Mount Sinai, whereas you will not see the one speaking unless he is a fleshly reality [*res carnalis*]. Likewise, there is something else that the prophet Zechariah says: "In that day the Lord will protect the inhabitants of Jerusalem. And he who will have offended will be on that day like David, and the house of David as that of God, and an angel of God in their sight."[21] With what he says—"and the house of David as that of God"—he certainly wanted it to be understood that he who would be accepted as God by all would be born from the house of David. When he said, moreover, "as that of God," and did not propose simply "God," he implied that the one who was to be born from the house of David would, in some respect, be less than God.[22] David attests to this, too, in the psalm when he says: "You have made him a little less than God"[23] Again, Micah said: "And you, Bethlehem Ephrata, are a small one among the thousands of Judah. Out of you shall come forth to me he that is to be the ruler in Israel, and his going forth [is] from the beginning, from the days of eternity."[24] Indeed, this—that is, "Out of you shall come forth to me he that is to be the ruler in Israel"—is said with respect to the body, with respect to which the prince would come in time. That which follows—"and his going forth [is] from the beginning, from the days of eternity"—implies the everlasting nature of divinity. For he attributes to divinity what is not appropriate to a mere man. Likewise, when David says in the psalm: "Your throne, O God, is forever and ever, the scepter of your kingdom is a scepter of uprightness, and you have loved justice and hated iniquity; therefore, God, your God, has anointed you with the oil of gladness above your fellows."[25] When he said this, I say, he

20. Is 40.5.   21. Zec 12.8.
22. Cf. Jn 14.28.
23. Ps 8.6. Vulg. reads, "a little less than the angels."
24. Mi 5.2.
25. Ps 44.7–8.

showed that the one to whom he spoke is both God and man. For when saying, "Your throne, O God, is forever and ever, the scepter of your kingdom is a scepter of uprightness," did he not clearly name him God? Next, when he said, "you have loved justice and hated iniquity; therefore, God, your God, has anointed you with the oil of gladness above your fellows," we perceive that he spoke to him as a man, for God does not have a god or a fellow. Likewise, David said in another place in the psalm: "O God, give to your king judgment and to the king's son your justice,"[26] and whatever other things are in the psalm. Tell me now, who is this son of the king? Solomon or Christ, who was to come from David himself and ought to be called his son?

MOSES: Certainly I do not want to weary you over this, for it is said of the christ,[27] as our sages have taught.[28]

PETRUS: Therefore, since you have agreed that this psalm concerns Christ, let us see whether those things which are read in the same place—"And he will continue with the sun and before the moon, throughout all generations";[29] "Let his name be blessed forevermore, his name continues before the sun";[30] and this, "And all the kings of the earth shall adore him; all the nations shall serve him"[31]—let us see, I say, whether all these things may be said of a mere man.

MOSES: Never. Rather, [they are said] of God.

PETRUS: It follows, then, that Christ is both man and God, as we say. Moreover, it follows that David knew this, with the Holy Spirit revealing it, and he foresaw the miracles that [Christ] would do. This is why he established this sort of a conclusion for the psalm: "Blessed be the Lord, the God of Israel, who alone does wondrous things, and blessed be the name of his majesty forever, and the whole earth shall be filled with his majesty."[32]

26. Ps 71.1.

27. I have left the term christ [*christus*] in lower case here where Moses is speaking, to name the messiah in a general rather than a specific sense.

28. See J. H. L. Reuter, *Petrus Alfonsi*, 51. A. Lukyn Williams also notes that Moses may have had in mind the reading of Ps 71.1 in the Targum: "O God, give the rules of Thy judgment to King Messiah, and Thy righteousness to the Son of King David." See his *Adversus Judaeos*, 236, n. 1.

29. Ps 71.5.   30. Ps 71.17.

31. Ps 71.11.   32. Ps 71.19.

Likewise, in the book *Dabre Iamin*, that is, *The Words of the Days*,[33] one reads that when David was thinking about building a house for the Lord, Nathan the prophet spoke to him in these words, in the Lord's persona: "And when you have ended your days to go to your fathers, I will raise up your seed after you, which shall be of your sons, and I will establish his kingdom. He will build me a house, and I will establish his throne forever. I will be to him a father, and he will be to me a son, and I will not take my mercy away from him, as I took it from him who was before you. And I will settle him in my house and in my kingdom forever, and his throne will be most firm forever."[34] Tell me, O Moses, I say, of whom is this prophecy said?

MOSES: Solomon.

PETRUS: That can never be. For when he says: "And when you have ended your days to go to your fathers," that is, when you have died, "I will raise up your seed after you," it is clear that it is not said of Solomon. For Solomon was already king while his father was still living.[35] If he had wished to say this about Solomon, certainly he would not have said, "which shall be of your sons," but rather, "which shall be of you." Moreover, what follows— "And I will settle him in my house and in my kingdom forever, and his throne will be most firm forever"—is clearly understood not to be said about Solomon. For neither was Solomon settled in the house of God (this is, in his kingdom), nor was his throne most firm forever. And since this is appropriate for God alone, then the one whom this concerns had to be man and God.

MOSES: Since, Petrus, you understand that all these things were said with respect to Christ, how is it that he said: "He will build me a house"? What does this house have to be, which Christ was to build?

PETRUS: To be sure, we understand that house to be holy Church, which Christ built upon a firm rock.

MOSES: And what did Nathan respond to David concerning the house which he said he wanted to build for the Lord?

33. Alfonsi refers here to First and Second Chronicles, which in Hebrew are known as *Dibre Haijamim.*

34. 1 Chr 17.11–14.

35. Cf. 1 Chr 29.20–23.

PETRUS: Clearly what David, speaking himself, said to Solomon his son: "The word of the Lord came to me," he said, "saying: You have shed much blood and fought many battles, so you cannot build a house to my name, after shedding so much blood before me. Behold, a son is born to you, a most quiet man, for I will make him rest from all his enemies round about, because he will be called Solomon,[36] and I will give peace and quietness to Israel for all his days. He will build a house to my name, and he will be a son to me, and I will be a father to him, and I will establish the throne of his kingdom over Israel forever."[37] And I concede that this really was said about Solomon, with respect to: "Behold, a son is born to you," and, a little after, "he will be called Solomon." Even David attests to this, speaking in these words concerning him to the children of Israel: "Among my sons, for the Lord has given me many sons, he has chosen my son Solomon."[38] And here, to be sure, David's speech to Solomon is altogether different from the one Nathan spoke to David about Christ. For here one reads: "A son is born to you and is called Solomon"; however, there one reads: "that I will raise up your seed after you, which shall be of your sons,"[39] and he bestows no name upon him. Moreover, he says there: "And I will settle him in my house and in my kingdom forever, and his throne will be most firm forever."[40] Here it says only: "I will establish the throne of his kingdom over Israel forever,"[41] which shows that as long as the kingdom of Israel endures, a king will not be wanting from Solomon's lineage, whereas the kingdom of Christ will always exist without end. But while the kingdom of Christ is unconditioned, the kingdom of Solomon was promised conditionally. Indeed, one reads about him in the books of Kings, where David speaks in this way to his son Solomon:

---

36. The Vulg. reads *Pacificus*, "Peaceable," not "Solomon." Perhaps one can explain the substitution, however, by recalling that Jerome proposed *Pacificus* as the Latin equivalent for the etymology of the name Solomon. See Jerome, *Liber interpretationis hebraicorum nominum*, ed. P. de Lagarde, CC SL 72 (Brepols: Turnholt, 1959), 71. This became a commonplace based on the assumption that the Hebrew form of Solomon, Shlomo, derives from the Hebrew word for "peace," *shalom*.

37. 1 Chr 22.8–10.   38. 1 Chr 28.5.
39. 1 Chr 17.11.   40. Ibid.
41. 1 Chr 22.8.

"That the Lord may confirm his words," he said, "which he has spoken of me, saying: If your children will guard my law[42] and walk before me in truth, with all their heart and all their soul, there shall not be taken away from you a man for the throne of Israel."[43] David himself also attests to this prophecy which we mentioned above, namely: "when you will have completed your days," etc. He attests, I say, that that was pronounced with regard to Christ. For hearing it and understanding it, just as we explained, but even then giving thanks to God, he said: "Who am I, Lord God, and what is my house, that you have brought me this far? But yet this has seemed little in your sight, Lord God, unless you also did speak of the house of your servant for a long time to come and you saw me in the law of a man exalted of the Lord God."[44] Indeed, when he said: "Who am I, Lord God, and what is my house, that you have brought me this far?" he said this about himself and his son Solomon. But what he said next: "But yet this has seemed little in your sight, unless you also did speak of the house of your servant for a long time to come," this truly he said in regard to Christ, who, he saw, would come from his house. But also by this passage, when he said: "and you saw me in the law of a man exalted of the Lord God." Since he said that, too, about Christ, he actually implied that he had to be exalted as both God and man.

42. Vulg.: "take heed of their ways."
43. 1 Kgs 2.4.
44. 2 Sm 7.18. The clause "and you saw me in the law of a man exalted of the Lord God" is absent from the Vulg.

NINTH *TITULUS*

MOSES: SINCE THEN, using many authorities, you show that the one whom you call Christ could be both God and man, with what authority, I ask you, can you show that he has already come, as you believe? For perhaps he has not yet come, but will only come at some future time.

PETRUS: There are actually several, O Moses, which clearly demonstrate that he has already come. For both the time when the prophets predicted that he would come has passed, and we know that he appeared during it, and besides this there are many other things we recognize in him and in his words and deeds, as was predicted by the prophets.

MOSES: In the first place, I ask you to show me when and how the prophets have spoken about that time and how to identify it.

PETRUS: Clearly we read that Jacob, speaking to his sons and individually blessing them when they were called before him, said: "The scepter shall not be taken away from Judah, nor a ruler from his thigh, until he come that is to be sent, and around him the nations will gather."[1] Moreover, I will not explain this prophecy in any way other than your ancient sages explained it. For they themselves said: "The scepter shall not be taken away," that is, the rod of the kingdom, "from Judah, nor a ruler from his thigh," that is, from the sons of his sons for the ages [*in secula*], "until he come that is to be sent," that is, Christ, whose kingdom it is, "and around him the nations will gather." And indeed we know that after Christ came there was no king or ruler of Judah any more. Therefore, we have to believe that this

1. Gn 49.10. Note that the Vulg. does not read, "around him the nations will gather" *(ad eum congregabuntur gentes)*, but instead, "he shall be the expectation of nations" *(ipse erit expectatio gentium)*. The author may have altered the passage here to reflect an alternate Jewish reading that can be found in Rashi. See J. H. L. Reuter, *Petrus Alfonsi*, 47, n. 2.

was established as the time of Christ's coming and that the one who came at that time was, without the scruple of any doubt, the Christ. Likewise, in the book of Daniel an angel spoke with Daniel in this way concerning the time of Christ's advent: "Seventy weeks have been established upon your people and upon the city of your sanctuary, that transgression may be finished and sin may have an end, and iniquity may be abolished, and the justice of the ages may be brought, and vision and prophecy may be fulfilled, and the saint of saints may be anointed. Know, then, and take notice: from the going forth of the word to build up Jerusalem again until Christ the ruler there shall be seven weeks and sixty-two weeks, and the streets shall be built again and the walls in the straitness of times. And after sixty-two weeks Christ will be slain [. . .] and the people with the leader that will come will destroy the city and the sanctuary, and the devastation of the end [will occur], and after the end of the war the appointed desolation. And he will confirm the covenant with many, in one week, and in half of the week the victim and the sacrifice will fail, and there will be the abomination of desolation in the Temple, and the desolation will continue even to the consummation and the end."[2] Certainly this prophecy, Moses, is obscure and difficult to understand, and there are many periods [*termini*] indicated there, yet nevertheless all of them were established in order to reveal the advent of Christ. At the outset, therefore, one must know that those weeks are weeks of years. Therefore, when it says, "Seventy weeks have been established upon your people and upon the city of your sanctuary, that transgression may be finished and sin may have an end, and iniquity may be abolished, and the justice of the ages may be brought, and vision and prophecy may be fulfilled, and the saint of saints may be anointed," when it says this, I say, it wants it to be known that seven times seventy—that is, four hundred ninety—years were appointed from the year of this same prophecy until the destruction of Jerusalem and of the Temple, which was accomplished by the Roman emperor Titus.[3] At the time

2. Dn 9.24–27. Note that there are several departures from the Vulg. text.

3. For the interpretation of these verses in medieval Jewish-Christian polemics, see especially Robert Chazan, "Daniel 9:24–27: Exegesis and Polemics," in

of its destruction, Christ had already come; he was the saint of saints and the justice of the ages, through whom every sin and iniquity was abolished and the entire prophecy was fulfilled. All the other things that follow, moreover, were expressed with respect to the determination and division of these four hundred ninety years. By what he said, "from the going forth of the word to build up Jerusalem again until Christ the ruler there shall be seven weeks," he hinted that from the time of this prophecy until Cyrus, king of the Persians, who was called a christ by God himself through Isaiah,[4] there were seven weeks of years, that is, forty-nine years, when by Cyrus's command Jerusalem began to be rebuilt. From its rebuilding and after the completion of this task, until Titus's assault on Jerusalem, four hundred thirty-four years passed, and this is just as he said, "sixty-two weeks will pass," that is, four hundred thirty-four years, "and the streets shall be built again and the walls in the straitness of times. And after sixty-two weeks Christ will be slain"; that is, after Christ is slain, "the people," that is, the Romans, "will destroy the city and the sanctuary with the leader that will come," that is, with Titus, "and the devastation of the end [will occur], and after the end of the war the appointed desolation." In what follows, however—"he will confirm the covenant with many, in one week"—that one week is actually seven years of siege.[5] For the city was besieged by the Roman army for seven years, and during those seven years those within it were hard pressed and afflicted, so that they had nothing with which they could offer sacrifice. And this is why he said, "in half of the week," that is, within a week, "the victim and the sacrifice will fail, and there will be the abomination of desolation in the Temple." Moreover, when he added, "the desolation will continue even to the consummation and end," he hinted that that captivity and desolation would be without end. Therefore, seven weeks until Cyrus, and sixty-two weeks from Cyrus to Titus, and one week of siege, actually equal seventy weeks.

Contra Iudaeos. Ancient and Medieval Polemics Between Christians and Jews, ed. Ora Limor and Guy G. Stroumsa (Tübingen: J. C. B. Mohr, 1996), 143–59.

4. Cf. Is 45.1.

5. In fact, the Roman siege of Jerusalem was only intermittent from 66 C.E. until the city walls were breached in 70 C.E.

MOSES: Inasmuch as you have defended the time of Christ's advent from the testimonies of the prophets, as much as could be done, I want you to explain those other things which, as you said, were revealed in him and his works and words and that also, as you assert, were predicted concerning him by the prophets.

PETRUS: We read in the book of Deuteronomy that Moses, when his death was imminent, spoke thus to the people of Israel: "The Lord your God will raise up for you a prophet like me from your nation and from your brethren. You will hear him, as you sought from the Lord your God in Horeb, when the assembly was gathered together, and you said: I will not hear the voice of the Lord my God any more, nor will I see this exceeding great fire any more, lest I die. And the Lord said to me: they have spoken all things well. I will raise them up a prophet like unto you from the midst of their brethren, and I will put my words in his mouth, and he shall speak to them all that I will command him. And [upon him] who refuses to hear his words, which he will speak in my name, I will be the avenger."[6] Who is he then, O Moses, who is he who the Lord said would be raised up like Moses and whom he commanded to be heard?

MOSES: Certainly he could have been speaking of Joshua, son of Nun, who arose after Moses and took his place.

PETRUS: In no way could that be about Joshua. Scripture speaks very clearly about him, as one reads in the book of Numbers: "And Moses answered the Lord:[7] May the Lord God of the spirits of all flesh provide a man, that may be over this multitude, and may go out and in before them, and may lead them out or bring them in, lest the people of the Lord be like sheep without a shepherd. And the Lord said to him: Take Joshua the son of Nun, a man in whom there is the Spirit, and put your hand upon him. And he shall stand before Eliezar the priest and all the multitude, and you will give him precepts in the sight of all, and part of your glory, that all the congregation of the children of Israel may hear him."[8] Since in fact here this so clear-

6. Dt 18.15–19.
7. The Vulg. reads, "And Moses answered him" (*cui Moses respondit*).
8. Nm 27.15–20.

ly concerned Joshua, why should that other prophecy, which is obscure—namely, this one, "the Lord your God will raise up a prophet," etc.—why, I say, should that statement be understood to apply to him? But also this one in which one reads, "you will give him part of your glory," as if to say, not all of your glory, by which it is revealed that there will be no one like Moses. And at the end of Deuteronomy: "And there arose no more in Israel a prophet like Moses."[9] This implies that "the Lord your God will raise up for you a prophet," etc., should not be said about Joshua, since there follows in the same passage, "like you." Also, in other ways this prophecy—which is, "the Lord will raise up for you," etc.—and those which were said concerning Joshua, differ. For in the former it has, "And upon him who refuses to hear his words [. . .] I will be the avenger," whereas one reads about Joshua, "He who will gainsay your mouth and not obey all your words, which you command him, let him die."[10] Therefore, it is clear in all these instances that that prophecy was not pronounced with regard to Joshua.

MOSES: With regard to whom, then?

PETRUS: With regard to Christ, who was like Moses, because, just like Moses, he himself gave a law.

MOSES: Now, then, show me how you can apply all the separate parts of the prophecy to him.

PETRUS: Indeed, the prophecy responds to the petition of the children of Israel. For they sought him, just as is written, on Mount Horeb, lest they hear any longer the voice of the Lord or lest they look with their vision [*visibiliter*] upon so great a fire and die. Against that, the Lord said to Moses, "I will raise them up a prophet like unto you from the midst of their brethren," as if to say that the one I will raise up will be of the lineage of the Jews themselves. But he will also be like you: that is, just as you have given a law, so, too, he also will give one. This is recognized, moreover, by the fact that he established the prophet in a unique way [*singulariter*] and in the highest degree [*per excellentiam*]. For if he himself would not give a law, he certainly would have said, "I will raise up prophets," not "a prophet." Indeed, God raised

9. Dt 34.10.
10. Jos 1.18.

up many prophets who announced his words, but none except Christ gave a law in a way analogous to Moses. "And I will put my words in his mouth,"[11]—which means that because they are unable to endure the force of my voice, I will speak to them through him under a veil of flesh. "And he will speak to them all the things which I will command him,"[12] as if to say clearly that he will say nothing but what I command and will. "Upon him who refuses to hear his words, which he will speak in my name, I will be the avenger."[13] That is, he will not slay or punish in the flesh in some other way one who has refused to perform his precepts, but I will avenge myself upon him mercifully according to my will. Since, then, Christ is born of the Jews' lineage and will be a lawgiver just like Moses, and has concealed the word of God under the veil of his flesh, he has himself taught nothing but what God the Father has commanded. He himself attests to this in the Gospel, when saying: "The word which you have heard is not mine, but his, the Father who sent me."[14] Since he did not himself will to be slain or punished in a bodily fashion, but instead preached mercy in all things, in fact nothing prevents the whole of the prophecy from having been said of him.

MOSES: There remains one more thing for which I want you to give me a reply. For since Christ, as you believe, was God and man simultaneously, why have you called him a prophet?

PETRUS: You seem to think that "prophet" is only a name for a human being, but that is not at all the case. Instead, he is called a prophet who states those things that have yet to come. One reads thus in Isaiah: "Behold my servant, I will raise him up, my elect, my soul delights in him. I have given my Spirit upon him, he will bring forth judgment to the gentiles. He will not cry out nor be praised,[15] neither will his voice be heard abroad. The bruised reed he will not break, and the smoking flax he will not quench. He will bring forth judgment in truth. He will not falter nor flee[16] until he bring judgment upon the

---

11. Dt 18.18.   12. Cf. Jos 4.10.
13. Dt 18.19.   14. Jn 14.24.
15. "Nor be praised" *(nec exaltabitur):* the Vulg. reads, "nor have respect to person" *(neque accipiet personam).*
16. "He will not falter nor flee" *(non deficiet aut effugiet):* the Vulg. reads, "He will not be sad or troublesome" *(non erit tristis neque turbulentus).*

land, and the islands will wait for his law."[17] But to whom better than to Christ can we apply this prophecy, O Moses? For he
himself was both the servant of God and his elect, in whom God
was well pleased. Indeed, this was said about him with respect to
the body. What follows, however—"I have given my Spirit upon
him"—was pronounced with respect to the soul. "He will bring
forth judgment," that is, the law, "to the gentiles." In fact, Christ
proclaimed the law which was confined to and hidden only
among the Jews. That is, he explained it, laid it open, and drew
out the marrow for this purpose: so that the gentiles could accept it. Then there follows: "He will not cry out nor be praised,
neither will his voice be heard abroad." And we know that Christ
was not clamorous, nor arrogant, nor did he desire vainglory;
rather, he loved humility above all things. "The bruised reed he
will not break, and the smoking flax he will not quench." Certainly we see that a bruised reed can be easily broken; however, smoking flax—that is, charred flax, but flax still containing
something smoking, that is, fire—can very easily be quenched.
But what can be better understood as a bruised reed or flax that
is almost quenched than the frailty of the sinner, who is serious-
ly damaged and almost quenched by sin? Christ, however, has
not broken the bruised reed and has not quenched the smoking flax, because he did not command that sinners who are already almost dead in their sins be slain. Instead, he tolerated
them mercifully and recalled them to repentance. The prophet
indicated this as well from the passages that followed, when he
added: "He will bring forth judgment in truth." Indeed, truth
and justice are one and the same thing. Whereas according to
the law of Moses the judgment and commandment was that
the sinner be slain, Christ led to truth and justice, however. He
drew out judgment when he commanded that sinners not be
slain but, what is still more just, that they be supported until
they should repent, when he said: "I do not desire the death
of the sinner, but that he be converted and live."[18] "He will not
falter nor flee until he bring judgment upon the land." Clearly
the prophet wanted Christ's death to be understood by "falter,"

17. Is 42.1–4.
18. Ezek 33.11.

whereas by "flee" he wanted his Ascension into heaven to be understood, as if to say: he will not die or withdraw from the land (that is, ascend to heaven) until he send the law upon the land. And to be sure, before he died according to the flesh or ascended to the Father in heaven, Christ established judgment upon the land when he gave us the law, that is, the Gospel. For that reason, he never really says he will not die, but "he will not falter," because Christ's death was not really a death but was instead a relocation and a faltering. To be sure, a man who dies does not live any longer, whereas Christ was resurrected on the third day and already lives in eternity. "And the islands will wait for his law." By the islands we understand the gentiles. The gentiles, however, awaited the law of Christ because they did not receive it from him but rather from his disciples, that is, the apostles. Nor is it he, but rather the apostles who will preach to the gentiles. Again, in Isaiah: "I the Lord have called you in justice, and taken you by the hand, and preserved you. And I have given you for a covenant of the people, for a light to the gentiles, that you might open the eyes of the blind and bring forth the prisoner out of prison, and those that sit in darkness and the shadow of death[19] out of the prison house. I am the Lord, this is my name. I will not give my glory to another nor my praise to graven things."[20] Isaiah proclaimed this, too, about Christ. For the Lord called him from the womb of the Virgin "in justice"; that is, Christ was born of the pure flesh of the holy and just Virgin without sin and the concupiscence of the flesh. He took his hand, which is a sign of protection and patronage, and he guarded him, just as he snatched him out of Herod's grasp when he was still a squalling infant. He led him into Egypt and returned him from there, freed him from the hands of the Jews who wished very often to stone him, and was his protector and guardian throughout his many other adversities. The Lord gave him "for a covenant of the people," namely, for the Israelites; that is, he gave him for this reason: so that he would disclose the truth of the law to the people of Israel. And the Lord gave

19. "And the shadow of death": absent from the Vulg. Note that it is also absent from the author's subsequent citation of this passage, below.
20. Is 42.6–8.

him "for a light to the gentiles," because the gentiles, once they had abandoned error and once the darkness of their unbelief was expelled, were bedewed with the light of Christ's law. He also sent him for this reason: to open "the eyes of the blind" and to "bring forth the prisoner out of prison, and those that sit in darkness out of the prison house." And Christ opened the eyes of the blind when he laid open the hearts of the unbelievers and revealed the light of the law, having driven away the shadow. He brought forth the prisoner out of prison because he frees and releases those believing in him from every captivity, even to this day.[21] Moreover, he brought forth those that sit in darkness out of the prison house because he drew forth those who were held in the dark prison of hell, when he himself descended to the lower depths. The Lord did not give his glory and praise to anyone other than Christ because to no other man did he join his divinity or bestow such great praise. Again, Isaiah: "Seek the Lord while he may be found; call upon him while he is near. Let the wicked abandon his way and the unjust man his thoughts, and let him return to the Lord, and he will have mercy on him, and to our God, for he is bountiful to forgive. For my thoughts are not your thoughts, nor are your ways my ways, says the Lord. For as the heavens are exalted above the earth, so are my ways exalted above your ways and my thoughts above your thoughts. And as the rain and snow come down from heaven, and return there no more, but soak the earth and water it, and make it to sprout, and give seed to the sower and bread to the eater, so shall my word be, which will go forth from my mouth. It will not return to me void, but it will do whatsoever I please."[22] And tell me, O Moses, how do you explain this entire passage? When is the Lord found, and when is he not found? When is he near and when is he distant?

MOSES: To be found and to be near are one and the same thing for God. He is near and he is found, however, by those who faithfully serve him.

PETRUS: The Lord clearly wants to be nearer to and offers

21. A reminder for Moses that the Jews will not be freed from their captivity until they accept faith in Christ.
22. Is 55.6–11.

himself more to sinners and to those who seem to be distant, than he does to the just and the faithful and, as you say, to those who are near. And the prophet also attested to this in another place, where he said: "Peace to him who is far off, and peace to him who is near, says the Lord."[23] Now what do we understand one "who is far off" to mean if not a sinner, and what do we understand one "who is near" to mean if not a just person? For when the prophet mentioned first the one who is far off and then mentioned afterwards the one who is near, he demonstrated in this way that God is nearer to the sinner than to the just person.

MOSES: We can also say that God is near on those ten days which are from the first day of the seventh month until the Day of Atonement, as has been said by our sages.[24]

PETRUS: And this is also a bad thing. Certainly, if the Lord is near and is found only on these ten days, then if a sinner who wishes to return to God seeks him at any other time and, being far from him, as it were, does not find him, then the fault will belong to God and not to the sinner when he cannot return to him.

MOSES: Our sages also say something else, namely, that God was near and could be found while the Temple of the Lord stood. Once the Temple was destroyed, however, he departed and then did not will to be found beyond it.[25]

PETRUS: They were very foolish in this matter as well. For even Moses spoke against this to the children of Israel: that if at some time they provoke God's wrath so that he disperse them as captives among the nations, if, nevertheless, returning to him they seek him at the end, without any doubt they will find him.

23. Is 57.19.
24. That is, from the first until the tenth of Tishri (from the festivals of Rosh Ha-Shanah until Yom Kippur, the ten Days of Awe). See B.T. *Ber.* 32b for the notion that since the destruction of the Temple the gates of prayer have been closed, but not those for weeping, while B.T. *Rosh HaShanah* 18a and *Yebamoth* 105a affirm that the individual can especially find God between the New Year (Rosh Ha-Shanah) and the Day of Atonement, or Yom Kippur.
25. One can find the claim in a midrash on Lamentations that the *Shekhinah* was removed from the world at the destruction of the Temple. See *Rabbinic Fantasies*, ed. Stern and Mirsky, 49. Cf. B.T. *Megilla* 29a, which avows that the *Shekhinah* dwelled with Israel in exile.

MOSES: Since you contradict both this one and that, when and how, then, do you assert that God is found or is near?

PETRUS: To be sure, the Lord was found and was near when he assumed flesh from the holy Virgin and dwelled among us in his presence [*presentialiter*]. Indeed, the prophet commanded that he be sought and invoked at that time when he said: "Seek the Lord while he may be found." For, with the Holy Spirit revealing it, he foresaw that this would occur in the future, which is why he also added in the following passages: "Let the wicked abandon his way and the unjust man his thoughts, and let him return to the Lord," namely, lest they think about him iniquitously or doubt that he is God on account of the flesh he has assumed; instead let them faithfully believe. For faith is in thought alone, and a human being's thought is indeed different from God's thought. Therefore, this also follows: "For my thoughts are not your thoughts, nor are your ways my ways, says the Lord." This is as if to say that you should not think that what you see and hear, namely, that a son is without a carnal father, is what you know to be beyond the customary order of nature [*contra usum*]. For I think one way and you think another way. You only think in a corporeal fashion, whereas I think spiritually. For I proceed along one way, and you proceed along another. You know no pathway but that which is customary [*in usu*], whereas I also know the one that is contrary to the customary order of nature because I can bring to pass whatsoever I will. And this is the meaning of "For as the heavens are exalted above the earth," etc., and, moreover, of that which follows: "And as the rain and snow come down from heaven, and return there no more, but soak the earth and water it, and make it to sprout, and give seed to the sower and bread to the eater, so shall my word be, which will go forth from my mouth. It will not return to me void, but it will do whatsoever I please." He added this, too, in order to demonstrate by an analogy to visible things what cannot so plainly be seen in the subtlety of divinity, and said that just as the rain will not return to heaven once it has fallen from heaven before it softens the ground and makes it fecund and to sprout, so, too, my Word, which will go forth from my mouth (that is, my Son whom I will send into the world in order to re-

ceive flesh), will not return to me void. Rather, before he re-
turns, he will do whatsoever I will. That is, just as I have dis-
posed, he will assume flesh, he will be scourged, he will die, he
will release his own from hell, and he will rise again and reveal
to those of less understanding the law that is hidden. And if by
his word (that is, his speech) God had wanted to be understood
as having spoken of himself, when he said, "my Word, which will
go forth from my mouth," he certainly would not have added,
"will not return to me," etc. For a word (that is, speech), once it
goes forth from the mouth, does not return to the mouth again.
With this it is clearly shown that he said "my Word" about the
person of the Son.

MOSES: You have already hinted with your words that snow
and rain return once more to heaven after they have descended
from heaven.

PETRUS: That is true.

MOSES: I would like you to show me how this can be proved
by reason.

PETRUS: First, to be sure, you have to examine where clouds
and rain come from, and then in that way you will more easily
discover what you seek.

MOSES: I beg you to make that clear for me.

PETRUS: Certainly you must see, O Moses, that when the sun
is directly above the sea and the earth, a certain humid vapor
arises from the sea and a dry vapor from the earth. These rise up
on account of the sun's heat just as steam [*fumus aquae*] rises up
on account of fire's heat. These two vapors, when they ascend,
mix with each other and create dense clouds. When the clouds,
however, reach a height of about sixteen miles, there they encounter a cold air which they cannot pass through, and in this
way they fall back to earth again, and this is where rains come
from. Moreover, God made the hollows of mountains so that
the rains would be stored there as if in a vault. He also made in
the very deepest recesses of the mountains certain small pores
through which, little by little, the water that is held there, hidden just as in a vault, is distributed, and these are the springs
from which all rivers flow. From the rivers, all the fish are nour-
ished, meadows and vines are irrigated, and both the crops of

men and [their] flocks of animals are watered; and they flow
past both large cities and small villages. And the proof of this
is that when rains are lacking the springs and rivers dry up, just
as we find Elijah saying in the third book of Kings: "But after
some time the torrent was dried up, for it had not rained upon
the earth."[26] The rivers, however, after they have flowed over the
earth for a long time, finally descend to the sea and join together with the sea waves. And thus, as we said above, the vapor of
the sea rises up on high once again and makes itself into clouds
once more. And there is not nor was there ever an end to this
ascent and descent from which God created the world, nor will
there be an end so long as it is pleasing to the creator of things.
Solomon attests to this, who says in Ecclesiastes: "All the rivers
run into the sea, but the sea does not overflow. Unto the place
whence the rivers come, they return, to flow again."[27]

MOSES: You have adduced many authorities from the prophetic books, to be sure, and you have explained them as you
pleased. But I would like you to show me just one with which
clearly one can prove plainly what you aver.

PETRUS: The hardness of your heart and that of those like
you is not something new. Neither did you believe, moreover,
when the prophets addressed you openly and without allegory,
which is why it is not surprising that the words of my explanation
seem absurd to you. Nevertheless, in order to cut short all your
pretexts and objections, let me now show you the one extremely clear authority from Isaiah himself. For Isaiah himself said
to you: "Behold, my servant will understand, he will be exalted
and extolled, and he will be especially high. As many have been
astonished at you, so shall his visage be inglorious among men
and his form among the sons of men. He will sprinkle many nations; kings will shut their mouth at him, for what was not told
to them, they have seen; and what they have not heard, they
have beheld."[28] "Who has believed our report? And to whom
is the arm of the Lord revealed? And he will grow up just like
a tender plant before him, and as a root out of thirsty ground.

26. 1 Kgs 17.7.
27. Eccl 1.7.
28. Is 52.13–15. Note a slight departure from the Vulg.

There is no beauty in him, nor comeliness, and we have seen him, there was no sightliness in him, and we have desired him [to be] despised, the most strange of men, and a man of sorrows and acquainted with infirmity, and his look was, as it were, hidden and despised, whereupon we esteemed him not. Surely he has borne our infirmities and carried our sorrows, and we have thought him, as it were, wounded[29] and as one struck by God and afflicted. But he himself was wounded for our iniquities; he was bruised for our sins. The chastisement of our peace was upon him, and by his bruises we are healed. All we like sheep have gone astray; every one has turned aside into his own way, and the Lord has placed upon him the iniquity of us all. He was oppressed[30] and afflicted, and he did not open his mouth. He will be led like a sheep to the slaughter, and he will be silent as a lamb before his shearer, and he will not open his mouth. He was taken away from distress and judgment. Who will declare his generation? For he is cut off from the land of the living. For the wickedness of my people I have struck him. And he shared his grave with the ungodly and his death with the rich, although he did no iniquity, nor was there deceit in his mouth; and the Lord was pleased to bruise him and to weaken him in infirmity. If he lays down his soul for sin, he will see a seed, and [its] time will be extended, and the will of the Lord will be prosperous in his hand. Because of the labor of his soul he will see and be filled. By his knowledge the just one will justify many, and he will bear their iniquities. Therefore, I will make him to participate in many, and he will divide the spoils with the strong, because he has handed his soul over to death and was counted with the wicked, and he has borne the sins of many and has prayed for the transgressors."[31] Clearly, Moses, I have above all labored over this prophecy in order to introduce it in the way it is found among you; by doing so I have abandoned, moreover, the correct but nevertheless variant translation of the blessed Jerome. I have done this, however, in order to remove all your

29. "Wounded" *(plagatus):* the Vulg. reads "a leper" *(leprosus).*

30. "Oppressed" *(coactus):* the Vulg. reads "offered" *(oblatus).* Note that there are several departures from the Vulg. in the remainder of this passage, as the author himself notes below.

31. Is 53.1–12.

pretexts. Because we apply this prophecy to Christ and you perhaps do not admit that, I would like you to tell me of whom you
think it was spoken.

MOSES: Actually, some of our sages assert that it was said concerning Jeremiah, because he was scourged, beaten, and impris-
oned, and he bore many other evils which would take too long
to enumerate.[32] But following others, we understand this to be
said concerning King Josiah, who, although he was a just and
saintly man, was slain not for his own sins but for the sins of the
people.[33]

PETRUS: Certainly, it cannot refer to either of them. For you
cannot apply the entire prophecy to either one. Now, if you understand it to be about Jeremiah: Jeremiah, to be sure, endured
scourges, prison, and great affliction, but he was not slain. Nor
when he was scourged did he remain silent. Neither did he bear
our sins, nor will you apply to him the other things the prophecy said. Regarding Josiah, you will find that nothing that is contained in the prophecy could have been said about him except
this: that he was a saint, and that he was slain for the wickedness
of the people.

MOSES: Of whom, then, do you think this prophecy was said,
to whom you can apply all of its parts?

PETRUS: Of Christ. For from what he said, "Behold, my servant will understand, he will be exalted and extolled, and he
will be especially high," we know that Christ, to be sure, was the
servant of God and one of great understanding, and he was exalted and raised especially high over all the servants of God. His
works were wondrous and stupendous, and he was never interested in glory. And so it is, "As many have been astonished at
you, so shall his visage be inglorious among men and his form
among the sons of men." There follows, "He will sprinkle many
nations." And indeed the Lord Christ rained a great rain, as it
were, on the Israelite nation when he came among them just as
among his own and showed them his works and his mighty
deeds. He sprinkled many other nations, however, when he watered them from afar, not with the presence of signs but with

32. Cf. Jer 11.19.
33. Cf. 2 Kgs 23.26–30.

their hearing and report just as if with a dew, and he rendered all their foolish ones silent with wonder. Therefore it is said: "Kings will shut their mouth at him, for what was not told to them, they have seen; and what they have not heard, they have beheld," just as it was told to the Jews about him, and they heard. Even the prophet himself, marveling, said this: "Who has believed our report? And to whom is the arm of the Lord revealed?" This is as if to say that the things that I predict will come to pass are so amazing, it will be difficult for anyone to judge that they should be believed—namely, that the arm of the Lord has to be revealed, that is, that his son has to be made incarnate and in this way visibly revealed to the world through the flesh that has been assumed. "And he will grow up," he said, "just like a tender plant before him, and as a root out of thirsty ground." To be sure, we see that from a thirsty ground (that is, from an arid soil) neither a rod nor a root can be generated without moisture. For moisture is like the very sun's masculine sex.[34] Christ, however, grew up like a root or a tender plant before the Lord from the dry earth, when God the Father begot him from the flesh of a virgin without a union with a man. What he added next—"There is no beauty in him, nor comeliness, and we have seen him, there was no sightliness in him, and we have desired him [to be] despised, the most strange of men"— he added in order to display his humility and contempt for worldly pomp. He said he was "a man of sorrows." Certainly he was a man of sorrows because he was not free from the snares of the malevolent in infancy, or in childhood or adolescence, nor from hardship, so that it was of great report and well known that he is "acquainted with infirmity." For here by that "infirmity" the prophet wanted nothing else to be understood than the afflictions and hardships that Christ endured in the world according to the flesh. There follows: "his look was, as it were, hidden and despised, whereupon we esteemed him not." The look of Christ, however, was hidden, as it were, because the splendor

---

34. I.e., it causes growth or generation. More commonly, it is the sun's heat to which this power is attributed. See Albert the Great, *De vegetabilibus libri VII*, 1.1.12.91–92, ed. Ernst Meyer and Charles Jessen (Berlin: Georgius Reimeris, 1867).

of divinity hid itself under his flesh, and he was unwilling to resist those assailing him (although he could have), which is why
he was despised and not esteemed, that is, not appreciated. And
"surely he has borne our infirmities and carried our sorrows,"
when he himself endured the sorrows and punishments which
were due our crimes. "And we have thought him, as it were,
wounded and as one struck by God and afflicted," that is, we
thought that the blow, that is, that scourge and that striking and
that beating, befell him on his own account, but this was never
the case. And this is as he said: "But he himself was wounded for
our iniquities; he was bruised for our sins." "The chastisement
of our peace was upon him," that is, he himself—as one com-
passionate and kind—sustained on our behalf the chastisement
and correction that we had to suffer to have peace. Therefore,
there follows, "by his bruises we are healed," namely, by the
bruises of the flails and of the wounds which he bore for us.
Similarly there follows: "All we like sheep have gone astray; every one has turned aside into his own way." Sheep, to be sure,
are simple, and the most senseless and wandering animals. And
we erred just like senseless sheep, because we did not know him,
who or what he was. "Every one has turned aside into his own
way," that is, hardly anyone believed his teaching, but each one
stayed on his old path. "And the Lord has placed upon him the
iniquity of us all," that is, the Lord forgives and washes away
through him (that is, through the baptism that he gave) the
original sin in which all are entangled. "He was oppressed and
afflicted, and he did not open his mouth. He will be led like a
sheep to the slaughter, and he will be silent as a lamb before his
shearer, and he will not open his mouth." None of this needs an
explanation; rather, it is clear to all. For Christ, when he was led
before Pilate and falsely accused, even beaten and cut with
blows, remained silent before Pilate himself, who was interro-
gating him with several questions, and hardly replied with any
word at all. But what follows next, "He was taken away from distress and judgment," is said through "endiadis,"[35] for he said

35. A figure of speech, when two words connected by a conjunction are used
to express a single idea; in this case, "distress and judgment" for "distressed
judgment."

"from distress" and "judgment" for "from a distressed judgment." And, certainly, we call a distressed judgment an unjust judgment. Assuredly, Christ was taken away from a distressed judgment, that is, he was seized because of a distressed and unjust judgment, although he had committed no crime. "Who shall declare his generation?" Certainly he pronounced this with respect to his divine generation, which is indescribable and ineffable, and by this he revealed that he would be God, from which it follows, "he is cut off from the land of the living." "For the wickedness of my people he was struck" is the same as what he said above, "he himself was wounded for our iniquities; he was bruised for our sins [. . .] And he shared his grave with the ungodly and his death with the rich." "With the ungodly" and "with the rich" means one and the same thing. For certainly the rich of this world are almost all ungodly. There was, however, a custom among the Jews that the ungodly and those killed for their crime be buried apart from the community of other human beings. And Christ was crucified and died with the ungodly, that is, with thieves, and he was buried outside a common graveyard, although he committed no iniquitous deed and there was no deceit in his mouth. But the Lord willed it so, just as is written in the following: "The Lord was pleased to bruise him and to weaken him," that is, to make him suffer. "If he lays down his soul for sin, he will see a seed," etc. We know that in fact in ancient times Scripture called a sacrifice that was performed for sin by the name of sin.[36] This is why here, too, the prophet said: If, Lord, you will lay down his soul (that is, Christ's soul) for sin, that is, as sin's sacrifice. That is: if he will be sacrificed for our sin, he will see a seed, that is, he will have a great seed and many heirs. And through the sacrifice of his body and his death Christ saw a great seed and had many heirs, and time was extended, and the will of the Lord was fulfilled in him. "Because of the labor of his soul he will see and be filled." This is as if to say, his soul will labor so much that it will be filled when it sees that labor, because it is so much; that is, it will appear to be too much. Just as is said, moreover, today: I have borne so much evil and

36. That is, it was known as a sin offering.

distress that I am sated with it. And Christ bore too many distresses and labors. "By his knowledge the just one will justify many," that is, through his knowledge the Lord, who is the just one, will reveal him to many to be just. Christ, however, was just, and the Lord reveals him to many to be just. But also that which follows, "he has carried their iniquities" is the same as what he said above—"Surely he has borne our infirmities and carried our sorrows." "Therefore," said the Lord, "I will make him to participate in many, and he will divide the spoils with the strong." And Christ participated in many because numerous people from among many nations believed in him. And he divided the spoils with the strong because, having divided the booty, as it were, he carried his portion away from the princes of hell, who had despoiled this world, when he snatched from there those who believed that he was the one who would come. There follows: "because he has handed his soul over to death." Clearly this recalls the reason why he participated in many, namely, that for the world's redemption he endured death, owing to his exceedingly great piety. And again what follows: "And he was counted with the wicked." And just as we described, Christ was reckoned with the wicked because he was hung with thieves. "And he has borne the sins of many," but not the sins of all, because he saved many but not all. Similarly, what follows: "And he has prayed for the transgressors." Christ, however, prayed for the transgressors when he prayed for those who were crucifying him, saying: "Father, forgive them, for they know not what they do."[37] Therefore, O Moses, both the time and all the other things that the prophets predicted concerning the Christ appeared in both word and deed in the one whom we believe him to have been. It is clear that in truth he has already come, and you should have no further doubt concerning this any longer.

MOSES: I understand well enough what you have said. But if this is the case, why have not all the other things that were written in the prophets about the christ been fulfilled in that man who you say has come?

PETRUS: Such as?

37. Lk 23.34.

moses: To be sure, the same Isaiah said of the christ: "And he will judge the gentiles and rebuke many people, and they will turn their swords into ploughshares and their spears into sickles. Nation will not lift up sword against nation, neither will they be trained any more for war."[38] And certainly these have not yet been fulfilled which, without any doubt, will be fulfilled after the coming of the christ. For even now, the nations still make war on one another.

petrus: You do not pay attention to how what you cited was said. For the prophet did not say that—"and they will turn their swords into ploughshares and their spears into sickles. Nation will not lift up sword against nation, neither will they be trained any more for war"—he did not, I say, say that in the way of reporting what the nations would do, but in the way of revealing what Christ would command. This is just as Zechariah says about him in another place: "And he will speak peace," he said, "to the gentiles."[39] Now just as here we understand it to mean that he will command peace, so, too, do we understand it there. And although he commanded it, it is not his fault if it was not fulfilled.

moses: Moreover, Jeremiah says: "In those days," that is, the days of the christ, "Judah will be saved, and Israel will dwell confidently." But this, too, has yet to be fulfilled, which ought to have been fulfilled after the advent of that man whom you call the Christ, if this was the advent of the christ. For Judah and Israel remain still in misery and captivity.

petrus: Surely that promise, O Moses, was made only to those belonging to Israel and Judah who would believe. Therefore, it was not fulfilled for those who were without faith. In the same way, after the people of Israel had been led forth from Egypt, because they had sinned and abandoned the commandments of the Lord, they did not enter the promised land which the Lord promised to Moses, saying: "I am come down to deliver my people out of the hands of the Egyptians, and to bring them out of that land into a good and spacious land."[40] Instead they all died in the desert.

38. Is 2.4.
39. Zec 9.10.
40. Ex 3.8.

MOSES: There is still something else that has not yet been fulfilled, which Isaiah prophesied would occur at the advent of the
christ. For he said: "The wolf will dwell with the lamb, and the
leopard will lie down with the kid. The calf and the lion and
the sheep will abide together, and a little child will lead them. The
calf and the bear will feed; their young will rest together, and
the lion will eat straw like the ox."[41]

PETRUS: O Moses, most foolish of all, do you understand that
literally [*simpliciter*] as he has pronounced the prophecy?

MOSES: Yes, even so.

PETRUS: The foolishness of your understanding,[42] assuredly,
is apparent in this. For if, as you say, the wolf will have peace
only with the lamb, and the leopard only with the kid, and the
lion only with the sheep and calf, what good is such an interpretation? For the wolf will disquiet the kid, and the lion the lamb,
and the leopard the sheep and the calf.

MOSES: How, then, do you interpret it?

PETRUS: To be sure, those beasts that live on prey and on flesh
we understand to symbolize ungodly men and robbers. Whereas
the prophet said about the rest of them (gentle and simple herd
animals) that Christ would command them to dwell and have
peace together. The prophet, however, hinted at what he wanted
to be understood to be about men in the following words, when
he added: "because the earth is filled with the knowledge of the
Lord."[43] Now, he did not say this with respect to the herd animals, which do not have a rational soul and cannot have knowledge of the Lord, that is, an understanding of the Lord. Rather,
to undermine your understanding of this prophecy, your sages
have said that there would be no difference between the modern age and the age of Christ, except that in his time you will endure captivity and every misery.

MOSES: Consider again still another of Isaiah's prophecies,
which we know has not yet been fulfilled. For he himself said:
"And the light of the moon will be as the light of the sun, and

41. Is 11.6–7.
42. "The foolishness of your understanding": lit., the foolishness of your
heart (*cordis tui . . . inscientia*).
43. Is 11.9.

the light of the sun will be sevenfold, as the light of seven days, in the day when the Lord will bind up the wound of his people."[44]

PETRUS: There is no people in the whole world more foolish than you, who think that God will increase the size of the body or the light of the moon or of the sun. For if the sun were only twice the size it is now—much less seven times—it would in fact burn up the whole world. And if its light were seven times greater, to be sure, it would stun our eyes with its exceeding splendor. Moreover, if the light of the moon were equal to the splendor of the sun, no one would be able to take his rest any more, because it would always be day. Therefore, by the increase of the lunar or solar light the prophet wanted one to understand the faith and glory of those who would believe in Christ, as if to say: their faith and glory will be many times greater and more brilliant than that of contemporaries. And the fact that the prophet was not speaking of the visible moon or sun, but rather of the glory and splendor of the faith of Christians, is attested in the following, when he added: "You will no more have the sun for a light by day, nor will the splendor of the moon cast light on you, but the Lord will be for you an everlasting light, and your God for your glory. Your sun will go down no more, and your moon will not decrease, because the Lord will be for you an everlasting light."[45] For if he were speaking of the sun or moon in their own right, surely what he said—"You will no more have the sun for a light by day, nor will the splendor of the moon cast light on you"—would contradict what he had said above, namely, "the light of the moon will be as the light of the sun, and the light of the sun will be sevenfold." Therefore, it is evident that the prophet is speaking here about the splendor and glory of the faith of holy Church, which is even indicated by the concluding portions, when he added: "But the Lord will be for you an everlasting light, and your God for your glory." This is as if to say you will never again lack brightness with the light of your faith, which is analogous to the passing sun or to the moon, since the

44. Is 30.26.
45. Is 60.19–20.

Lord will illumine you eternally with the glory of his light. But also what follows: "Your sun will go down no more, and your moon will not decrease." If this, I say, is understood literally as it is written, namely, that the splendor of the sun and the moon will exist without cease, then there will be no day or night, no month or year, since all these occur as a result of changes of the sun and moon. Therefore, not without reason we understand this passage spiritually, to concern the light and glory of our faith, which will neither decrease nor disappear.

MOSES: What is the meaning of what Isaiah says next: "Then will you see and abound, and your heart will wonder and be enlarged, when the multitude of the sea will be converted to you, the strength of the gentiles will come to you, the multitude of the camels will cover you, the dromedaries of Midian and Ephah: all they from Sheba will come, bringing gold and frankincense and announcing praise to the Lord"?[46] These things, too, have yet to be consummated.

PETRUS: In fact, they were consummated at the time of the second Temple, which Ezra constructed according to Cyrus's command, as the prophet Haggai attested, who said: "Thus says the Lord, the God of hosts: yet one little while, and I will move the heaven and the earth, and the sea and the dry land. And I will move all the nations. And what all nations have desired will come, and I will fill this house with glory, says the Lord of hosts. The silver is mine and the gold is mine, says the Lord of hosts. Great will be the glory of this last house, more than of the first, says the Lord of hosts. And in this place I will give peace, says the Lord of hosts."[47] Haggai hinted that the things that Isaiah had said were yet to come actually had to be fulfilled there in the Temple, which had already begun to be rebuilt in his time.

MOSES: It can be as you say.

PETRUS: But tell me, O Moses, why is it that Haggai said: "Great will be the glory of this last house, more than that of the first"? In what sense was the glory of the last house greater than that of the first, when those precious decorations which were in the first were not in the last? For the ark of the Lord

46. Is 60.5–6.
47. Hg 2.7–10.

was not in the second [Temple], nor did they use the rational in it,[48] nor did the fire which consumed the sacrifices come there from heaven, nor was there an anointed one or a prophet at that time nor, similarly, many other things.

MOSES: We know nothing about this, certainly, except what we have heard from our sages, but they said only that the second house lasted ten years longer than the first.

PETRUS: This is in fact no glory.

MOSES: Then, without any doubt, Haggai lied.

PETRUS: Far from it. But in this respect the glory of the last house was great, more so than that of the first, because Christ came when it was still standing. His advent was a glory greater than all the aforementioned items have. But we can also understand that this same house may be called "last" and "first" in a much more subtle way, if you please, namely, because of its beginning and end. For since Christ, through whom divinity dwelled in that house as well, appeared toward its end, the glory in the last was greater than the first. For all the things that Isaiah pronounced and Haggai attested were fulfilled with the advent of Christ. At his coming, the multitude of the sea and of the earth was converted to him, and the heaven, the earth [*tellus*], and the seas were moved. They were moved, I say; that is, the inhabitants of the heavens and the earth and the sea rejoiced, and from all the directions of the earth they brought various offerings to Jerusalem for the praise of Christ himself.

MOSES: Why should I bring any further objection to you, when you explain all my authorities according to your own desire?

PETRUS: Because the truth has firm columns on which it is supported.

48. "Rational" (*rationale*): i.e., the high priest's oracular breastplate, so called at Ex 25.7.

TENTH *TITULUS*

OSES: I WANT YOU to return to the subject matter and, I beg you, explain to me the other parts of your faith. Since you believe, then, that Christ was both God and man, why did he allow himself to be crucified and why did he not release himself from the hands of the Jews? How was the power of his omnipotence so diminished?

PETRUS: He could have protected and safeguarded himself well enough, if he had wished, but he endured this of his own free will for the sake of the salvation of his own, although it was unwelcome to the flesh that was of this world. For the Word of God assumed flesh for no other reason than to free from the devil's captivity those who believed in him and who would yet believe in him.

MOSES: From your response, certainly, many questions arise. First, what is the devil; second, why did human beings fall into his power; third, why did God free human beings from his control when he had permitted them to fall under it; fourth, why, when he wanted to redeem them, did he not accomplish this by his power, but instead preferred to become incarnate and to suffer?

PETRUS: Since you have asked many questions at once, and one cannot respond completely to many at the same time, I want you to ask them separately, if you please, and then I will respond with what I think.

MOSES: At the outset, then, I would like to hear about the devil, and what he is.

PETRUS: The devil, O Moses, is a very subtle and spiritual matter [*res*], and he previously belonged to the orders of good angels. Two of the chief angels of his order are called Huza and Hazazel[1] in Hebrew, whereas they are called Haroth and Ma-

---

1. A great deal of confusion reigns in rabbinic sources over the meaning of the term or name Azazel. But in the first book of Enoch (6.4), Azazel (or Azael)

roth in the Arabic language.[2] And this devil was burdened by his sin and iniquity and was rendered somewhat heavier, as it were. Thus, having fallen from the summit of the heavens, he descended below gradually, and his habitation is here below the firmament.

MOSES: In fact it is written among us that Huza and Hazazel are devils, and are called leaders among them, but here I would rather hear with pleasure how you can demonstrate through philosophical reason that they exist, or how they exist.

PETRUS: At the outset, you have to know that there are nine parts to that art which is called necromancy [*nigromantia*].[3] The first four of these treat the four elements, and how we can operate in them naturally [*phisice*], whereas the remaining five treat only of what can be effected by the invocation of evil spirits. These evil spirits are called devils by humans.

MOSES: In fact, perhaps these devils were never, as you say, good angels, but were always evil spirits.

PETRUS: This is certainly untrue. For God made only what is good, since one reads in the truest Scripture: "God saw all the things he had made, and they were very good."[4] But they became evil because they performed evil.

MOSES: Since we know already that the devil exists, both

---

is one of the leaders of the angels who desired the daughters of men. Huza (or Uzza) is identical with Shemhazai, who is another angel fallen with Azazel. See Louis Ginzberg, *The Legends of the Jews*, 1: 149–51.

2. Qur'an 2.102.

3. Necromancy was listed among the various mantic or divinatory arts, whose origins were attributed to the devil or demons (see Isidore of Seville, *Etymologiarum siue Originum libri XX*, 8.9.3). Hugh of St. Victor identifies eleven such arts, which include necromancy, geomancy, hydromancy, aeromancy, and pyromancy. Necromancy deals with infernal things—that is, with conjuring up spirits of the dead especially. Geomancy involves earth, hydromancy water, aeromancy air, and pyromancy fire; these four arts, then, establish a correspondence to the four principal elements. See Hugh of St. Victor, *Didascalicon de studio legendi* 6.15, ed. Charles H. Buttimer (Washington, DC: The Catholic University of America Press, 1939), 133. I am unaware, however, of other attempts to divide necromancy into nine parts or sub-disciplines, as Petrus Alfonsi attempts to do. For a good discussion of necromancy, see Richard Kieckhefer, *Magic in the Middle Ages* (Cambridge: Cambridge University Press, 1993), 151–75. For a discussion of the place of necromancy in Alfonsi's conception of the liberal arts, see also María Jesús Lacarra Ducay, "La renovación de las artes liberales en Pedro Alfonso," 136–37.

4. Gn 1.31.

from the test of experience and from the approbation of the
sages, we ought to have no further doubt that he exists, nor do
we require a more protracted discussion on this question. Let
us put it aside then, and let us inquire why man fell under his
influence [*arbitrium*].

PETRUS: Since, then, God created Adam to his image and
likeness, for this reason he created him to be both composite
and simple, that is, superior among creatures: composite, indeed, so that he would inhabit the world and have power and
authority over it, and be susceptible to dissolution; whereas [he
created him] simple, so that when he was pleasing to the creator, he would cross over into the celestial homeland of the angels, without the death of the flesh. Since, I say, God created
him such as this, when the devil, who was dwelling in the lower
air near the ground, saw this, he envied him and sought his condemnation, so far as he was able, when he inspired his heart so
that he would violate God's commandment and eat of the forbidden fruit in order that, because of this, man would fall from
his dignity, just as he himself fell.

MOSES: Before you say anything else, Petrus, I would like you
to tell me why it is that you say that Adam was made both composite and simple. For these seem to be contraries, and you also,
when we debated the resurrection of the dead, denied that a
body could be both simple and composite at the same time. But
it is another contradiction that you said that he was created susceptible to death and created in such a way that he could cross
over to the homeland of the angels without death. For by the
one he is shown to be mortal, whereas by the other, immortal.

PETRUS: You know that all animals are composed of four elements. Moreover, they differ among themselves with respect
to the variety of these same elements that are unequally united
in their composition, according to their qualities and quantities. From this, moreover, the dissimilarity of diverse species appears. Seeing that the heat of those very elements from which
they are composed is opposed to the cold, the moist to the dry,
the void to the full, the heavy to the light, and the thin [*subtili-
tas*] to the thick, and that all the remaining qualities that exist
in them are contrary to one another, for this reason the things

composed from them are always changing: that is, they grow
and they are diminished, they grow warm and they grow cold,
and they are affected by the other accidents in turn. Illness,
however, arises from the fact that some of these qualities incline
so much toward the expulsion of the others, that if one grows
a little bit, the other is diminished a little bit. Whereas if one is
abundant beyond measure, the other diminishes so much that
it is not able to oppose it adequately, the links are dissolved,
those that are united are separated, and the composites are destroyed. This dissolution is called death. In truth when God created Adam, it pleased him to create him such that he would
be able both to die and not to die. Therefore, he made him
from the more refined elements and fashioned him in every respect equally proportioned, and he did this so that the qualities
of these elements would in no way have the power of overcom-
ing one another.[5] Moreover, he was created in such a way that
he was able not to die, and for this reason I have called him
simple and immortal. Indeed, he was immortal in this manner,
just as other simple [creatures] are all immortal. Some animals
provide evidence of this since, because they were created more
equally proportioned from the elements than others, undoubtedly they live longer. Whereas because he [Adam] was made
from the four [elements] subject to dissolution, for this reason I
have said that he is mortal and composite.

MOSES: What you say pleases me. But since, as you say, he was
able both to die and not to die, why did mortality overcome immortality, to the extent that until now every human is mortal?

PETRUS: This is what I was determined to explain, and this
is the reason why Adam fell into the devil's power. When [the

---

5. The twelfth-century scholar of Chartres, William of Conches, for example,
held that when still in Paradise, Adam's complexion "was perfectly temperate,
as he had equal shares of the four qualities." As a result of his sin and disobedi-
ence, however, Adam and his descendants have departed from a balanced, temperate complexion, and the human body subsequently suffered corruption. See
William of Conches, *Dragmaticon* 6.13.2–3, ed. Italo Ronca, CC CM 152 (Turnholt: Brepols, 1997). A translation appeared as *A Dialogue on Natural Philosophy
(Dragmaticon Philosophiae)*, trans. Italo Ronca and Matthew Curr (Notre Dame,
IN: University of Notre Dame Press, 1997). See also Honorius of Autun, *De philosophia mundi* 23 (PL 172: 55D).

devil] incited his heart to transgress the creator's obedience, he considered it. Whereas after he considered it, he chose it. After he chose it, he desired it. After he desired it, he did it. Moreover, when he did it, he sinned. In fact, after he sinned, he lost the balance that he had (and thus the immortality) and received mortality altogether, as is the nature of composites, to the extent that it could not again be separated from him. This is why he received a definition of such a kind that he was said to be rational and mortal, and in truth he and everyone who proceeded from his seed had this same nature. And it is certainly just that if one thing comes forth from another, it will receive the likeness of its nature. Whereas since Adam's soul had a more subtle and stronger nature than the body, because he offered assent to that sin and did not resist it when he could have, so every soul[6] that has joined itself to a body begotten from that corruption has been unable to pass over to the summit of heaven (which was its nature) when it departed from the body, on account of that sin. Instead it remained in the lower air here near the ground. Because the soul fell as a stranger, as it were, to the place that was his, that is, belonged to the devil, on account of this the devil had power over it, and his desire, which he had desired himself, was fulfilled. Whereas because in fact Adam's sin was double—namely, spiritual and corporeal: spiritual, because he elected to obey the devil rather than to believe God, which pertains to the spirit; corporeal, however, because he took delight in the sweetness of the forbidden fruit, which belongs to the body—clearly for this reason he sustained a double punishment, that is, the death of the flesh and the death of the soul.

MOSES: You have explained both in a skillful and logical [*ordinate*] manner, it seems to me, why Adam (and indeed every human being) fell under the devil's influence on account of his sin. But I would also like this to be made clear to me, if you know the reason: why and how Adam lost that balanced nature which he had in his complexion [*compositio*] because of his physical transgression of a commandment.

PETRUS: You know, then, that since Adam was made equally proportioned from all the elements, he had to have a bal-

6. Reading *omnis anima* (A) for *omnia anima* (B).

anced temper of dispositions: of anger and sorrow, of eating and drinking, and others, none of which are overabundant or diminish in a human being except from an overabundance or diminution of qualities. When, in fact, the devil counseled him to violate the command of his Lord, he himself pondered over it so that he elected to do it, and his soul did not forbid it as it could have done. Then, from that point on, he began to sin and to cast off his [complexional] balance so that he lost that temper, and although he did not need to—rather, it was forbidden to him—he longed to eat and gradually developed the need, and ate, and then he lost [complexional] balance altogether. If he had thought about this at the outset, whether what he heard was good or bad, he would only have considered it, and, moreover, he would not have elected to do it; neither would he have sinned, without any doubt, nor lost [complexional] balance. For example, just as when someone is neither too joyful nor too sad, but has a balanced proportion of each, if he hears some rumor about himself over which he is able to become angry or not, if he wishes, when he thinks about it in such a way that what he heard would make him distempered [*aegre ferat*], indeed the red bile from which anger proceeds is produced in him from a thought of this type, and thus he becomes heated and angered.[7] The more heated he becomes, the more bile is produced, until he is completely angered, and in this way that measured and tempered nature of sadness and joy that he had before is destroyed. Whereas if he does not reflect upon that rumor so that it annoys him, the bile is not produced; neither does the man become heated or angered, nor is a tempered nature separated from him.[8]

MOSES: To be sure, we believe that Adam sinned because of the serpent's counsel, and that every human being is given up to death for his sin. For our sages have attested that there were many human beings who would not have died at all but for the serpent's counsel and Adam's sin. We do not believe, however,

7. Reading *irascitur* (A) for *erascitur* (B).
8. For a discussion of Alfonsi's use of medical sources and concepts to explain Adam's fall, see Irven M. Resnick, "Humoralism and Adam's Body: Twelfth-Century Debates and Petrus Alfonsi's *Dialogus contra Judaeos*," *Viator* 36 (2005): 181–95.

that the souls of the saints descended to hell after death. I beg
you to explain why [they should do so], if you have some authority concerning this.

PETRUS: I will clarify this for you in brief, but, nevertheless,
I will introduce no very clear authorities for it. In Genesis one
reads that Jacob, after having gathered his sons and daughters
together to comfort him over his son Joseph, was unwilling to be
comforted, saying: "I will go down to my son into hell, mourning."[9]

MOSES: Certainly, Jacob said this with respect to the body.
For he wanted "hell" to be understood to mean the ground in
which everyone is buried, as if to say: until I die and am buried
in the ground with my son, I will never cease to mourn over his
death.

PETRUS: What you say is not true. For he knew that his son
had not been buried in the ground; rather, he thought that he
had been devoured by some wild beast. Therefore, he said this
with respect to the soul: "I will go down to my son into hell,
mourning," as if to say, because my son is dead I will die, and,
mourning, I will go down to hell where his soul and the souls
of all the dead are. Even David attested to this in the psalm,
when he said: "Who is the man that will live, and not see death,
who will rescue[10] his soul from the hand of hell?"[11] With what
he said—"Who is the man that will live, and not see death"—he
implied that there is no human being who will not die. By this,
however—"who will rescue his soul from the hand of hell"—he
hinted that there was no soul in his day that could be saved from
the hand of hell. So, too, Hezekiah, although he was a good and
holy man—just as he himself attests in his prayer when he said:
"I beseech you, O Lord, remember, I pray, how I have walked
before you in truth and with a perfect heart, and have done
what is good in your eyes."[12] Even though he was so holy, I say
that nevertheless he revealed that he himself had to descend to

9. Gn 37.35.

10. "Rescue" (*eruet*), where the Vulg. reads *salvans*.

11. Ps 88.49.

12. 2 Kgs 20.3. "Good in your eyes" (*bonum est in oculis tuis*), whereas the
Vulg. reads, "what is pleasing before you" (*quod placitum est coram te*).

hell when, as we read in Isaiah, he spoke in the following words: "In the midst of my days I will go to the gates of hell."[13]

MOSES: If it is as you claim, then the souls of the patriarchs and the prophets and all the other saints who died were confined in one and the same place with the souls of the ungodly, before the death of the one whom you call Christ.

PETRUS: Actually, it is true that all were in shadow or darkness, but they were not all in a place of punishment (that is, torment), for each one was requited according to his merits; nevertheless, all were in hell and subject to the authority of the devil. None of the dead from Adam until Christ's death avoided the halls of hell. And we perceive this from the words of Moses, who, although he admonished the children of Israel to fulfill earnestly the commandments and proclaimed to them that they would possess rewards for doing so, never promised them any of the felicity of paradise, for it was already known to all at that time that none would enter there before the death of Christ.

MOSES: I do not think that Moses avoided speaking of paradise for the reason you have said. Rather, he knew that he could admonish them to obey God's precepts or deter them from their iniquities more readily by [referring to] visible goods, which they greatly desired, or by [referring to] present evils or difficulties which they feared, than if he were to speak to them about future torments or about the felicity of heaven, about which they were ignorant.

PETRUS: Your opinion is wrong. For if he urged them on with a double reward or a double punishment, he would admonish them just so much more to avoid evil and embrace the good. Besides, if you wish, I will show you that even according to your faith concerning this very matter the souls of the saints were in hell and under the authority of the devil before Christ's death.

MOSES: To be sure, I desire nothing other than the truth.

PETRUS: At the outset, then, I ask you, where have the souls of the saints been, since you believe that they were not in hell?

MOSES: Certainly, they have been in heaven.

PETRUS: Answer this, too, I beg you, whether you have ever

13. Is 38.10.

read or heard how high the power of those who work the art of necromancy can rise.

MOSES: Only so far as the firmament.

PETRUS: And can anything cross over that?

MOSES: It is surprising that you ask that, since you hear it said not only by wise men but also by old women in a proverb: "You have only as much [power] as the devil has in heaven."

PETRUS: Now then, I want you to tell me whether you believe that what one reads in the first book of Kings—namely, that Samuel was raised by a woman who had a divining spirit[14]—was a fact or a fantasy?

MOSES: It is shown to be true in many ways. In one, because the book clearly talks about how he rose up from the earth. She herself responded truthfully concerning the nature of his form and his age and apparel, and how she spoke by divine inspiration [*ex parte dei*] to all the things Saul asked, and there was nothing false in whatever she said. Second, unless Saul knew that it was in the woman's power to raise Samuel, he would not have asked that he be raised. Third, our sages assert that God forgave Saul his sin upon his death, based on Samuel's discussion with Saul. From what he said, "tomorrow you and your sons will be with me,"[15] they proved that Saul went into a place of rest with Samuel.

PETRUS: It is disagreeable to debate any longer whether this is true or false. But if it is as you claim, how could he be raised by the art of necromancy if he was [already] in heaven? But if he was not in heaven, then undoubtedly he was resting in hell under the authority of the devil.

MOSES: You have ambushed me well and overcome me, and it has been adequately demonstrated up to this point how man came into the power of the devil.[16] It remains for you to explain, then, why the Lord released him from there, since he was allowed to fall.

PETRUS: Once the human race was damned, then, by the ser-

---

14. Cf. 1 Sm 28.7–12.

15. 1 Sm 28.19.

16. Cf. B.T. *Shabbat* 152b–153a, where it is said, concerning Samuel, that for twelve months after death, the body exists and the soul can ascend or descend. After twelve months, the soul ascends but does not descend again.

pent's counsel, and damned, I say, from the sin of the first parent, Adam, and punished, as we say, with a second death, since there were many holy men who fell into the devil's snare having committed no sin of their own beyond that ancient sin (and natural sin, as it were), the Creator of the human race saw this and, moved by pity [*pietas*] and mercy, willed that they be freed from there.

MOSES: Since, as you claim, he was moved with such pity over them, why did he suffer them to be confined there for so long, until the time of the one whom you call Christ?

PETRUS: To be sure, he did not do this based on some form of justice, but only from his pity and absolute goodness; and absolute goodness, as we said at the beginning of our discussion, ought to have neither measure nor limit.

MOSES: And why, as I said above, since he wanted to redeem them, did he not accomplish this with his power, but preferred instead that his Word become incarnate and suffer?

PETRUS: It was in fact the most perfect wisdom to release them in this way, just as was found in his other ancient deeds. When previously, as you yourself know, he prepared to lead the people of Israel out of Egyptian slavery and wished to slay the firstborn of the Egyptians with an evil spirit, while keeping his own [people] safe, he commanded them to sacrifice a lamb or a kid for each individual house and to daub the entryways[17] of the homes with its blood, so that when the evil spirit came it would pass over the house daubed with blood. But although he wanted to safeguard them, could he not have done so without this act?

MOSES: Certainly he could have.

PETRUS: Why, then, did he require this sort of liberation?

MOSES: Clearly it is his wisdom that assigns some cause for the individual things by which he wishes to lead them to their outcome, just as he wanted to redeem them from that death by means of the sacrifice of a lamb or kid. We, however, cannot perceive all these causes of things. For the mysteries of God are so profound and inscrutable that no one can penetrate them.

PETRUS: Why, then, do you express surprise when asking why

17. Adopting the variant reading *ostia* in place of *hostia*.

the Lord sent his Word to become incarnate and to die for the redemption of humanity?

MOSES: And why did he not redeem them from that sin of Adam with the sacrifice of some animal, just as in the law he commanded that some sheep be sacrificed for sin?

PETRUS: O most stupid of all men, where could so many sheep be found? For certainly it would have been necessary to sacrifice as many sheep as there were people from the beginning of the world itself, and as many as there would be in the future even until its consummation. Besides this, that sin that had seized both the body and the soul could only reasonably be removed by a sacrifice that had both a body and a soul.

MOSES: Therefore, since he wanted them to be redeemed by such a sacrifice, why could that sacrifice not have been accomplished through some prophet or any other holy man? Why instead did he permit his Word to receive flesh and to undergo death?

PETRUS: Because it was necessary that the man who would die to redeem us from such a sin (and so great a sin) be immune from every sin; for if he were not, he would need to redeem his own sins by his death. Such a one could not be found who was merely a man. For the nature of the body is not able to guard itself against sin, as God attests in Genesis even when saying that a man's mind regularly inclines to wicked deeds from youth.[18] Also, Solomon said in Ecclesiastes: "There is no man on earth who does good and does not sin."[19] Therefore, it was God's reason and wisdom that his Word receive a human body, to guard it free of all contagion and sin, so that he who was so clean and free of every vice could redeem that general transgression, and he who was drawn from the One who is the beginning of all things could remove the first sin of all. Indeed, he was begotten without a carnal father to remove the offense of him who was created without a father and, moreover, so that on the day of judgment God would reasonably condemn those who were liberated from the devil's snare by his son's death, when they in turn withdrew from him by their own iniquity.

18. Cf. Gn 8.21.
19. Eccl 7.21.

MOSES: Since you claim that the one whom you call Christ died of his free will for the redemption of humanity, why do you condemn his killers and why do you assert that they are guilty of sin when they only fulfilled his will?

PETRUS: Certainly, if they had done this with that intention—namely, to fulfill his will—and if they had believed that by his death they would escape from the power of the devil, undoubtedly they would have incurred no sin. Whereas since they denied him and slew him from envy, this is why they are guilty of such a great crime, and this is why neither in the present age nor in the future will they display compassion or remorse [*tribulatio*], for as long as they remain in this wickedness. Let me show you by an analogy that they are guilty and have been condemned deservedly, and you yourself will judge that it is right.

MOSES: Certainly if, when I hear it, it is right, I will judge that it is right.

PETRUS: Once a certain man had one boat, and it was his intention to burn it, in order to harvest the nails from it and to make charcoal from its planks. While he was deliberating over this, however, an enemy of his came to the boat at night, and, not knowing his intention, he burned it from hatred. When the morning came, however, the aforementioned man found the nails of his ship on one side, and the charcoal on another, just as he wanted. And another example: There was a certain stone house that belonged to a certain man, which he wanted to dismantle so that he could make for himself another building from its stones. By chance, an enemy of his tore it down one day so that not one stone remained on another stone,[20] and he did this not to fulfill his will—of which he was ignorant—but from hatred. When, however, the already mentioned man came to his house on the next day, he found that what he had thought to do and wanted to do had already been accomplished. Since in fact neither the one who burned the boat nor the one who tore down the house acted to fulfill the will of his enemy, but only acted out of envy, how will you judge them?

MOSES: To be sure, I judge that they are guilty and should be punished.

20. Cf. Mk 13.2; Lk 19.44.

PETRUS: For the same reason, they are guilty and subject to judgment who slew Christ—not in order to fulfill his will, but from the poison of hatred and envy.

MOSES: Without any doubt they would be guilty if they acted in the manner which you describe. Yet they never acted in this way, but rather slew him with a just judgment.

PETRUS: And what crime did they impute to him, since they delivered him over to death?

MOSES: That he was a magician and that he led the sons of Israel into error by the magical art. In addition to this, he called himself the Son of God.

PETRUS: It is not at all surprising that they spoke these as well as other lies, even though he had come to redeem them. For Hosea prophesied this concerning them: "Woe to them, for they have departed from me. They shall be wasted because they have transgressed against me. And I redeemed them and they have spoken lies against me."[21] Besides this, where was he able to learn so much about the art of magic that with it he changed water into wine,[22] fed five thousand people with five loaves,[23] healed lepers[24] and those suffering dropsy,[25] and restored movement to the lame,[26] hearing to the deaf, speech to the mute, sight to the blind,[27] and, what is greater still than all of these things, raised the dead,[28] and performed all the other miracles, too many to enumerate here?

MOSES: Our sages say, certainly, that he learned it in Egypt.[29]

21. Hos 7.13.
22. Cf. Jn 2.1–11.
23. Cf. Mt 14.13–23; Mk 6.31–46; Lk 9.10–17; and Jn 6.1–15.
24. Cf. Mt 8.2–4; Mk 1.40–44; Lk 5.12–14; 17.11–19.
25. Cf. Lk 14.2–4.
26. Cf. Mt 9.32–33; Lk 11.14.
27. Cf. Mt 9.27–31; Mk 8.22–26; 10.46–52; Lk 18.35–43; and Jn 9.1–11.
28. Cf. Mk 5.35–43; Lk 7.11–15; and Jn 11.
29. For the claim that magic was introduced from Egypt, see B.T. *Shabbat* 104b (and see *supra*, p. 106, n. 30). The notion that Jesus had magical powers is present in the *Toledot Yeshu*, where it is suggested that he acquired these when he stole (and misused) the ineffable name of God. The charge that Jesus learned the magic arts in Egypt can, however, be located at least as early as the second-century pagan philosopher Celsus's *On the True Doctrine* 2.2. See *On the True Doctrine: A Discourse Against the Christians*, trans. Joseph Hoffmann (New York, Oxford: Oxford University Press, 1987), 57. See also Hoffmann's *Jesus Outside the Gospels* (New York: Prometheus Books, 1984), 46–50. In possibly a late

PETRUS: Do your words confirm, then, that at that time in Egypt there were those who performed the same deeds?

MOSES: That can be so.

PETRUS: Why, then, were their deeds not made known and reported, just as his were? Moreover, why did the wise men of Egypt receive his teaching and his law, if they knew him to be a magician?

MOSES: I really do not know how to answer you on this. For I have not heard that they ever believed in him, or how or when they may have done so.

PETRUS: Let us put aside these things for a moment and let us inquire into his specific deeds, so that we may inquire whether they were performed by magic art or some other natural science [*phisica*], or rather by the power of God.

MOSES: You speak well. And I do not care much to investigate his lesser deeds. For if you demonstrate that his greater deeds were performed by the power of God, I will not have any doubt about the lesser ones.

PETRUS: You speak wisely, and, as you say, I agree to examine whatever has to be investigated first.

MOSES: First of all, I want you to explain to me how the lepers were cleansed, and how the blind were illuminated.

PETRUS: You know that a leper cannot be cured in any way other than by medicine, or by the power of God.[30] If by medicine, then he is purged either by potions taken internally or by ointments applied externally.[31] Since, however, no person saw

---

twelfth-century Jewish polemical text from western Europe one also encounters the claim that Jesus learned the magical arts in Egypt. See Frank Talmage, "An Hebrew Polemical Treatise. Anti-Cathar and Anti-Orthodox," *Harvard Theological Review* 60 (1967), 339. In counterpoint, perhaps, later Christian polemics would commonly link Jews and magic. See, for example, Anna Foa, "The Witch and the Jew: Two Alikes that Were Not the Same," and Ronnie Po-Chia Hsia,"Witchcraft, Magic, and the Jews in Late Medieval and Early Modern Germany," in *From Witness to Witchcraft: Jews and Judaism in Medieval Christian Thought,* ed. Jeremy Cohen, Wolfenbütteler Mittelalter-Studien 11 (Wiesbaden: Harrassowitz Verlag, 1996), 361–74; 419–33.

30. Jewish polemicists were accustomed to point out that prophets of the Old Testament also cured leprosy by invoking divine assistance (see 2 Kgs 5.1–14), and therefore they, too, could perform the same miracles that Christians ascribed to Jesus. See, for example, *The Polemic of Nestor the Priest*, 1: 64.

31. In his *De natura rerum*, the thirteenth-century author Thomas of Cantimpré mentions one such ointment that, applied externally, is said to be effective

him administer any medicine, but he cured them in an instant with only a word, then it is in fact clear that it was done by the power of God.

MOSES: Do we not read that the magician Firminus cleansed one leper?[32]

PETRUS: It is certainly a lie that he cured him, whereas in fact he himself deceived men's eyes with his magical art and caused to appear real what was not there. A proof of this fact is that after a period of time the sick person relapsed into the same illness, and although on the outside his skin appeared to another person to be clean, nevertheless he never lost the illness internally, as he said himself.[33] In addition, however, one reads in

---

against leprosy. He notes, "A mole burned to ashes and sprinkled with the white of egg and placed on the face is a remedy against leprosy." Thomas of Cantimpré, *De natura rerum (Lib. IV–XII): Tacuinum sanitatis*, codice C-67 (fols. 2v–116r) de la Biblioteca Universitaria de Granada, comentarios a la edición facsimil, ed. Luis García Ballester, vol. 1 (Granada: Universidad de Granada, 1974), fol. 29v, p. 272. His contemporary, Albert the Great, notes, too, that certain poisons, taken internally, can also be effective against leprosy. See his *Quaestiones super de animalibus*, 7, q. 31, ed. Ephrem Filthaut (Monasterii Westf.: Aschendorff, 1955), 185, 69.

32. Perhaps the Firminus mentioned in Augustine's *Confessiones* 7.6.8–10, who is described as skilled in astrology and magic. There is, however, no mention of his healing a leper. Another possibility, suggested to me by the Warburg Institute's Professor Charles Burnett, is that "Firminus" may be a corruption of "Firmus," a Latin equivalent of the Arabic name "Thabit." If this is the case, then this could be a reference to Thabit ibn Qurra (d. 901), an astronomer and mathematician, some of whose scientific works were translated into Latin by Gerard of Cremona in the twelfth century. No certain identification seems possible, however.

33. It is unclear whether Alfonsi means here that the necromancer eliminated only the external signs of leprosy, while its internal cause (rooted in the imbalance of the humors) remained, or whether he is referring to the common notion that leprosy is not only a disease of the body but also an affliction of the soul stemming from immorality and depravity. For a contemporary medical discussion of leprosy, see *Tratado médico de Constantino el Africano. Constantini Liber de elephancia*, ed. and trans. Ana Isabel Martín Ferreira (Valladolid: Universidad de Valladolid, 1996). For common medieval notions of leprosy, see Saul Nathaniel Brody, *The Disease of the Soul: Leprosy in Medieval Literature* (Ithaca: Cornell University Press, 1974); also, Geneviève Pichon, "Essai sur la lèpre du haut moyen age," *Le moyen âge* 90:3–4 (1984): 331–56. For the link between leprosy and depravity, especially sexual depravity, see Joseph Zias, "Lust and Leprosy: Confusion or Correlation?" *Bulletin of the American Schools of Oriental Research* 275 (1989): 27–31; and Stephen R. Ell, "Blood and Sexuality in Medieval Leprosy," *Janus: Revue internationale de l'histoire des sciences, de la médecine de la pharmacie et de la technique* 71: 1–4 (1984): 153–64.

the necromantic art that a leper will never truly be cured by it. Concerning the blind, however, or indeed those who were born blind, natural science [*phisica*] rejects that medicine can make them see. In fact, the magician Assitha attests that light is not truly restored to them by necromantic art.[34]

MOSES: That can be so. But what will you say about the dead, since Assitha professes the same thing—that he can raise them and that a man can speak with them—and he reveals the manner in which it can be done in his book. And, on the other hand, what will you say about what one reads in the book of Kings,[35] how Samuel was raised by the woman with a divining spirit, as we said?

PETRUS: Actually, it is true that Assitha claims this [in his book], just as you say; but with respect to the resuscitation of the dead there is an enormous difference between an act of God and one that occurs by magical art. For the dead who are raised by some magician are unable to walk further than the length of their shadow, but when they reach its end they return to the ground. Those, however, who are raised by the power of God drink and eat, and they walk along in whatever manner and however far and however long as it pleases God, so that those whom Elisha[36] and Elijah[37] and Christ raised live just like the rest of mankind.

MOSES: Since it has been clearly demonstrated up to this point that, just like the other prophets, that man accomplished all he did not by magical art, but rather by the power of God, I want you to tell me why he presumed to call himself the Son of God and not a prophet.

PETRUS: Certainly he did so because he was truly the Son of God. Since we demonstrated that above with many authorities, when we described him as being both God and man, it is not necessary to offer additional proof here. But if you want us once again to enter into a strict disputation, I will demonstrate to you by reason that he spoke the truth when he called himself the Son of God.

MOSES: If you please.

---

34. Like Firminus, Assitha has not been identified.
35. Cf. 1 Sm 28.7.   36. Cf. 2 Kgs 4.32–37.
37. Cf. 1 Kgs 17.17–24.

PETRUS: Then, can one who effects something by God's power, effect it without God's will?

MOSES: It seems to me to be necessary that one who does something by the power of God only effects it according to the will of the same God.

PETRUS: And one who works through the power of God and works his will, does it not follow that he is God's friend and his faithful servant?

MOSES: Certainly that follows. For in our reading we found that the holy prophets who performed miracles in days past, like Moses and Elijah and Elisha and many others who accomplished many miracles in their lives, were beloved by God and faithful to him.

PETRUS: And it is necessary that one who is God's friend and faithful to him not say anything that is false about God or on behalf of God.

MOSES: That is true.

PETRUS: Since, then, Christ, as was proved above, performed miracles by God's power and will, and it follows from this that he was his friend and faithful servant, one concludes without a doubt that he never made a false claim about God or on his behalf. And since this is the case, then he called himself the Son of God truly.

MOSES: What you said is reasonable [*ratio est*]. But with great astonishment I wonder about this because, although at that time there were many men endowed with great intellect and wisdom, they did not perceive him to be such. If they had known this, why did they reject his faith and teaching and, by crucifying him, knowingly incur the damnation of their souls?

PETRUS: Clearly they did this from envy, just as we declared, namely, because they were afraid of losing their rank and reputation on account of him. And we find something analogous to this at the time when Jeroboam was made king of Israel. Indeed, once Solomon had died, his kingdom was divided into two, as Scripture attests, and his son Rehoboam obtained one part, and his servant Jeroboam[38] obtained the other part. After having taken counsel with his nobles, however, Jeroboam made

38. Cf. 1 Kgs 11.26.

two golden calves, which his people adored, lest, if they were
to go up often to Jerusalem to pray and offer sacrifice (as was
the custom) perhaps they would remain there sometimes and
take the side of Rehoboam, and Jeroboam would lose his rank.
This is just as this same Scripture teaches when it says: "And Jeroboam said in his heart: Now the kingdom will return to the
house of David, if this people goes up to offer sacrifices in the
house of the Lord in Jerusalem, and the heart of this people
will turn to their lord Rehoboam, the king of Judah, and they
will kill me and return to him. And finding out a device, he
made two golden calves and said to them: Go no more to Jerusalem. Behold your gods, O Israel, who brought you out of
the land of Egypt."[39] Although, however, both Jeroboam himself and his leading men [*proceres*] were endowed with much
wisdom—on the one hand, because of Solomon, who preceded
him and who, according to Scripture's testimony, was the wisest
of all men (both of those who went before him and those who
followed after), and, on the other hand, because of that peace,
which was great in the time of Solomon himself,[40] which provided a great opportunity to learn wisdom—in fact it is clear that,
just as we said, they did this from envy and out of fear of losing
the kingdom. Therefore, you ought not to be surprised if the
doctors of the law and the scribes slew Christ from the poison of
envy, since they feared that they would lose their glory and rank
on account of him.

MOSES: What you say appears true. Nevertheless, I still wonder greatly (although I have asked about the same thing elsewhere), I wonder, I say, since he was as powerful as you believe,
why did he not avenge himself immediately?

PETRUS: Beyond question, he acted in this way owing to his
great goodness and mercy. And we perceive this from his words
[spoken] while he was hanging on the Cross, saying: "Father,
forgive them for they know not what they do."[41] This shows that
he loved them beyond measure, even though they acted wickedly against him, as the prophet Zechariah attests: "And they

39. 1 Kgs 12.26–28.
40. Cf. 1 Kgs 5.12.
41. Lk 23.24.

ELEVENTH *TITULUS*

MOSES: UP TO THIS point, it has been shown well enough that that man accepted death of his own free will to redeem the human race. Now, however, I want to discuss with you how he was resurrected on the third day, just as you said in the exposition of your faith. And indeed it could very well be that, since (as you say) the fullness of divinity dwelled in him,[1] and he restored other dead people to life, that he revived himself. But in this regard I ask you whether he was both God and man after he was resurrected, just as he was earlier, or not?

PETRUS: Undoubtedly, I believe that he was. For when his soul was released from his body to descend to hell to free good men from there, still divinity itself never withdrew from the soul; therefore, divinity remained with it always, even when it returned to the body. This is why then and now and for all eternity he will be both God and man.

MOSES: I reckon that it is enough that you believe this to be the case. But there remains one more thing I want you to explain to me. For since he received flesh for no other reason than to free the sons of Adam from the yoke of the devil, after (as you say) he fulfilled this as he willed, why again did he burden himself with the body's weight?

PETRUS: Indeed, Christ's body was subtle and entirely pure from every sin, and he did not contract any sin either by himself or from his first parent, Adam. And since this was the case, did he ever have to die at all, since even Adam died only because of sin, and, in addition, since divinity dwelled in him?

MOSES: No.

PETRUS: Since, therefore, he accepted death not on account of any sin that he committed but rather only in order to save his own, did he not deservedly have to be revived [from death]?

1. Cf. Col 2.9.

239

MOSES: The order of the argument clearly demands this. But why did he hurry so to be raised up and why did he not wait to be raised up at the end of the world,[2] along with the other good people who had died?

PETRUS: For indeed the other dead committed many sins in this world. In fact, they received death, namely, the punishment for sin, for Adam's transgression, and this is why they could not be raised until it pleased God to do so. He, however, took neither sin from Adam nor anything else, as we said. Instead, he gave himself over to death on one day voluntarily and for our redemption, whereas on the next day he descended to hell to lead good men out of there. When, then, he had completed all the tasks for which he had come, and there was nothing else that he had to do, so to speak, he was deservedly resurrected on the third day. Besides, even Enoch[3] and Elijah,[4] because they were saintly and worthy men (just as both we and you believe), are still alive, and although they have to die at the end of the world, nevertheless they will be resurrected immediately because of their sanctity. Since this is the case, ought not the body that was the holiest of all and the purest from sin be raised immediately, as he willed? Moreover, it was necessary for him to be raised for this reason: that just as when he descended to hell he freed the dead from the authority of the devil through his death, so, too, by his Resurrection he freed those still to come from the tyranny of the devil because when they hear that he was resurrected, they believe, and in this way they escape from his yoke.

MOSES: What you say is reasonable. But can you provide some authority from the prophets, that he had to be raised?

PETRUS: Certainly I can. For David said in the Psalms: "You will add days to the days of the king, his years even to the day of generation and generation."[5] Could this prophecy be said of any king except Christ? The prophet wanted to be understood by the "days of the king," to be sure, that defined period when Christ lived in the world before the passion. When he said, how-

2. That is, at the general resurrection.
3. Gn 5.24 implies that Enoch was taken up into heaven, whereas Sir 44.16 claims that he was "translated into paradise." See also Sir 49.16.
4. Cf. 2 Kgs 2.11.
5. Ps 60.7.

ever, that days must be added to the days of the king, which he pronounced without limitation, he understood the time after his Resurrection. He also indicated that this would be without end when he added: "his years even to the day of generation and generation." In Isaiah, too, one reads: "Now will I rise up, says the Lord, now will I be exalted and now will I lift up myself."[6] And the Lord wanted these three to be understood in this way: for when he said, "now will I rise up," he spoke of the Resurrection of his body from death; when, however, there follows, "now will I lift up myself," he hinted at his ascent to heaven; whereas the third, which is, "now will I be exalted," he added with regard to the exaltation and glory of those who believe in him.

MOSES: Since you have mentioned the Ascension, and I have been inclined to ask you about this for some time, I beg that you explain to me now, if you please, how you believe this occurred. For reason debars a weighty thing from being supported by or ascending above a light one.

PETRUS: Actually, it is my belief that he ascended to heaven. For I believe that the power of his omnipotence was so great that, however it was done, it was possible to be done, because it pleased him. To be sure, if I were to treat this with some believer, I would say no more. Whereas because you are without faith, and understand only what is so obvious as to be nearly palpable, I will respond to you a little more explicitly, both for this reason and because I desire that thereby you will believe something of the good.

MOSES: I demand that you do so.

PETRUS: Certainly you know that the goose and the hen, the sparrow and the lark, were all created from the four elements?

MOSES: Of course I know that.

PETRUS: Tell me, then, why do the sparrow and the lark rise up when flying, whereas the goose and the hen cannot do the same thing?

MOSES: Because the former have a small body and are lighter, and the latter are larger and, for that reason, heavier.

PETRUS: If lightness depends on size, why does the vulture or

6. Is 33.10.

the eagle rise up higher than all others when flying, since it is
larger than all others?

MOSES: Because its body is composed of the more subtle elements.

PETRUS: And although it is light and subtle, how is it that its
body can lift off?

MOSES: Undoubtedly, [because of] spirit, without which not
only could it not fly, but it could not be moved at all.

PETRUS: Since, then, Christ's body after the Resurrection
was extremely light and subtle—indeed, since at death it lost
all weight and thickness, a proof of which is that it no longer required either food or drink—since, I say, it was such as this and
it had with it both spirit (that is, soul) and divinity in addition
(which, as Moses attests, has dominion over and surpasses all
the spirits of the flesh), could it not ascend to heaven when it
pleased? As far as Elijah is concerned, whose body acquired no
subtlety from death and nevertheless ascended on high in the
presence of his disciple Elisha,[7] how do you believe this to have
been accomplished both according to reason and according to
science [phisica]?

MOSES: To be sure, Elijah fasted a great deal and ate very
little, so that his body acquired so much lightness and subtlety
that it could rise up into the air, where the angels received him
and carried him off, as it pleased God.

PETRUS: Therefore, since Christ's body was made subtle both
by death and by the fact that after the Resurrection it was not
necessary for him to eat or drink, and in fact he contained within himself the fullness of divinity, which is above the angels, why,
then, was he unable to ascend to heaven, just as we say he did?
But there is also a reason why he ascended [to heaven]. For if
the Lord called the place where Moses stood holy, when God appeared to him in the burning bush, owing to his proximity to it
for one hour, and he ordered Moses to remove his shoes owing
to its sanctity, saying: "Remove the shoes from your feet, for the
place whereon you stand is holy ground,"[8] then was not the body
of Christ, in which the fullness of divinity dwelled not just for a

7. Cf. 2 Kgs 2.11.
8. Ex 3.5.

moment but perpetually, the holy of holies? Since such was the
case, did he have to remain behind in the squalor of this world
after the Resurrection? Rather, just as we affirm by right reason,
he abandoned it and rose up into heaven.

MOSES: You have proved this with a clear argument, and you
have introduced a good analogy. But is one able to find any authority concerning his Ascension in the prophets?

PETRUS: Certainly one will be able to. For we read in Genesis that God spoke of this to Abraham, although he did so in a
mystery [*occulte*]. For it is written: "And he brought him outside
and said to him: Look up to heaven and count the stars, if you
can number them. And he said: So will your seed be. And Abraham believed God, and it was reputed to him unto justice."[9] But
tell me, Moses, what is the meaning of what he said: "And he
brought him outside"? Why did he do this? Was Abraham unable to know inside as well as outside that he was unable to number the stars? Or was God unable to speak to him inside as well
as outside, if he wished? Likewise, when he said: "So will your
seed be." Why did he not say: "I will make your seed just like the
stars of heaven, and your seed will not be numbered"? Just as he
said in another place: "I will make your seed as the sand of the
sea; if anyone can number the sand of the sea, so will your seed
be numbered."[10]

MOSES: Certainly, I know no other reason for this, other than
that it pleased God to speak in this way.

PETRUS: I want you to understand the entire passage, and I
want you to know that Scripture did not employ any word without reason. The Lord caused "he brought him outside" to be
written for two reasons. One was to show him the location of
heaven, which is indicated by this passage: that is, "Look up to
heaven." Whereas the other reason was to show him the multitude of the stars, and this is why he said: "count the stars, if
you can number them." Moreover, what comes next, "thus will
your seed be," is expressed in Hebrew with an expression that

9. Gn 15.5–6.
10. The author conflates Gn 13.15 and Gn 32.12. In the Vulg. the first passage compares Abraham's seed to the dust of the earth, whereas the second
compares it to the sands of the sea.

in Latin represents both "hither" [*huc*] and "thus" [*sic*], namely,
[using] "co" (כֹּה), which signifies both a location and an analogy. Now if he wanted to express it in such a way that it would
only signify location, certainly he would have said "henna" (הֵנָּה);
whereas if only to represent "thus" [*sic*], he would have expressed
it as "cacha" (כָּכָה). Therefore, by the fact that he employed "co"
(כֹּה) he wanted to be understood there both the place in which
Abraham's seed (namely, Christ, after his Ascension) would be,
and the multitude of his seed.

MOSES: I know that what "co" (כֹּה) represents in Hebrew,
Latin represents with "sic," but I do not think that it ever signifies place [*locus*].

PETRUS: Certainly it does. For one reads in Exodus that Moses saw "an Egyptian man striking one of the Hebrews, his brethren. And when he had looked hither and thither, and saw no
one there, he slew the Egyptian and hid him in the sand."[11] Now,
where "hither and thither" [*huc atque illuc*] is expressed in the
Latin, in the Hebrew you find "co" and "co" (כֹּה וָכֹה). But also as
confirmation of this opinion, there follows in the same passage:
"And Abraham believed God, and it was reputed to him unto justice." Now, why did Abraham believe God in this promise more
than in other promises that God had made to him?

MOSES: Actually, he believed in all of them, since he was never without faith.

PETRUS: And why does Scripture not say that he believed in
those specific promises, just as it does here? Or, since he always
had faith, why was it not silent here as well in the same way, just
as it was silent about this in the other places?

MOSES: I do not know, but this is what it says.

PETRUS: Did we not say above that Scripture did not employ
any expression without reason?

MOSES: Tell me, then, why it said this.

PETRUS: Actually, because that promise concerning the ascent of his seed into heaven is miraculous [*contra usum*] and
incredible, and therefore in order to demonstrate his sanctity it
added: "Abraham believed God." In fact, because it would not
be surprising were he to doubt it, nonetheless he did not doubt

11. Ex 2.11–12.

it but believed, and therefore it concludes: "and it was reputed to him unto justice." But David also spoke in a psalm of Christ's Ascension when he reported what was promised by the Lord concerning his seed. "His seed," he said "will endure forever, and his throne as the sun before my gaze and as the moon perfect forever, and an ever-faithful witness in heaven."[12] Was this promise made in regard to someone from David's seed other than Christ, or only for Christ?

MOSES: Since no advantage arises for me from contradicting it, I do not deny that it was truly made on behalf of the christ. Based on this there is proof that a condition always accompanies the promise that was made by the Lord to David concerning his seed in some way other than concerning the christ. This is just as one finds in the third book of Kings, when David, since the days of his death were already approaching, said to his son Solomon, chastising him: "Take courage and be a man," etc.[13] Then he immediately added the reason why he was chastising him, saying: "If your children will take heed to their ways and walk before me in truth, with all their heart, and with all their soul, there will not be taken away from you a man on the throne of Israel."[14] That, however, was a promise made to him concerning the christ, for if his children sinned certainly they would be punished. Yet nevertheless what was promised had to be fulfilled, just as one reads in the psalm: "And if his children forsake my law, and do not walk in my judgments, if they profane my justice and do not keep my commandments, I will visit their iniquities with a rod and their sins with stripes, but my mercy I will not part from him nor will I make that which comes forth from my lips to be in vain."[15]

PETRUS: You have spoken well and you have shown well that you understand the Scriptures and have expressed nothing contrary to them. But how will Christ remain in eternity if he is not God, and how will his throne be just like the sun or the moon in the sight of the Lord, and how will he always be a faithful wit-

---

12. Ps 88.37–38.
13. 1 Kgs 2.2.
14. 1 Kgs 2.4.
15. Ps 88.32–34. Note that the Vulg. differs somewhat from this passage.

ness in heaven unless he is in heaven? Certainly the psalmist indicated that Christ would ascend to heaven. He could not do this, however, as we believe, unless he were both man and God. In fact, the logic of the passage demands this, it seems to me.[16] Again, on the same topic, David said elsewhere in the Psalms: "Arise, my glory; arise, psaltery and harp; I will arise with the dawn. Be praised above the heavens, God, and your glory above all the earth."[17] Certainly David hints here at the Resurrection and Ascension of Christ, and at certain other things. For when he says, "Arise, my glory," he indicates Christ's Resurrection, as if to say: Arise from death, Christ, you who are my glory. He introduced the latter portion, however, that is, "arise, psaltery and harp," owing to the joy and gladness that would come from Christ's Resurrection. These were indicated well by the psaltery and harp, since instruments of this sort are employed at a time of prosperity and happiness. This is as if to say that when Christ rises again every joy and happiness arises with him. In fact, one knows from the third [statement], which is "I will arise with the dawn" [*exsurgam diluculo*], when it ought to say "at dawn" [*in diluculo*], that David himself had to be freed from the darkness of hell with the rising Christ. For here we understand "dawn" to mean "light," just as in many places where the noun is "evening," we are accustomed to understand "darkness" and "night." This is as if clearly to say that when Christ rises, even I will rise with him from darkness into glory and great light. The fourth [statement], however, which states, "Be praised above the heavens, God, and your glory above all the earth," adds this concerning the exaltation and Ascension of Christ into heaven. From this Ascension glory has to come upon him across the entire earth, as if to say: You will ascend and you will be exalted above the heavens, and from this, glory will accrue to you throughout all the earth. Whereas in reality it said, "God," we necessarily understand Christ, who was both man and God. For God, understood simply,[18] does not move from place to place, and undoubtedly he neither descends nor ascends, nor is he exalted.

16. In Migne, this last statement is attributed to Moses.
17. This passage conflates Ps 56.9 and 56.6, as they appear in the Vulg.
18. "God, understood simply": *purus enim deus.*

MOSES: I confess, what you have said about the Ascension suffices. But you touched on still one more item in the exposition of your faith, namely, that he will come to judge the living and the dead on the day of judgment. I require neither an argument nor a reason for this matter. For if, as you believe, he is both God and man, I admit that it is enough that he is the judge of the world. Still, do you have some authority from Scripture concerning this?

PETRUS: Certainly I have. For we read in the book of Daniel: "I beheld until thrones were set in places, and the Ancient of Days sat."[19] And later in the same place [he said]: "The court sat, and the books were opened."[20] Then in the same vision [he added]: "I beheld then in the vision of the night and, behold, one like the Son of Man came with the clouds from heaven, and he came even to the Ancient of Days, and they presented him before him, and he gave him power and honor and a kingdom, and all the peoples, tribes, and tongues will serve him. His power is an everlasting power that will not be taken away, and his kingdom will not be destroyed."[21] Certainly, the Ancient of Days who sat is God the Father. When he said, "The court sat, and the books were opened," the judgment is indicated that will come at the end of the world, in which the merits of individuals written in books, as it were, will be separated. He who came with the clouds of heaven, however, is Christ, who rightly is not called "the Son of Man" in an absolute sense, but "like the Son of Man," because he was not born from a carnal father and mother but instead from the Virgin and God the Father. With this—that once judgment was prepared and the books were opened, the Ancient of Days gave him power and honor and a kingdom, and promised him the service of all peoples, tribes, and tongues—it is in fact clear that judgment over all is granted to him at the consummation of the world. Moreover, this—that is, "his power is an everlasting power that will not be taken away, and his kingdom will not be destroyed," which applies only to a divine kingdom, and what precedes it, "like the Son of Man he

19. Dn 7.9.
20. Ibid.
21. Dn 7.13–14.

TWELFTH *TITULUS*

OSES: UP TO THIS point, we have debated sufficiently individual parts of your faith, but you mentioned one thing more in the beginning of the debate, namely, that at the hour of your baptism you believed the apostles. I require that that belief be explained to me: namely, what it is; whether you believe merely that they were good and saintly men, or that what they preached was true; and whether you believe what they themselves believed.

PETRUS: In fact, I believe both that they were saintly men and that all that they preached was true, and I struggle to do all that they preached, as far as I am able.

MOSES: Now you have fallen into a trap from which you cannot be set free. For when I inquired at the beginning whether you observe the law of Moses as it was given by him, which you seemed to me to have transgressed, you in fact replied that you fulfill it truly and observe it and walk with a straight step along its righteous paths. Moreover, he whom you call Christ preserved it in all instances, just as he himself attested when he said that he came not to destroy the law but to fulfill it.[1] The apostles, however, whom you assert you believed, destroyed it and commanded things contrary to its precepts. Which is why, when you say that you believe in them and that their preaching is true in all respects, you seem to believe both the one thing and its contrary.

PETRUS: Clearly the apostles were true disciples of Christ. Whatever they preached they certainly did through Christ, and they did not destroy the law of Moses but rather fulfilled it.

MOSES: And how can we know that they preached those things through Christ, when it is well known that they only preached after his death?

1. Cf. Mt 5.17.

PETRUS: But how can we doubt that, when we know that they preached nothing but Christ and his precepts? Proof of the fact that they preached him and his precepts is that in order to spread his faith they, barefoot, sought out strange and distant lands, and they almost all suffered thirst, hunger, nakedness, cold, and at the same time heat, distress and toil, the lash, and murder for the sake of his confession. Now how could they endure these things for him and be disobedient to or opposed to his precepts?

MOSES: If, as you say, the apostles did not disagree with Christ, and Christ did not in any way depart from the law of Moses, then why were the apostles opposed to Moses?

PETRUS: And in what thing are they found to be opposed [to him]?

MOSES: In all things.

PETRUS: You have gone too far. For they preached fasting, alms, and mercy. They commanded one to love God above all else and to love one's neighbor as oneself. And in addition they forbid murder, fornication, theft, false witness, envy, and the other vices, which both reason abhors and Moses forbids. How, then, do you say that they were opposed to Moses in all things?

MOSES: If they agreed with Moses in the things mentioned above, why did they disagree with him in certain others?

PETRUS: In what?

MOSES: First is that circumcision which God gave as a commandment to Abraham[2] and Moses, which both Christ, whom even you say was circumcised,[3] and the apostles laid aside—indeed, they even forbid that it be done.[4]

PETRUS: We ought first to look into this circumcision—why it was commanded and what use it has—and then we will better understand whether what the apostles did was just or unjust.

MOSES: That is acceptable.

PETRUS: Tell me, then, what useful purpose could the circumcision in which you believe serve, or why was it commanded to be performed only on the eighth day?

2. Cf. Gn 17.9–14.
3. Cf. Lk 2.21.
4. Cf. Acts 21.21.

MOSES: I know no reason for the eighth day except that it pleased God. It did, however, serve a useful purpose, because it was an occasion of salvation.

PETRUS: It follows from your words, then, that anyone who is circumcised on any day will be saved, and so it was commanded to be performed on the eighth day in vain and without benefit. But it is also fitting to ask something else—whether circumcision requires something else in addition for salvation, or whether it alone can confer salvation.

MOSES: Certainly it requires something else, because for salvation to be perfect it is necessary, in addition to circumcision, to fulfill the law of Moses, and, if it please you, you can hear the manner in which it may be done. For if someone both has been circumcised and has guarded the entire law, undoubtedly he will be saved. If, however, he has been circumcised but has presumed not to observe the law in some respects, he will suffer punishments for the transgression, but nevertheless he will pass over from that to salvation. But if he has guarded the entire law but was not circumcised, he cannot be saved at all despite all the punishments he suffers.

PETRUS: Where do you get this belief, when God never promised that to either Abraham or Moses, and none of the prophets ever said this?

MOSES: We understand this, indeed, from the words which the Lord said to Abraham: "The male, whose flesh of his foreskin will not be circumcised, that soul will be lost[5] out of his people."[6] With this he implies that one who has been circumcised will not perish, but will be saved instead.

PETRUS: But, according to the explanation of this authority of yours, he who has not fasted on the tenth day of the seventh month,[7] although he be circumcised, nevertheless will have no salvation. For thus is it written in Leviticus: "Every soul that is not afflicted on this day will perish among his people."[8] If he will

---

5. "Lost" (*disperiet*): the Vulg. reads "destroyed" (*delebitur*), whereas some MSS of the *Vetus Latina* retain Alfonsi's reading.

6. Gn 17.14.

7. I.e., on Yom Kippur, the Day of Atonement.

8. Lv 23.29.

perish for this, undoubtedly circumcision will avail him nothing.

MOSES: This certainly seems to be reasonable [*ratio*].

PETRUS: What do you say, then, about Adam, Seth, Enoch, Methuselah, Noah and his son Shem, and the many others who were never circumcised but who we believe have been saved nevertheless?

MOSES: They lived before circumcision was commanded, and for this reason they could be saved without it.

PETRUS: And what do you say about Job and his companions, who lived after the commandment of circumcision and, although they were uncircumcised, were saved nonetheless?

MOSES: In fact, they did not belong to the people to whom the commandment of circumcision was given.

PETRUS: What, then, caused all those mentioned above to be saved?

MOSES: I really do not know, but I think it was their good faith and the sacrifices that they employed.

PETRUS: What, then, do you say of Ishmael, to whom the commandment of circumcision was given but not the law, and whose progeny still to this day are circumcised?[9] Now, are they not saved by that circumcision? If you say that they are, then circumcision alone confers salvation apart from the fulfillment of the law of Moses. But if you say that it does not, then you contradict yourself, since above you said that circumcision is the cause of salvation.[10]

MOSES: What you say is reasonable.

PETRUS: What do you think, too, about Jewish women, who cannot be circumcised and yet are still believed to be saved?

MOSES: They are saved because they are born from men who were circumcised.[11]

9. In fact, circumcision is not explicit in the Qur'an, nor is it a legal requirement in Islam. It is part of customary practice *(Sunnah)*, however, and frequently observed.

10. In fact, Moses said above that both circumcision and observance of the Mosaic law are necessary. Alfonsi misrepresents his view here, just as he misrepresents the Jewish understanding of circumcision by interpreting it typologically as a sign for Christian baptism.

11. This was also a conclusion drawn by Albert the Great. See his *De sacramentis*, tr. 2, q. 4, 4, ed. Albert Ohlmeyer (Monasterii Westf.: Aschendorff, 1958), 20–21.

PETRUS: Then what do you say about Sarah and Rebekah, Rachel and Leah and Zipporah (Moses' wife, who was a Midianite) and Ruth, who all, as you believe, were saved and who nonetheless were not born from the Jews? For if they will not be saved, certainly their husbands, who were both saints and prophets, would not have them as wives or produce children in them.

MOSES: To be sure, I do not know what response to give you concerning this, because it was never disclosed to me. Explain to me, however, the benefit of circumcision, if you know it.

PETRUS: Circumcision was actually given for this reason: so that the people [*gens*] of the Lord could be differentiated from and recognized from among other peoples.[12] It was commanded to differentiate this people better, then, and for another reason: namely, so that no one would take a wife from another tribe.[13] And indeed this is the whole [purpose for the] commandment: because Christ had to come from the seed of Abraham and from the law of Moses and from the tribe of Judah, namely, so that when he came, it could be recognized that he himself was Christ, and so that no one would rise up from another people who would claim to be the Christ and thus lead the world into error. And, to be sure, we have two arguments to show that circumcision was commanded to distinguish the people, and not, as you say, for salvation. One is that it was commanded to be performed on the eighth day and not earlier. The reason for this is that a boy is not separated from his mother before the eighth day, and so there was no fear that he would be confused with others. It is commanded, however, that the woman be washed and cleansed from her pollution on the eighth day.[14] Before that happens, the boy is circumcised lest, once his

12. It was commonly held by Christian exegetes that God imposed the requirement of circumcision upon the Jews to differentiate them from their gentile neighbors. For example, see Alfonsi's contemporary, Bruno of Segni, and his *Expositio in Genesim*, cap. 4, where he remarks, "Judaeis quoque circumcisionis signum a Domino datum est, quo a cunctis gentibus discernuntur . . ." (PL 164: 174C).

13. Cf. Nm 36.7–8.

14. A parturient is unclean for seven days when the child is male; for fourteen days when female (see Lv 12.1–5). At the end of this period, she is required to undergo ritual ablution. For a discussion, see Hyam Maccoby, *Ritual and Morality*, 49–50.

mother has been taken away, he be exchanged or confused with others. Another is that for the forty years when the children of Israel tarried in the desert, none who were born there were circumcised. When, however, they came to inhabitable land, so that they not mix with other peoples, the Lord immediately commanded them through Joshua to be circumcised, just as they discover who read the book of Joshua himself.[15] You said that circumcision is the cause of salvation. Yet certainly circumcision was not its only cause, but rather a good faith, sacrifices, and upright deeds— both before and after circumcision was given. This is just as is evident in the cases of Adam, Seth, Enoch, Methusaleh, Noah and Shem, Job and his companions, and the Jewish women, who were all saved without circumcision but with a correct faith and good works. But all of the aforementioned types of salvation conferred salvation only on those who, having the capacity for discernment, believed that Christ had arrived, and believed that they could be saved only through him. Since Christ—the savior whom they expected—really came to fulfill the law of Moses, he wanted himself to be circumcised so that it would be clear from this that he had to come from the seed of Abraham and from the law of Moses and from the tribe of Judah, just as we proclaimed. Therefore, now that all the things for which circumcision was given were fulfilled, no one needs circumcision any longer, because there is no more distinction according to race [*genus*].[16] For whoever betakes himself to the law of Christ, and regardless of his race or language wishes only to be faithful, exists on the same level with other Christians. In addition, as soon as baptism came, since it is itself the universal form of salvation for men and women, circumcision was no longer necessary for salvation. Therefore, since it has been shown in all [these] ways that circumcision is not necessary after the advent of Christ, you can clearly understand from this why the apostles never commanded that it be performed.

MOSES: Even if they did not command it, why did they forbid that it be done besides?

PETRUS: Certainly they did so for this reason: so that people would not think that circumcision confers salvation just as bap-

15. Cf. Jos 5.2–9.
16. Cf. Col 3.11.

tism does, or that circumcision confers salvation together with baptism, and so fall into error just like the Nestorians and Jacobites, who think that a person can only be saved by both,[17] and just like you yourselves, who, if someone from outside the bloodline [*de externa progenie*] wants today to convert to your law, command that if he is a male, he be circumcised first and baptized after that, whereas if a female, you command only that she be baptized.[18]

MOSES: Your remarks imply that we did not employ baptism until after Christ's advent, as if we learned it from Christ himself.

PETRUS: If not from him, then from whom did you learn it?

MOSES: From Moses.

PETRUS: That is false. And we have two arguments for this: One, when the Lord gave a commandment to Moses concerning foreigners, saying: "And if any stranger wishes to dwell among you, and to keep the Passover [*phase*] of the Lord, all his males should first be circumcised, and then he will celebrate it with due religious observance: and he will be as one that is born in the land."[19] Certainly, if baptism were necessary then, he would have commanded it as well as circumcision, and since it is not present here where it especially ought to be if what you say were true, and Moses did not mention it anywhere else, you cannot in any way prove that you learned it from him. A second argument is that your sages—certainly those who came before Christ—never said anything at all about this baptism, by which they reveal that you did not receive it from Moses. In fact, those who lived after Christ's advent learned baptism from him and so, commingling it with circumcision, they led the people into error.

17. "Jacobites": in general, those Eastern Christians who rejected the decisions of the Fourth Ecumenical Council at Chalcedon (451 C.E.) and who were ostracized as "monophysites." "Nestorians": a title applied to followers of the fifth-century heretical patriarch Nestorius, whose christology is sometimes identified as "dyophysite." For the claim that the Jacobites circumcise their children like the Jews, see *supra*, p. 152, n. 25. It is unclear, however, why Alfonsi also associates Nestorians with the practice of circumcision.

18. According to Jewish law, a male proselyte must both be circumcised and undergo ritual immersion; a female undergoes only ritual immersion. This ritual immersion represents an analogue to baptism for Petrus Alfonsi.

19. Ex 12.48.

MOSES: You have replied in a way that seems proper concerning circumcision. But what will you say about the Sabbath day, which in many places the Lord commanded through Moses to be observed, and which he himself commanded on his own behalf when speaking to the children of Israel at Mount Sinai? And the commandment for its observance was written on the stone tablets, such that the Lord said, "Remember to keep the Sabbath day holy"[20] And in the following passages he added the reason, saying: "In six days God made the heaven and the earth and the sea, and all things that are in them, and rested on the seventh day; therefore the Lord blessed the seventh day and sanctified it."[21] And in addition he commanded that he who did not observe it be stoned;[22] however, the apostles repudiated it and commanded that another day be observed.

PETRUS: To be sure, just as you said, the Lord commanded that that day be observed as a remembrance of the creation of the world, but it also symbolized another thing that was still to come.

MOSES: And what is that that had still to come?

PETRUS: The advent of Christ, who completed all his works which he accomplished while he lived in the world on the sixth day, that is, Friday, when he accepted death on our behalf. On the seventh day (that is, the Sabbath day), however, he rested, and indeed he brought relief from the pains of hell to all those who, believing in him, died before his death. Once that was completed for which Sabbath observance was a sign, however, it was not necessary to observe it any longer.

MOSES: According to your explanation, if Sabbath observance was a sign of his act, as you say, then once it was completed it should be observed all the more: on the one hand, as a remembrance of the creation of the world, and, on the other, for the saints' relief from the pains of hell.

PETRUS: Certainly the reality is not what you think. For your ancestors who lived before Christ's advent observed the Sab-

20. Ex 20.8.
21. Ex 20.11.
22. Cf. Nm 15.32–36.

bath as a remembrance of the world's creation, as you said, and because they believed that on the same day they ought to enjoy relief from the pains of hell, through the Christ. In truth, after Christ's Resurrection (which was the basis of Christian faith, and faith is the basis of salvation; although all salvation derives from Christ's death, still without faith it confers no benefit), after Christ's Resurrection, I say, it was no longer necessary for all those believing in him to observe the Sabbath but to observe Sunday[23] instead, namely, the day of the Resurrection, which was the basis of their salvation.

MOSES: And why did they not observe both, namely, the Sabbath as a remembrance of the world's beginning, and the other day as a remembrance of their salvation?

PETRUS: We said that the Sabbath was observed as a remembrance of the world's beginning, whereas in fact its observance was on account of the creation of things which was completed then, just as is written: "And on the seventh day God completed his work, which he had made, and he rested from all the work which he had done."[24] In fact, because this same day was the first day for the damnation of souls, and this because of Adam, who sinned on the evening of the preceding day (namely, at the twelfth hour), whereby he fell from glory to damnation, after which the salvation of souls came from Christ's Resurrection, now the day of damnation ought not to be celebrated any longer, but rather that day that was the beginning of salvation. And I can show this to you, if you like, with an example. For a certain king constructed a certain city, in which he erected precious buildings. He planted shrubs and vines everywhere and introduced streams of water into its midst, on this side and that, and made it fertile and overflowing with all delights, and gave it to a certain people to dwell in. But in this same city there was a certain enemy of the king who invoked the right, I know not how, that as often as anyone left it, he became the enemy, and, laying an ambush, he seized him and thrust him into a dark prison cell. The king, however, who had founded the city, prom-

23. "Sunday": *dies dominica*, the Lord's day.
24. Gn 2.2.

ised to its inhabitants that a time would come when he decided to free them from that enemy. Moreover, he required no other payment or remuneration from them other than that they should venerate that most honored day on which the city had been completed, and for the sake of this, moreover, he would free them from the aforementioned enemy on the same day. They celebrated it for a long time, just as the king commanded them. When some time had passed, however, he had compassion and pity [*pietas*] for them and determined to free them from their captivity with his presence [*presencialiter*]. Therefore, he sent his son, who, once he had vanquished the enemy, freed the captives from his power. And once they were freed from the yoke of the enemy, the aforementioned king set the city in order in such a way that it was never again necessary to fear captivity from that enemy. But tell me, O Moses, which day ought to be celebrated: the one on which the city was completed but on which the people fell into the power of the enemy, or the one on which it was set in order in such a way that it no longer feared to be made captive by him?

MOSES: Undoubtedly, that day when it was set in order in this way.

PETRUS: Clearly, we ought to celebrate Sunday for the same reason, on account of Christ's Resurrection, which, just as we said, was the basis of faith and salvation, especially since whosoever believing in him died before the death of Christ, but were subject to the darkness of hell earlier, were certainly saved by him when he died. In fact, those who believed after the Resurrection both are saved by his death and have not known hell [*tartara*] for all that. This is the reason why the apostles commanded that that day in particular and not the Sabbath day be observed, even though our Lord Jesus Christ observed it. But he only did this to fulfill the law of Moses, which he safeguarded, and because the day of the Resurrection had not yet come.

MOSES: And what do you say about the festival of the Passover which the Lord commanded to observe—to sacrifice a lamb on it and to eat it with unleavened bread and bitter herbs[25]—which all of the apostles neglected, commanding instead another feast

25. Cf. Ex 12.1–28; Dt 16.1–8.

and one with a different order, since the one whom you call Christ never, so long as he lived, intended to celebrate it?

PETRUS: At the outset, O Moses, to be sure, we must carefully examine the rites and the basis for the rites for which the Passover [*phase*] was commanded in Egypt, and then why, afterwards, it was commanded a second time in the desert.[26] When we have done this, we will see whether we ought to celebrate the festival of the Passover after Christ's death, or not.

MOSES: That seems proper.

PETRUS: Certainly, these are its rites and religious observances: One is commanded to select a lamb or kid on the tenth day of the first month, and to guard it until the fourteenth day. It is also commanded that it be a male and young and without any blemish, and that it be sacrificed by the entire multitude of the children of Israel on the fourteenth day between the two evenings, and that its blood be placed on each post and on the lintels of the houses (and this only in those houses in which it had to be eaten). Indeed its flesh was not eaten raw or boiled in water, but only roasted on a fire. Moreover, it was commanded that the entire thing be cooked on the fire whole—with the head and feet and intestines—and then hastily eaten during the night, and its bones were not broken, and so, too, it was eaten with unleavened bread and bitter herbs.[27]

MOSES: It is actually just as you said.

PETRUS: Tell me, then, for what reasons were these rites commanded?

MOSES: I do not know, except that the Lord wanted it done this way. Concerning the blood, however, I know that it was commanded to be placed on the post of each house and upon the lintels for this reason: so that when the evil angel came to a house daubed with the blood he would pass over it.[28]

PETRUS: Have I not often said to you above that no word goes forth from the mouth of the Lord without reason?

MOSES: You tell me, then, why they are commanded to observe these rites.

26. Cf. Lv 23.5.
27. Cf. Ex 12.3–10.
28. Cf. Ex 12.22–24.

PETRUS: Certainly the lamb of Egypt and its rites were a figure and symbol for the Lamb of God that had to be sacrificed, that is, for Christ. For just as the Lord's faithful ones were preserved through that lamb from the power of the angel who slew the bodies, so, too, through Christ those believing in him were redeemed from the devil, who damned the souls, and the lamb was pointing, as it were, to the one who would come after it.

MOSES: What you have said about the lamb seems correct, but how can you apply the aforementioned rites of the lamb to Christ, whom you call "the Lamb of God"?

PETRUS: Very well in every respect. For just as the lamb was commanded to be selected on the tenth day of the month and to be guarded until the fourteenth day, so, too, on the tenth day of the month (namely, on the day of the [new] moon) your sages took counsel concerning keeping a watch on Christ. Indeed, on the preceding Sunday Christ came to Jerusalem to celebrate the Passover there, and the entire people received him with happiness and great pomp and honor. Because of this the envy and malevolence of the sages grew even more, and one took counsel with another concerning keeping a watch on him and slaying him on the day following.[29] That counsel, however, was covered up and concealed until the fourteenth day. And just as the lamb was commanded to be a male and young and without any blemish, so, too, Christ was both a male and young and was without any blemish, that is, without sin. It was commanded, however, that a sheep or a goat, and not a cow, be selected as the sacrificial victim, although of these animals it was the cow that was commanded to be offered as a sacrifice under the law.[30] This was done for this reason: so that when the sheep or the goat was seized, it would not resist as the cow does, and this was a sign, moreover, that when Christ was seized, he did not resist or defend himself, as he could have. The fact that it was commanded to be sacrificed by all the multitude of the children of Israel (although it was enjoined specifically on each one, even though they would not all make one sacrifice, but each household and family would make its own sacrifice) indicates that the

29. Cf. Jn 11.47–53.
30. Cf. Nm 19.6–9.

entire multitude of the Jews slew Christ. For even though not all were present, all nevertheless offered their assent.[31] Truly, [the fact that it is sacrificed] by the fourteenth day and [eaten] between the two evenings has to show that there are two evenings to the day. One is when the sun begins to descend from the mid-point of heaven, whereas the other occurs when it gives way entirely to the night. And Christ expired on the fourteenth day and between its two evenings, at the ninth hour, as you yourselves believe. By the two evenings your two captivities can also be understood, namely, the Babylonian and the one of Titus. And Christ died between the two evenings, because his death was after the Babylonian captivity and before the captivity of Titus. And the fact that the lamb's blood was commanded to be daubed on each post and on the lintels of the houses in the sign of a cross signifies the blood of Christ that was poured out upon the Cross. And just as the blood of that lamb, as we said, safeguarded the Lord's faithful ones from the death of the body, so, too, the blood of Jesus Christ redeemed his faithful witnesses from the death of the soul. And just as the blood [of the lamb] protected no houses except those in which the lamb was eaten, which is why it was commanded to be placed only on those, so, too, the blood of Christ that was poured out on the Cross saves no one but him in whom the Lamb of God is present, namely, him who eats the body of this same Christ. In addition, just as the lamb was commanded to be eaten during the night, so also was Christ seized at night, so that he could not be freed or defended by the people. Moreover, just as it was not to be eaten raw or boiled in water but only roasted on a fire, so, too, Christ was condemned—not without a judgment but without a

31. Here Alfonsi seems to anticipate an increasingly harsh assessment of Jewish guilt for the Crucifixion, which appeared among a number of Christian thinkers in the twelfth century and later. He suggests that it was not only the Jewish leaders who were responsible, but the entire community gave its assent, even those who were not present at the time. For developments in the apportionment of blame and guilt in the Crucifixion, see Jack Watt, "Parisian Theologians and the Jews: Peter Lombard and Peter Cantor," *The Medieval Church: Universities, Heresy, and the Religious Life. Essays in Honour of Gordon Leff*, ed. Peter Biller and Barrie Dobson (Woodbridge, Suffolk, UK, and Rochester, NY: The Ecclesiastical History Society, 1999), 55–76; Jeremy Cohen, "The Jews as Killers of Christ from Augustine to the Friars," *Traditio* 39 (1983): 1–27.

just judgment—just like meat that is roasted on a fire that is neither completely raw nor well-cooked. But it was also commanded for the same reason to be eaten quickly and with unleavened
bread. For just as, when unleavened bread is made, one never
waits until the flour [*pasta*] rises but instead makes it quickly,
so, too, in Christ no righteous judgment was awaited, but instead he was hastily condemned. The bitter herbs with which
the lamb was commanded to be eaten signify that calamity and
bitterness come from that unjust condemnation. Moreover, the
fact that [the lamb] was commanded to be cooked whole and
complete (with the head, feet, and intestines) and that after the
meal its bones were not to be broken, implies that no limb of
Christ was cut off at his death, but instead he was hung with all
his limbs [intact]. And after his death none of his bones rot-
ted, or experienced any other decay, but instead he rose again
whole and complete. Therefore, you see that, just as was predicted, that lamb of Egypt and its rites were a figure and symbol for the Lamb of God, that is, Christ. If we have passed over
some rites and left them unexplained, if you investigate atten-
tively, you will be able to apply them similarly to Christ.

MOSES: Although, Petrus, you have explained the Passover
of Egypt as was proper, I want you, if you please, to say why a
second time in the desert the Passover was commanded to be
performed.

PETRUS: Clearly this was done for no reason or purpose other than as a remembrance of the Egyptian Passover, and to declare why Christ, the Lamb of God, had to be sacrificed. But also
Christ always celebrated the Passover so long as he lived: on the
one hand, in order to fulfill the law of Moses; and on the other
hand, because those rites were not yet fulfilled. In fact, after the
whole [of the rites] was fulfilled by his death, it was no longer
necessary for that Passover to be performed, but only that Pasch
which was ordained for us by our apostles. For it is correct for
us to substitute for the day of the salvation of bodies the day of
the salvation of souls, which is more deserving of veneration.
For as the greater happiness arrives, the lesser withdraws, just as
when the sun rises, the stars' brightness flees. But we ought to
put aside the remembrance of the first one for the sake of the

remembrance of the one that follows, just as the Lord promised through the prophet Jeremiah: "Behold," he said, "the days are coming, says the Lord, when it will be said no more: The Lord lives that brought forth the children of Israel out of the land of Egypt, but: The Lord lives that brought the children of Israel out of the land of the north."[32]

MOSES: Certainly, that promise will be fulfilled with the christ's advent.

PETRUS: It is true that it had to be fulfilled with Christ's advent, but since it has been proved that Christ has already come, then the prophecy was fulfilled when he came. Thus it must be understood in this way: we ought no longer to recall that the Lord brought forth the children of Israel out of Egypt, but instead from the land of the north, that is, from hell, since the devil is understood by the north, the land of which is [his] dwelling and hell, just as the prophet Joel said: "I will remove far from you the one who is from the north, and drive him into a land impassable and desert; with his face towards the east sea, and his hinder part toward the utmost sea, and his stench will ascend, and his rottenness will go up, because he has acted proudly."[33] In fact, I do not care to explain how we can understand the devil by the north, for your sages have explicated this well enough.[34] Besides, how do you say that you celebrate the Passover, when you do not offer sacrifice or have an altar or a priest who will do it? Do you think that you can fulfill the Passover merely with the herbs and unleavened bread that you eat? In reality, sometimes you even change the day of the Passover and defer it until the day following, because you never celebrate it on Monday, or Wednesday, or Friday. I want you to explain to me why you do this.

MOSES: I do not know why, other than that our sages ordained it so, and Gamaliel above all.

PETRUS: And do you know why Gamaliel did so?

MOSES: No.

PETRUS: Indeed, Gamaliel was a holy man and a faithful

32. Jer 16.14–15.
33. Jl 2.20.
34. See B.T. *Sukkah* 52a; Ginzberg, *Legends of the Jews*, 3: 160.

Christian.[35] And because he knew that on Monday the Jews initiated a plan by which Christ could be condemned, and, moreover, on Wednesday the silver was given for the betrayal of Christ, and that on Friday Christ was fixed to the Cross, because, I say, he knew this and did not want any joy to be expressed on those days, for this reason he forbade them from celebrating the Passover on those days and enjoined that it be deferred until the day following. He did not want to reveal this secret, however, to everyone.

MOSES: After you have condemned the festival of the Passover, which takes precedence over and surpasses all others (and for which it is commanded that he will perish who has not observed it)[36] it will be pointless for us to debate the other, lesser [festivals], since you can condemn them much more easily. I want you to answer me, however, concerning the fast on the tenth day of the seventh month, which God commanded be observed for the atonement of our sins, so much so that he said that he who does not observe it perishes from his generation, and your apostles put it aside.[37]

PETRUS: First, I want you to tell me whether the fast alone suffices for anyone for the elimination of sins, or whether repentance is required with it.

MOSES: Clearly, there can be no expiation without repentance.

---

35. Gamaliel: a name shared by six sages who were descendants of Hillel. Gamaliel the elder (fl. first half of the first century C.E.), according to legend, instructed Paul in Torah (see Acts 22.3). His grandson, Gamaliel II, was a leader of Palestinian Jewry at the end of the first and beginning of the second century, president of the reconstituted Sanhedrin, and occasional disputant with Christian believers. He also helped develop the symbolic Passover meal and story—the *haggadah*—as a substitute for the sacrificial system that had been observed before the Temple's destruction. For Gamaliel II, see Shamai Kanter, *Rabban Gamaliel II: The Legal Tradition* (Chico, CA: Scholars Press, 1980). Petrus Alfonsi's "Gamaliel" seems to be a legendary figure based on at least these first two rabbinic leaders. It is important for him, however, that this rabbi of the Talmud should have recognized Christ as messiah, and therefore changed Jewish Passover practice because of the Crucifixion. In this way, the Talmud is understood to contain concealed evidence for Christian truths.

36. In fact, Ex 12.19 and Nm 9.13 only state that one who does not properly observe the Passover will be cut off from the people. This is also the case for Lv 23.29, in the next note.

37. Cf. Lv 23.27, 29.

PETRUS: Again, I ask you about the power of its expiation. In what do you claim it consists—in the fast day or in the repentance?

MOSES: In both.

PETRUS: Answer this also: if someone has repented, having omitted the fast, and has died in this condition, whereas another person has likewise died after having fasted but not having repented, which of them, rather [than the other], will have salvation?

MOSES: Undoubtedly, the one who repented.

PETRUS: Therefore, we can affirm that the power of its expiation consists in repentance and not in the fast, as Isaiah attests when he says: "Is this not rather the fast I have chosen? Unfasten the bonds of mercilessness. Loose [. . .] the bundles that oppress."[38]

MOSES: What, then, does the fast avail?

PETRUS: To be sure, it is the beginning of every good, which is commanded in order to weaken the human body and to restrain it from the vices.

MOSES: According to your words, anyone who will have fasted and done penance together, on any day whatsoever, will have the remission of sins.

PETRUS: That is true.

MOSES: Why, then, did God expressly command a day for this fast?

PETRUS: So that on the day that was determined, all would gather together and, fasting, would do penance.

MOSES: And why have your apostles dismissed all this?

PETRUS: Because Christ came, who has fulfilled the whole law, and he fasted for forty days.[39] For that reason the apostles, namely, his disciples, commanded forty days in place of one, because forty days of the fast avail more than one, and a penance of forty days is more beneficial than a penance of one day.[40]

MOSES: You have treated the fast as was correct, but what will you say about the sacrifices which the Lord commanded to be

38. Is 58.6.
39. Cf. Mt 4.2; Lk 4.2.
40. E.g., the forty days in the Lenten observance.

performed with an ox, a goat, or a sheep, which your apostles omitted, commanding instead that a sacrifice be done only with bread and wine?[41]

PETRUS: All the sacrifices which were commanded and ordained in the law of Moses were nothing but a figure and symbol of the principal sacrifice that was to come; and [they were commanded] so that the gentiles both would accustom themselves to sacrifices and would acknowledge through them that, just as these customarily washed away sins, so, too, the greatest sin could be removed through the greatest sacrifice. As Christ, namely, our holy of holies and principal sacrifice, came, however, and was sacrificed for our redemption, it was not necessary then for those ancient sacrifices to be performed. For when that one is present for which some symbol existed previously, then the symbol could be removed without contradiction. Therefore, since Christ himself came, we now employ that sacrifice which the apostles ordained for us, or, rather, which Christ himself gave, namely, bread and wine. And this sacrifice is analogous to the sacrifice that Moses called a "toda" (תּוֹדָה) sacrifice[42] when commanding it in the law, that is, a sacrifice of "praise," and which he commanded be performed with bread and wine only, as a figure of ours. David, too, knowing in advance that that [sacrifice] would come, and condemning all the others on its behalf, said in the psalm: "Shall I eat the flesh of bullocks? Or shall I drink the blood of goats? Offer to God the sacrifice of praise."[43] With this he suggested that all of the other sacrifices ought to be put aside, and that that sacrifice which is called a sacrifice of praise ought to be performed. And this is indeed our sacrifice of praise. For when performing it we praise God for the benefit which he bestowed upon us when saving us through his Son Jesus.

MOSES: And what do you say about those meats [carnes] that Moses forbade to be eaten in the law,[44] and which your Christ did not eat? Your apostles, however, not only did not forbid that they be eaten, but they themselves ate them.[45]

PETRUS: Since all things that God made are good, as Scrip-

---

41. I.e., they substituted the Eucharist for the older sacrifices.
42. Cf. Lv 7.12.
43. Ps 49.13–14.
44. Cf. Lv 11; Dt 14.
45. Cf. Acts 10.9–16.

ture attests when it says that "God saw all the things he had made, and they were very good,"[46] and that God said to Noah and his sons, "Everything that moves and lives will be food for you, even as the green herbs have I delivered all things to you,"[47] and since both Abraham and Isaac and the rest of the patriarchs ate everything that they wanted until Moses (and so, too, did Moses before he received the law), then why were the meats forbidden to be eaten in the law of Moses?

MOSES: Because at the beginning of the world men were still wild and bestial, as it were, they could not be admonished too quickly to obey the precepts of the Lord. Knowing this with a certainty, the wisdom of God never intended to give them all the precepts at the same time. Rather, gradually, he gave one to Adam, namely, so that he would not presume to eat of the fruit which he forbade;[48] another to Noah, namely, not to eat meat with blood and not to commit murder;[49] and, moreover, he commanded both sacrifices and circumcision for Abraham.[50] When Moses came, however, and God wanted the children of Israel to unite with him and wanted to differentiate them from the gentiles, he commanded his precepts for them, as it pleased him, and forbade unclean meat, lest they be polluted by it. In fact, he gave them a sign for the distinction between clean and unclean.

PETRUS: And this uncleanness which you have mentioned concerning the meat, is this itself a body or a reality which accrues to a body?

MOSES: Neither. Rather, it is some spiritual reality that comes down into a body, and yet it attributes neither growth nor diminution to it, but is such that it forbids what was never forbidden to it before, and it unites itself to the body in four ways. In one way, when it cleaves to the body from its creation and never separates from it: for instance, when it is derived as an inheritance from the father and mother, as we see in the pig and in other prohibited meats. In a second way, when it is united to a body in which it was not present earlier but [from which]

46. Gn 1.31.
47. Gn 9.3.
48. Cf. Gn 2.17.
49. Cf. Gn 9.3–6.
50. Cf. Gn 17.10; 22.13.

afterward it is not separated, as is seen in the dead and in lepers. In a third way, when something cleaves to a body from a supervenient cause, and separates[51] from it afterward because of an act, just as those who touch the dead are unclean until they have been cleansed with a sprinkling of ash.[52] And in a fourth way, when it joins itself to a body for another reason, and withdraws without any act, as they who touch some carcass [*morticinum*] are defiled for the entire day, but they are cleansed when the sun sets without any purification. Because these meats were unclean, then, they were forbidden by Moses for this reason: namely, so they not make unclean those who eat them. But also they were forbidden for another reason, as our sages assert, lest they introduce a hardness of heart or a dullness, which would inhibit understanding.

PETRUS: Certainly in the past these two vices, namely, uncleanness and hardness [of heart], befell bodies from meats, when bodies were still ensnared in that general sin and did not possess the fullness of the Holy Spirit. As Christ came, however, and cleansed the bodies of believers by baptism and infused the fullness of the Holy Spirit, now the person's body cannot be defiled or dulled by any meat. Even your sages attest to this, who said that after the advent of Christ all meats ought to be permitted and eaten.[53] But also on account of this they said that the meat of a pig is called "hazir" (חֲזִיר), that is, "changeable," since after the advent of Christ it had to be changed from inedible to edible.[54] Moreover, this argument can be provided for all unclean things. But even Moses attests to the acceptability of the meats in the future, after Christ's advent, when speaking to the people of Israel with these words: "When the Lord God will have enlarged your borders, as he has said to you, and you want to eat the flesh that your soul desires, and if the place which the Lord your God

---

51. Reading *se iungitur* (B) as *sejungitur* (A).

52. Cf. Nm 19.11; Lv 11.24.

53. The midrash to Ps 146.7 ("The Lord will loose the bonds") reports that "some say that of every animal whose flesh it is forbidden to eat in this world, the Holy One, Blessed be He, will declare in the time-to-come that the eating of its flesh is permitted." See *The Midrash on Psalms*, trans. William G. Braude (New Haven, London: Yale University Press, 1959), 2: 365–66.

54. Perhaps an allusion to the verb חזר, meaning "to turn around" or "revolve." But Alfonsi's definition here requires quite a stretch.

will choose, that his name should be there, be far off, you will kill from the herds and flocks that you have, as he has commanded you, and you will eat in your towns, as it pleases you. Even as the roe and the hart are eaten, so will you eat them. You will eat both the clean and the unclean alike."[55] Before the advent of Christ, the borders of Israel were indeed narrow, because they did not have the entire land that the Lord had promised them through Moses. The Lord, however, enlarged the borders of Israel after Christ's advent, when the apostles preached his law throughout the entire world. But even the place that the Lord chose so that his name would be there is now far off, because that ancient Temple of the Lord has been destroyed. Therefore, now one can eat all meat without transgression, whether clean or unclean, just as you please. Moreover, what I have said up to this point, O Moses, certainly I have done to satisfy your desire. Whereas if I wished to defend myself in another way, actually I would say that we have a new law, and it is not at all opposed to the law of Moses. For one of the Lord's commandments is not opposed to another, but rather when the period of one commandment has been fulfilled, he gives another commandment, as it pleases him, just as we saw for the commandment that the Lord gave Noah concerning the eating of meats. For after Moses came, and the period of [Noah's] commandment had been fulfilled, then he granted to Moses himself another commandment, namely, one forbidding meats. Once again, after its period was fulfilled with the advent of Christ, behold, he restored that ancient commandment which had been given to Noah, namely, the one concerning the admissibility of meats. And indeed the Lord promised through Moses himself that a prophet—that is, Christ—had to be raised up just like Moses, who would give a new law just as Moses did, as we said above. Again, Isaiah prophesied in this manner concerning a new law that he foresaw had yet to come: "And in the last days the mountain of the house of the Lord will be prepared on the highest mountaintop, and it will be exalted above the hills, and all nations will flow to it. And many people will go, and say: Come, and let us go up to the mountain of the Lord, and to the house of the God of Jacob, and he will teach us his ways, and

55. Dt 12.20–22.

we will walk in his paths, for the law of the Lord will come from
Zion and the word of the Lord from Jerusalem."[56] O Moses, what
is this mountain of the house of the Lord? For if you want to
speak of Mount Zion, where the house of the Lord was (namely,
the Temple), reason contradicts you, because it was not situated
on the highest mountaintop, since there were around it other
hills higher than it, nor could it be that at some time it would be
raised up above the hills. Moreover, what is the meaning of what
he said: "And many people will go, and say: Come, and let us go
up to the mountain of the Lord, and to the house of the God of
Jacob, and he will teach us his ways, and we will walk in his paths,
for the law of the Lord will come from Zion and the word of the
Lord from Jerusalem"? Now, what are the ways of the Lord or his
paths, or what is the law that would come forth from Zion and
the word that would come forth from Jerusalem? For he did not
say of the law of Moses, which is known to all, "He will teach us
his ways," nor did that ancient law go forth from Zion, but rather
from Mount Horeb. And it was not from Jerusalem, but from Sinai instead, that Moses announced the word of the Lord. Therefore, the prophecy must be understood in this way: undoubtedly,
holy Church is the house of the Lord. Indeed, kings were wont
to be compared to mountains, and prophets to hills. The mountain, however, upon whom the Church itself was constructed is
the king of holy Church, namely, Christ, and he was prepared on
the highest mountaintop and was raised up above the hills because he was elevated and honored above all kings and above all
prophets. And deservedly the prophet said both of holy Church
and of Christ: "All nations will flow to it," that is, to Christ. This is
because many from all the nations have believed in him, saying:
"Come, and let us go up to the mountain of the Lord," that is,
to Christ, whom the Lord established as king of all, "and to the
house of Jacob," that is, to holy Church. "And he will teach us
his ways," that is, the teaching of his law, "and we will walk in his
paths," that is, in the observance of his law, which is a new law, just
as we call new roads "paths." Moreover, what follows—"the law of
the Lord will come from Zion and the word of the Lord from Jerusalem"—implies that the law of Christ would come forth from

56. Is 2.2–3.

Zion and his word would come forth from Jerusalem. For the Holy Spirit, whose advent was the foundation of the law, came upon the apostles in Zion and [the law] was given by him and preached through him. And both the apostles and Christ himself preached in Jerusalem before anywhere else, and the preaching went forth from there throughout the whole world. Therefore, it is patently clear that Isaiah prophesied concerning the new law. In the same way, Jeremiah said this about the new law: "Behold, the days will come, says the Lord, and I will make a new covenant with the house of Israel, and with the house of Judah, not according to the covenant I made with their fathers, in the day when I took them by the hand to bring them out of the land of Egypt."[57] Now in Latin where we have "new covenant," in Hebrew you find "berith hadasa" (בְּרִית חֲדָשָׁה), which means "new law," as Moses attests in the many places where he calls the commandments of his law "berith" (בְּרִית). Moreover, Jeremiah himself implied that he said "new covenant" for "new law" when he added: "not according to the covenant I made with their fathers, in the day when I took them by the hand to bring them out of the land of Egypt." For clearly here he is speaking of the covenant (that is, that law) which the Lord gave Moses in the desert after he had gone forth from Egypt.

MOSES: We have debated long enough and sufficiently concerning our law and yours in a mutual exchange, and you resolved all my objections, just as was proper, and I could set forth nothing against you. But I have reserved one more thing for you in a storehouse, as it were. I am confident that, when I have arrayed it against you, you can be vanquished without a defense, because you will find that there can be no response to it.

PETRUS: And what is this matter that is so great and of such power and force, from which you anticipate so much for yourself and menace me until now?

MOSES: Actually, it is this: that you act against God and all the prophets, namely, that you cut down a tree in a grove, and then afterwards you seek out a carpenter, who chisels it, sculpts it, and forms it into the appearance[58] of a man, smoothes it and paints

57. Jer 31.31–32.
58. Reading *species/speties* (A) for *spenties* (B).

it, and you place the image in a very high place in your churches and adore it. Wherefore, even Isaiah expressed your rebuke and reproach, with these words: "The carpenter has stretched out his rule, he has formed it with a plane, he has made it with corners, and has fashioned it round with the compass, and he has made the image of a man, as it were, a beautiful man dwelling in a house."[59] And later, on the same topic: "They do not consider in their mind nor know nor have the thought to say: I have burned part of it in the fire, and I have baked bread on its coals, and I have broiled meat and have eaten, and of its residue shall I make an idol? Shall I fall down before the trunk of a tree? Part of it is ashes. A foolish heart adores it, and he will not save his soul nor say: Perhaps there is a lie in my right hand."[60]

PETRUS: To be sure, the truth is not what you think. For we do not fashion idols or adore them; instead we make a cross and place upon it the image of a man, and by the cross we designate an altar, and by the image we designate the sacrifice which takes place on the altar. For just as animals were sacrificed on an altar, so, too, even upon a cross was the Lamb of God sacrificed. And just as no one cared what happened to the rest of the stones from which the altar was constructed, so, too, we do not care what happens to the rest of the cross or the image placed upon it. And just as Solomon and others, when prostrating themselves before the altar, never adored it but rather adored God only, so, too, even we, when genuflecting before the Cross, never adore the Cross or the image placed on it, but instead we adore God the Father and his Son Jesus Christ.

MOSES: What you say would certainly be reasonable if you had in every place that Cross on which the Lamb of God was sacrificed, but it is not, since you have another cross, on which the Lamb [of God] was never placed.

PETRUS: In fact, we cannot have that Cross in every place.[61] This is why it is neither astonishing nor wicked if we make other crosses in its image [similitudo], so that those who have not seen

59. Is 44.13.
60. Is 44.19–20.
61. In fact, medieval Christians generally accepted that the True Cross had been rediscovered by the Empress Helena, with the aid of a Jew, and that the Church of the Holy Sepulchre in Jerusalem contained this holy relic. On

Christ's Cross may at least look upon others which were made in its likeness and recall and understand the sacrifice[62] that was made on it. In the same way, the sons of Gad and the sons of Reuben constructed an altar across the Jordan in the image of that altar in Jerusalem, so that their children and wives, who could not go up to Jerusalem, might look upon it for a testimony only and as a reminder of the other one, just as you can find written in the book of Joshua.[63]

MOSES: Certainly, God gave a great deal of his wisdom to you and illuminated you with a great reasoning power [*ratio*] that I am unable to vanquish. Instead you have confounded my objections with reason.

PETRUS: Undoubtedly, this is a gift of the Holy Spirit, whom we receive in baptism, who also illuminates our hearts, lest we presume to believe something that is false. If you believe what we believe and have yourself baptized, you will enjoy the same illumination of the Holy Spirit, so that you will recognize what things are true and repudiate those that are false. Now, then, since I have pity upon you, I implore God's mercy to illuminate you with the fullness of his Spirit and to give you a better end than beginning. Amen.

---

this legend, see H. Quillet, "Croix (Adoration de la)," in *Dictionnaire de théologie catholique*, ed. A. Vacant and E. Mangenot (Paris: Letouzey et Ané, 1908), 3: 2342–45. For the legend in Christian anti-Jewish polemics, see Ora Limor, "Christian Sacred Space and the Jew," in *From Witness to Witchcraft: Jews and Judaism in Medieval Christian Thought*, ed. Jeremy Cohen, Wolfenbütteler Mittelalter-Studien 11 (Wiesbaden: Harrassowitz Verlag, 1996): 55–77.

62. Reading *sacrificium* with Migne for *sacrificii* (A).

63. Cf. Jos 22.9–34.

INDICES

GENERAL INDEX

'Ā'ishah. *See* Aissa
'Alî. *See* Haly
Aaron, 131–32, 174
Abdallah ibn-Salām. *See* Abdias
Abdias, 152
Abner de Burgos. *See* Alphonse of Valladolid
Abraam, 133
Abraham, 131, 133, 148, 153, 157, 243–44, 250–51, 253–54, 267
Abraham bar Hayya, 3, 11
Abraham ibn Ezra, 11, 14
Abū Bakr, 154
Abū Ma`šar, 156
Abû Tâlib. *See* Abytharius
Abytharius, 162
Acha, king, 133
Adam, 129, 131, 148, 157, 177, 187, 222–25, 227, 229–230, 239, 240, 252, 254, 257, 267
Adelard of Bath, 20, 60; works of, *De opere astrolapsus*, 18
Adversus Iudaeos literature, 3, 4, 8, 35
Agobard of Lyons, 29–30
Ahaz, king, 178–80, 182
Aissa, 154
Akiba, 101, 110
Alan of Lille, 34, 169
Albert the Great, 33, 55, 211, 234, 252
Albert, Bat Sheva, 30
al-Bīrūni, 23
Aldaz, José Aragüés, 18
Alexander Nequam, 48
Alexander of Hales, 33
Alfonso I, king, 3, 13, 22, 40
Alfonso VI, king, 3

al-Hāshimi, 23
al-Khwârizmî, 18–20
al-Kindi, 23
Al-Ma'mūn, caliph, 22
Alphonse of Valladolid, works of, *Mostrador de Justicia*, 28
Alphonsus Buenhombre, 28
al-Qirqisānī, Ya'qūb, 30, 50
Alvárez, Lourdes Maria, 12
Amédée de Lausanne, 146
Amon, 102, 157–58
Amos, prophet, 115, 142, 152
Amram, 45
Anania, 110
Ananias, 70, 99, 100
Angel of Death, 94
angels, 94; Azazel, 220; Gabriel, 154; Haroth, 220; Hazazel, 220–21; Husa, 220–21; Huza, 221; Maroth, 221; Metatron, 50; Sandlfon, 50; Shemhazai, 221
anger, definition of, 66
apostles, 12–13, 40, 114, 203, 249–50, 254, 256, 258, 262, 264–66, 269, 271
Arabic, language, 11, 23, 221; science, 17; script, 23; translation from, 22, 25
Arabs, 19, 151, 157–58, 161
Aren, city of, 55–63
Aries, zodiacal sign, 55, 58–61, 158
Aristotle, 67, 84
arithmetic, 20
arts, liberal, 20–21, 41; *quadrivium*, 20–21; *trivium*, 20
Ashtor, Eliayahu, 10
Assitha, 235

277

reason, 8, 13, 15, 26, 29–31, 34, 39,
41, 46, 48, 50, 52–53, 58, 71–73,
75–76, 78, 80–84, 90, 97, 102, 117,
120, 122, 127, 130–31, 135, 137–
39, 146–47, 155, 162, 164–65, 167,
171, 185–86, 207, 221, 230, 235,
241–42, 250, 259, 270, 273
Rebecca, 253
Red Sea, 69
Regensburg, 15
Rehoboam, king, 236–37
Reinhardt, Klaus, 21, 28
Rembaum, Joel E., 33
Resnick, Irven M., 54, 224
resurrection, Jewish doctrine of the,
15, 42, 120, 122–23, 129, 131–32,
135–38, 162, 222, 240
Reuben, 33, 273
Reuter, J. H. L., 18, 21, 24, 26, 84,
104, 151, 181, 192, 196
Rhazes, 84
rhetoric, 20
Rhineland, 7
Richards, Jeffrey, 6
Riley-Smith, Jonathan, 7
Robert of Ketton, 25
Roman, army, 198; emperor, 197; em-
pire, 4; Senate, 4
Romano, David, 20
Romans, 5, 198
Ron, Zvi, 175
Rosenthal, Erwin I. J., 14
Rosenthal, Judah M., 33
Rosh Ha-Shanah, 205
Rouen, 15
Ruth, 253

Saadia Gaon, 32
Saba, 142, 218
Sabbath, 98, 103, 110, 139–40, 143–
44, 256–58
sages, Jewish, 32, 41, 43, 45, 48,
50–51, 53, 64, 68, 71–72, 90, 95,
97, 99, 102, 107, 111, 113, 119,
121–23, 128, 132, 137, 144, 175,
188, 190, 192, 196, 205, 210, 216,

219, 222, 225, 228, 232, 255, 260,
263, 268
Sallām ibn Mishkam, 153
Salmon ben Yeruham, 30–31
Samaria, 182
Samaritans, 151
Samsó, Julio, 11
Samuel ben Meir, 14
Samuel of Morocco, 27–28
Samuel, prophet, 133, 152, 228, 235
Sancho Ramirez, king of Aragon, 9
Santiago-Otero, Horacio, 21, 23, 28,
48, 84
Saperstein, Marc, 31
Sapir Abulafia, Anna, 14–15, 147
Sara, 253
Saracens, 24, 42, 146, 150, 155–56,
164
Saragossa, city of, 9, 22
Saturn, planet, 87, 158; Saturn, stat-
ue of, 158
Saul, king, 133, 228
scapegoat, 107
Schmitz, Rolf, 34
Schoonheim, Peter L., 67
Schubert, Kurt, 33
Scorpio, zodiacal sign, 57
Scriptures, sacred, 14, 34, 44, 49–50,
69, 73–75, 80, 86, 97, 130–31,
133, 138, 162, 167–68, 171, 176,
180, 187–88, 199, 213, 221, 236–
37, 243, 244–45, 247, 267
Secrets of Secrets [*Secretis secretorum*], 172
Sela, Shlomo, 11
Sennacherib, 70, 121
Sepphora, 253
Septimus, Bernard, 157
Sergius, 152
Seth, 131, 252, 254
Shatzmiller, Joseph, 11, 16
Shem, 34, 252, 254
Shi'ūr qōmāh, 30
Signer, Michael A., 7, 11
Simon the Pious, 49
Simonsohn, Shlomo, 7
sin, original, 212; venial, 42

INDEX OF BIBLICAL CITATIONS

New Testament

INDEX OF TALMUDIC CITATIONS

INDEX OF QURANIC CITATIONS